OLDER

The Unauthorized Biography of George Michael

Nicholas and Tim Wapshott

SIDGWICK & JACKSON

First published 1998 by Sidgwick & Jackson

an imprint of Macmillan Publishers Ltd
25 Eccleston Place, London SW1W 9NF
and Basingstoke

Associated companies throughout the world

ISBN 0 283 06317 3

3 5 7 9 8 6 4

A CIP catalogue record for this book is available from
the British Library.

Typeset by SetSystems Ltd, Saffron Walden, Essex
Printed and bound in Great Britain by
Mackays of Chatham plc, Chatham, Kent

For Louise and Elizabeth

Contents

Acknowledgements

No biography can capture wholly the richness of a subject's life. Even an autobiography, perhaps in particular an autobiography, will only tell a partial truth. However, it is possible to assemble a large body of evidence about a person's life and, through friends, family and colleagues, to build a picture of the person which is faithful and true. Even with a subject like George Michael, who jealously guards his privacy, an accurate portrait can be drawn. Inevitably this has meant relying on many sources who have allowed their memories of him to be recorded on condition that they are not identified. To all those who have helped us but wish to remain anonymous we would like to extend our warm thanks.

A great number of figures in the music industry have provided invaluable memories and insights into George Michael's life and music, among them Simon Bates, Trevor Dann, Richard Digance, Charles Stuart-Smith, Matthew Bannister, Shelagh Macleod, Peter Webber and Lesley Robinson. Among those who helped us with details of the court case, we would like to thank those representatives of Sony who provided background information. We are also grateful to Michael Barwick, Charles Burgess, Joan Burns, David Crisp, Martin Dix, Martin Elliott, Alan

Acknowledgements

Goodridge, Helen Healey, Doug Hearney, Caroline and David Hogan, Stephen Kilminster, David Koppel, Caradoc King, Eric King, Rachel Lockhart, Fiona Macleay, Yvonne Negron, Matthew Parris, Eileen Peters, Kelly Powell, Shane Sexton, Amanda Slayton and Michael Welsh for their help. The passages from George Michael and Tony Parsons's *Bare* are quoted with the kind permission of A.P. Watt. Thank you also to Morrison Leahy Music Limited.

Our literary agent David Godwin and Susan Hill, our editor at Macmillan, have encouraged and cajoled us to bring this book to fruition and their constant support has been of great assistance. Louise Nicholson and Elizabeth Bennett have been tireless props during the writing of the book, for which we offer our profound thanks.

Introduction

It would be easy to mistake George Michael's rise to fame as just one more rags to riches story in the annals of music history. It is, as far as these things go, a near perfect example. George Michael, born Georgios Kyriacos Panayiotou, the intelligent son of a Greek-Cypriot immigrant, dreams of a life in the music business and every evening writes songs alone in his bedroom, to the detriment of his schoolwork. When he leaves school with no job in sight, he starts a band and before long his career takes off. The verve of his delivery and the freshness of his songs ensures that he soon reaches stardom. After years of success as one of a pop duo, he gracefully abandons his partner and sets off on a solo career, which reaches a pinnacle with a triumphant world tour. The album accompanying the tour breaks all sales records and leaves George Michael, by now a handsome, sophisticated young man, one of the richest singers in the world.

There, however, the fairy-tale takes an odd twist. The relentless rise, a parody of a successful career in show business is suddenly cut short by a long and acrimonious dispute between George Michael and his record company, Sony. The details of the disagreement, over the promotion of an album, are soon overshadowed by Michael's declaration that he will not record any more songs until he is released from his contract.

The case strikes to the heart of the uneasy relationship between a creative recording artist and the often faceless businessmen who control his work. The situation reawakens the memory of similar battles between artists and their patrons down the years. It was hard not to imagine that Michael had knowingly taken on the persona of Bette Davis, the fiery Hollywood actress who had waged a permanent and often hysterical campaign against the exploitative confines of the Hollywood studio system. If he did not model himself upon Davis, he might well have learnt from her example. She won her freedom, but at a high price. And so would he. Still he kept at it with admirable patience and composure.

In all he attended the High Court in the Strand, London, for seven months, though he remained at home during some of the more detailed court discussions concerned solely with points of law. His dignified composure throughout those trying times won him loyal support from his fans and a healthy respect in the music industry. Many other artists wished they had the determination, and the money, to fight a similar case. Although it was never likely that George Michael would win his case, while it lasted it offered the prospect of all recording artists renegotiating their recording agreements – a prospect which alarmed a few record companies outside of Sony.

The battle was inevitably billed as David versus Goliath, with George Michael cast as the boy with the sling. To this end it put a strain both on Michael, whose lonely disposition meant he could not share the mental pressures of waging such a case, and on Sony, whose relationship with its artists lies at the centre of its profitability. Although the company needed to stand firm, they did not wish to seem domineering or unfair to a creative talent lest the others contracted to it took fright.

The verdict in the case was almost a foregone conclusion. The agreement with Sony was deemed fair and fairly entered into. Sony could rightly now demand that Michael complete his seven-record contract. It was profoundly unlikely that a British judge would ever undermine the fundamental principles of contract law. Yet, even with the case lost, the battle was not over. Michael would buy his freedom from Sony by granting them a share of the profit in his future recordings and the free exploitation of his back catalogue.

And along the way the case exposed for the first time and with great clarity the complexity and the veniality of the global recorded music industry. Not since The Beatles took each other to court in advance of their break-up had the music industry been laid so bare. Those outside the business were surprised to discover from the detailed breakdown of earnings from top-selling albums how little a star like Michael retained. It also destroyed the picture of pop stardom as a glamorous occupation. Michael demonstrated that record company demands for time to be set aside for publicity work ate into an artist's working year and stifled creativity. And the Byzantine world of contracts and agreements, and the management and ownership of rights, revealed pop stars as sometimes little more than bonded labour in a dubious international trade.

Michael's case was doomed from the start, yet, despite pleas from his friends to call off the expensive action, Michael pressed on. When Sony's agreement with Michael was upheld by the court, Michael did not buckle. He stood by his determination never to work for Sony again and this led eventually to a compromise, in which Michael's songs would be used by other companies but Sony retained a financial interest in his future work. It showed an extraordinary degree of persistence and an unusual quality of character to get his own way in such uncomfortable circumstances. It showed that, as well as being a singer of substance, he is someone who understands the importance of business, a rare quality among the performing talents of the music industry.

Michael's private life has always been the cause for speculation. When that finally gave way to the stark fact that Michael was homosexual, highlighted by his arrest in a Beverly Hills public lavatory, the singer was left to wonder what such a revelation would do to his career.

After two careers in music, in Wham! and as a solo artist, George Michael set out to become master of his own destiny, with a free-ranging contract to write and perform the songs he chose. To that extent his life has come full circle, for he began with everything within his grasp, writing songs and singing them to himself in his bedroom in his parents' home.

1

New Lives

George Michael was born just as the Sixties were getting into their stride. The year 1963 saw the old order in Britain giving out its last gasp. In June, the month that George Michael was born, the government of Harold Macmillan was reeling from the Christine Keeler scandal. Jack Kennedy, the young, handsome American President, flew into Berlin where, with the words 'Ich bin ein Berliner', he declared himself against the cruel division of the city into its communist and capitalist halves. That same month the leader of the Catholic Church, old Pope John, died and was succeeded by Pope Paul. The Russians sent the first woman up into space and, perhaps most significant of all the events of 1963 for the baby Georgios, The Beatles recorded their first album, *Please, Please Me*. Pop music would never be the same again.

The boy who would become George Michael was born Georgios Kyriacos Panayiotou on 25 June 1963, in his parents' humble home, a small flat above a launderette in Finchley, a north London suburb. His father, Kyriacos Panayiotou, like many living in that part of north London, was a Greek Cypriot who had arrived in Britain ten years earlier, a penniless refugee from the Mediterranean island of Cyprus.

Young and hardworking, the teenage Kyriacos Panayiotou was determined to escape the impending civil war
and the poverty of his Cypriot upbringing and make
something of his new life in Britain. He would turn away
from his past and change his name to Jack Panos. And he
was determined that the lives of his children would be in
every way better than his own meagre childhood.

Jack Panos was one of seven children from a working-
class family of Greek Cypriots. He lived with his parents,
his three brothers and three sisters, in the remote village of
Patriki on the north-eastern spur of Cyprus, in the Famagusta region. It was not an eventful place. Although a war
was raging about them, as the Allies gradually took back
Greece and its islands from the Germans, it did not greatly
affect life in Patriki. The villagers of Patriki, like those in
the rest of the Mediterranean in the Forties, mostly
scratched a living, tending their own land to eke out what
they earned as farm labourers with home-grown vegetables. And the better off might aspire to a goat, for
milking. When the men had gone off into the fields to
work, tending the orange and lemon groves, and the
children were packed off to school, the streets were
deserted. There was little to do in the dusty village except
hide from the scorching sun.

Though poor, the people of Patriki, like most Cypriot
communities, were close-knit, supportive of each other
and proud. They lived like their parents and grandparents
in a way which had barely changed from one century to
the next. There was no such thing as social security or a
welfare state. Instead, those still of working age supported
their older close relations, who in turn spent their days
looking after the children and the very old in extended

families. The commonplace hardship of everyday life fostered in the people of Patriki a gritty determination to make the best of a poor life. And those who dared transgress the unwritten laws of the village could be met with fierce opposition fed by fiery tempers.

About 33km south of Patriki was the seaport of Famagusta, the nearest centre of civilization in a spartan landscape. For the people of Patriki it was a place to sell their surplus produce. But, through its fishing industry and the large ships which docked there, it represented to Kyriacos and his young friends a window to the wider world. It was the island's major port, where local industry exported cotton and local brandy to mainland Greece. Famagusta was no place for children and Kyriacos was rarely taken there, but he knew that the port would one day be his gateway to a better, more rewarding and more secure life.

For as innocent as Kyriacos's rural childhood seemed in the Forties and Fifties, it was lived out against a background regularly littered with the grim realities of first a world war, and then a country caught up in long periods of bloody civil war. Throughout its history the island had been heavily fought over because of its unique geo-strategic importance, sitting at a crossroads between Asia and Africa. The population now is largely of Greek origin but Turkish (amongst other) claims on the island over the centuries have led to sporadic territorial and ethnic strife. The Famagusta region sat in the middle of what became in 1974 the Turkish section in the north, occupying a third of the island.

When Kyriacos was growing up, gun and tracer fire in the mountains often interrupted the tranquillity of the countryside and served as a constant reminder of the troubles facing Cyprus. When he left school in the mid-Fifties Kyriacos started work locally as a waiter, but he never thought that his future was in Cyprus. Instead, when he was just eighteen, he saw his chance for a better life and grabbed it. Britain, having pulled itself out of the post-war depression, had attained a new affluence and, in a bid to find cheap labour to undertake the mostly menial jobs proving hard to fill, appealed for immigrants from outlying parts of the fading empire such as Cyprus and the West Indies.

For the teenager, the toughest part of leaving Cyprus was totally cutting himself off from his family. He wondered how he would cope without them and, for that matter, how they would cope without him. His income as a waiter, though small, was already a notable contribution to the family's joint income. Still, he did not face his sea voyage to Britain alone. His cousin, close friend and his senior by one year, Dimitrios 'Jimmy' Georgiou, would be leaving with him. Dimitrios had served his apprentice-ship as a local tailor but also saw little future for himself on Cyprus and had successfully applied for British immigra-tion. Like so many immigrants before them, the two men persuaded a Greek merchant ship captain to let them work their passage to Britain, where they arrived at London docks with less than £1 in their pockets between them. But while they had no money, they were rich in optimism.

Arriving in London in 1953 saved them from fighting in the imminent civil war. Had they stayed in Cyprus they would have faced serving their time in National Service when the turmoil and troubles started, continuing for the next fifteen years. Emigrating together brought the two cousins closer than ever and a very strong bond was formed between them. Like their fathers before them, they became best friends. Later their own sons, Georgios and Andros Georgiou, would follow their example. As they had no money, they threw themselves on the mercy of a network of Greek-Cypriot friends and relations in north London, who were happy enough in the short run to put them up and feed them. But their hosts were not well off and it was essential that the two young men quickly found jobs. They were both ready to work hard, filled with hopes for a better life. Deciding to find work together, they were soon junior waiters clearing tables. They worked all hours for little pay, but the money seemed good to the two young men, who were richer than they had been so far in their lives. They taught themselves English, a struggle at times, but they were both determined to fit into their new country. Kyriacos even changed his name. As so many English people found it difficult to pronounce his Greek name, while keeping it for official purposes, he was happy to Anglicize it for everyday use to Jack Panos. (Eventually he would change his name by deed poll.)

On their rare nights off from the restaurant the two young men played hard and went out dancing to rock 'n' roll. They liked a good time and soon became caught up in the new crazes enjoyed by British teenagers. Chief among their favourite stars was the 'King of Rock 'n' Roll' Elvis Presley, and they listened to many other American rockers, among them Jerry Lee Lewis, Buddy Holly, the Everly Brothers and Roy Orbison. They also liked the rather tamer British talent, such as Ruby Murray, Shirley Bassey, Helen Shapiro, Adam Faith, Tommy

Steele, Russ Conway, Lonnie Donegan and The Shadows, fronted by Britain's so-called Presley pretender, Cliff Richard.

Of course, one of the great things about the milk bars and dance halls where you could listen to rock 'n' roll was that there were girls around. Kyriacos was handsome, with a mop of jet-black hair which he wore like Elvis, greased back with a quiff at the front. So it was to the strains of rock 'n' roll mix, at a dance in north London, that Jack met the young woman who was to become his wife. Lesley Angold Harrison was a working-class girl from Archway, north London, who lived with her family in Lulot Street, one of a labyrinth of streets between Holloway and Highgate.

Jack Panos liked Lesley's English prettiness; Lesley liked Jack's air of the exotic. After the first meeting they began dating and before long they found themselves engaged to be married. After a modest wedding in Holloway, they began their new life as Mr and Mrs Panayiotou in a small two-bedroomed rented flat above a launderette in Finchley. It was a modest beginning. The shabby terraced building looked out over a dismal yard, then over the equally dreary backyards of a row of nondescript shops. The flat was basic but Lesley worked hard to quickly make it home. They had little money between them. Even after they were married, Jack always sent money home to his family in Cyprus. Still, it was not long before Lesley became pregnant. Yioda Panayiotou was born in 1959.

The extra mouth to feed put a strain on the family and Jack was now obliged to work seven nights a week to meet the family budget. Hence he could not help that he was a largely absent parent, although he made a point of spending time at home in the few hours' break from the restaurant between lunch and dinner.

Two years later Lesley gave birth to another girl, whom they named Melanie. While Lesley remained at home, Jack's hard work started to pay off a little: he was made an assistant manager at the restaurant. But while the promotion brought some extra money, it meant extra responsibility and even longer hours away from his family. With two children already, their two-bedroom flat was beginning to seem cramped. Then the next year, in 1962, Lesley announced that she was expecting their third child.

In Britain it was to be a dramatic summer, but in Finchley the excitement of the autumn of 1962 passed Lesley by. Heavily pregnant and with two small daughters on her hands, she was too busy even to listen to the radio. The Cuban missile crisis, the jailing of the Russian spy William Vassall, the arrival of satire on British television in the shape of *That Was The Week That Was*, the rocking of the Macmillan government with the Profumo scandal and the recording of the first Beatles record, 'Please, Please Me' were of little consequence to Jack and Lesley Panayiotou. They waited for their new baby, Jack secretly hoping for a boy after two daughters. Their waiting came to an end on 25 June 1963 with the arrival of a boy, to be named Georgios Kyriacos. Today, nothing marks the fact that 73 Church Lane is the birthplace of a music legend.

The first few years were happy and uneventful for Georgios. Nothing was to change much until 1969 when the family was uprooted in the first of many subsequent moves, as the Panayiotou family gradually became more prosperous. Having worked hard for others for more than a decade, Jack felt he knew the restaurant business well enough to risk the security of an employee's modest wage for the chance of greater independence and reward. He gave up his job and with two other equal partners opened a small restaurant of his own, the Angus Pride in Edgware, Middlesex. The business was soon profitable and before long Jack found himself better off. But now he worked longer hours than ever, turning up to unlock in the morning and sometimes not leaving until the last customer made his way home. Often he was not in bed before the early hours. The restaurant was open seven days a week and there was not enough in the business to employ anyone to cover for him, so he was continually away from his growing family.

Still, he did make time to develop a strong bond with his children, in particular his son Georgios. In his autobiography, *Bare*, George Michael says that he always respected his gentle father and that he never had any reason to fear him. But he was sorry that he did not spend more time with him. As a young boy he had longed to go on long walks in the park like other boys did with their fathers.

As soon as the new restaurant was established, Jack Panos decided to move out of the cramped confines of 73 Church Lane. The Panayiotou family moved slightly northwards to the lower middle-class surroundings of Burnt Oak, in Edgware, and a semi-detached house with a garden, which Jack bought with a mortgage of £4,000. This was the first time that Georgios, now aged six, had enjoyed the delights of a garden and, like all small boys, he liked getting up to his knees in mud. And he developed an early interest in natural science. Family and friends remember him exploring the garden, covered in dirt, rooting around under bushes, his short legs and shorter trousers filthy in mud, as he collected ants, worms and other insects for closer inspection.

An often recounted Panayiotou family story tells how, shortly after moving to Burnt Oak, very early one Sunday morning and still in his pyjamas, the intrepid would-be naturalist went out into a nearby field to collect specimens. And while he grappled, poked and prodded his way through the grass, he sang to himself, blissfully unaware that he was being watched by a neighbour. Lesley, shocked when she was informed her son was not in the house, went running out to bring him in. As he grew older, his interest in nature and wildlife flourished, a passion that, he later explained, stemmed from a family visit to Whipsnade Zoo made when he was about four. All he could remember about it was that it was the first time that he had seen a goat.

By the dawn of the Seventies, Jack Panos was enjoying the fruits of his labours and as soon as he could afford it he returned to Cyprus to show off his wife and children to the family he had left behind. It was an emotional homecoming, with Jack seeing his family in Cyprus for the first time in fifteen years. Jack was now well established in Britain and, inspired by his example, the rest of the Panayiotou family decided that they should join him. In time, he helped all but one of his six brothers and sisters to move from Cyprus to Britain.

George Michael remembers three family trips to Cyprus during his childhood, all taken with Jack's cousin Dimitrios and his young family. Jack and Dimitrios remained close friends, even though they had gone their different ways. Dimitrios had also married and, having returned to his trade as a tailor, moved with his new wife to south London to start a family. Despite the distance between them, the cousins made a point of seeing each other every Sunday, taking it in turns to make the journey.

It was not possible to visit Cyprus every year. Modest holidays taken in Britain were much more feasible, such as trips to the coast at Birchington, in Kent, to stay with relatives of Lesley. Sometimes they would venture the four or so miles to the funfair at Margate.

Being the youngest of the family and the only boy, Georgios was spoiled by his mother and sisters. While he enjoyed all the attention and joined in with the games his sisters used to play, he also learned to get his own way. He became a fussy eater and refused to eat school dinners, preferring instead to take peanut butter and strawberry jam sandwiches, an unlikely combination introduced to him by some American neighbours.

The Panayiotous were a traditional family, who combined the spirit of Jack's Greek upbringing with Lesley's honest working-class values, both of which stressed the importance of the family and encouraged the belief that nothing should be taken for granted. Although they felt comfortably off, Georgios was expected to make his contribution. Instead of being given pocket money as of right, he was rewarded with cash for doing odd jobs around the house.

Georgios was always drawn to music. And one day, much to his delight, he discovered in the garage an old, forgotten gramophone and three records, two singles by the Supremes and one by Tom Jones – they swept him away. It was the beginning of his love affair with pop music. In his autobiography, George Michael says: 'I was totally obsessed with the *idea* of records; I loved them as things and just being able to listen to music was incredible.'

Jack and Lesley were happy to encourage Georgios's fascination with music and, in 1970, for his seventh birthday, they gave him a portable cassette-recorder. It came with a hand-held microphone, which gave him the chance to record himself singing favourite songs and he started recording pop music from the radio. Before long his love for pop music evolved into an obsession.

At the age of ten George Michael bought his first record, by Carly Simon. It was a strange time to become obsessed with pop. With the extraordinary, innovative Sixties left behind, British pop and rock became derivative, theatrical, pompous and silly. Originality gave way to cheap mimicry. The pop music industry turned to glitter and overnight, over-made-up pop stars wearing outrageous flared costumes, sitting atop towering platform boots, were sparkling and screaming for attention. Unapologetic pastiche became the fashion, with cod rock 'n' roll acts like Mud and Showaddywaddy recording all the old rock hits for a new generation. And there was the usual crop of cringe-making novelty records to top the charts, from 'Back Home' by the England World Cup Squad to *Dad's Army* star Clive Dunn singing 'Grandad' and Rolf Harris's sentimental 'Two Little Boys'.

Then there was David Bowie, who showed that there could be substance beneath the dazzling make-up and outrageous costumes. He influenced the George Michael generation with three of the decade's biggest selling albums, *Hunky Dory* (1971), *The Rise and Fall of Ziggy Stardust and the Spiders From Mars* (1972), which stayed in the charts for 105 weeks, and *Aladdin Sane* (1973). And alongside Bowie was the increasingly flamboyant Elton John. While Bowie appealed only to the young, Elton was enjoyed by all ages. He could play hard thumpers like 'Crocodile Rock' but could easily switch to gentle ballads like 'Your Song', 'Rocket Man', 'Daniel' and 'Goodbye Yellow Brick Road'.

Like most young people in those days, young Georgios was drawn to glam rock, though David Bowie was not an especial favourite. He liked The Sweet and in particular their hit 'Blockbuster'. But most of all Georgios admired Elton John. Perhaps he saw a model for his own life in Elton John, one of the most successful singer/songwriters in the world. Behind the outrageous glam-rock façade of Elton John was a shy, modest and anxious Reginald Dwight from the outer-London suburb of Pinner – a gap-toothed tubby young man who had transformed himself with self-discipline and determination into a world-famous pop superstar. Georgios studied Elton John's music, his style and his showmanship and learned from the example.

It is little wonder, perhaps, that since achieving his own pop stardom George Michael has cited Elton John as one of his most important and lasting musical influences. And, when asked to pick his favourite performer from child-hood he names John. However much the young Georgios dreamt of being a pop star, he could not have imagined that there would be a time when he would share the top of the bill with Elton and that they would record a No. 1 song together. Nor that the two men would become close friends and confidants.

Georgios's dreams of becoming a pop singer led him to regularly sing into his tape-recorder and make up new songs, borrowing styles from the charts of the time. But there was little evidence that he had any particular talent for singing or for composition. He did, however, show some early promise as a musician, when, at the age of seven, he was encouraged by his parents to learn the violin. He persisted with violin lessons for six years. Though he has since admitted that he had no interest in the instrument and he found learning it a chore, his early contact with music proved most valuable.

Equally tedious as violin for the young Georgios were the private Greek lessons his parents, and in particular his father, encouraged him to take every Saturday morning. Together with his two sisters he was driven in a small van to a dingy classroom in Willesden, where their teacher only spoke to them in Greek. Most of the other pupils were being brought up in a home where there were two Greek-speaking parents and Greek was the everyday language. But to Georgios and his sisters, who had an English mother and whose father was largely absent, it was a largely unknown language. During the lessons Georgios would scribble out notes, but little Greek penetrated his brain and he made no discernible progress. He would often appeal to his parents to let him give up, but it took two years of lessons – and two years of valuable Saturday time – before they eventually relented. As far as he was concerned, the attempt to learn Greek was a total waste of time.

Apart from attending the hated Greek lessons, he was taught little about Greek traditions, surprisingly for the son of a first-generation immigrant. Georgios made very few concessions to his father's Cypriot background, although from time to time, at family weddings and special occasions, he glimpsed a little of the formidable culture which had nurtured his father's roots. At these parties he saw his father spring to life, dancing traditional dances to music played on the Greek bouzouki, a member of the mandolin family, with a glass balanced on head. Apart from admiring his father's agility, such antics left Georgios unmoved. But as time went on and he spent more time on holiday in Cyprus among his father's family, he began to understand a little more of what it was to be a Cypriot Greek.

On one such holiday, when he was ten, Georgios discovered that Greek-Cypriot justice was fast and furious. His family was staying with the Dimitrios Georgiou household when Georgios and his slightly older cousin Andros took to stealing – and were caught. As he explained many years later, 'We completely rifled this shop. It was a game a lot of kids play – you steal something and the next day go back for something bigger. It started off with sweets and progressed to a thirty-two-box carton of toy cars.' What was particularly stupid was that Georgios didn't even like playing with toy cars. The prank earned Georgios a severe thrashing from his father, who was ashamed and angry that his son would behave so badly among his own people. It was one of only two occasions that Georgios was hit by his father – the other some time later for being greedy when he whined that he wanted a torch.

There is little to suggest that George Michael is part-Greek today. Despite the trips to Cyprus and the half-hearted Greek lessons on Saturdays, he has largely turned his back on his Greek roots. He has joked that the only thing that links him to Greeks is the fact that he is hairy. But Michael readily acknowledges that one lasting influence of being the son of an immigrant, the absence of his father, who needed to establish himself in a new country, ensured that more than other children he came under the influence of his mother. He would always turn to her for advice about his life. As he has explained, 'My father was the typical Greek who comes to London and works twenty-four hours a day, so his views were never impressed on me when I was very young. I always saw it through my mother's eyes in terms of what I should be after.'

Until her death in 1997, Lesley Panos remained Michael's closest friend and the main influence upon his life. As her only son, she treated him with special affection and he returned it in full measure. She stood between him and his father's often blunt ways. He was brought up by her as someone special and he thought of her in the same terms. It was she he was to turn to whenever he wanted to break away from the traditional working life expected of him by his father. It was she who backed him when he decided to follow his instincts and try to make a career in the music industry. It was the close bond between them which inhibited him from forming close friendships with girls. It was to protect his mother's feelings that he persistently refused to be drawn on his private feelings about love and sex. And it was his mother's love which inspired so many of his love songs. After her death, he would explain, 'My mother's soul is in every song I have ever written.'

It was Jack Panos's hard work and business acumen, however, which drove the family. His success in the restaurant business meant that by the early Seventies he was able to move once again to a larger, more opulent house in a smarter neighbourhood. The new home in

Radlett was a large detached house in the depths of leafy Hertfordshire. It was far removed from the humble rented flat above the launderette where he had started life in Britain. And a higher income also opened other avenues to the Panayiotou family. Jack and Lesley began to consider sending Georgios to a private school, in order to give him the good education they had never had. Georgios, however, had other ideas. He felt that moving to a private school would remove him from his friends and somehow turn him into a product of a system, which he thought of as affected. So, much to his parents' horror, he refused even to sit the entrance examination.

The new house in Radlett was in a poor state of repair and it took the best part of a year for workmen to make it habitable. In the meantime, the Panayiotou family lived above Jack's restaurant, where a daily diet of steak and thick-cut chips followed by sticky Greek puddings and endless helpings of ice cream quickly changed Georgios's shape. Always a chubby child and much taller than most boys his age, the new diet caused him to balloon. This added to his insecurities, for he also thought he was ugly. The run-up to puberty did not find George Michael in best shape. He had dark bushy eyebrows, unruly frizzy black hair and, because he was short-sighted, he wore uncompromising heavy-rimmed spectacles.

The planned move to Radlett inevitably interfered with Georgios's schooling. While living above his father's restaurant, he began his secondary education by going to the local Kingsbury High School, but after completing only his first year Georgios had to start at a new school.

By the mid-Seventies Jack Panos's business took off. He had added a second restaurant on the Edgware Road, in north-west London, and soon opened others. It was a dream come true, a poor Greek Cypriot who, through hard work and application, becomes a self-made millionaire. And while Jack accepted the burdens of a successful entrepeneur, he was determined to reap the benefits. His family were given the best of everything and Jack indulged himself with the trappings of wealth, including a racehorse. Years later, when George Michael was himself a self-made millionaire, he helped his father buy the ultimate present, his own racehorse stud-farm.

The children, too, were indulged like never before. In 1975, Georgios was given a drum-kit for his twelfth birthday, an extravagant present. It was every boy's dream and was the most expensive thing he had ever been given. But before long it lay ignored and forgotten. Whatever else the young Georgios was to become, it would certainly not be a drummer. The same year the family moved again, to the affluent surroundings of Bushey, in Hertfordshire. It was everything Jack and Lesley had dreamed about – leafy, spacious and private. But to Georgios, who was on the verge of becoming a teenager, it seemed as dull as hell.

Georgios could not disguise his lack of enthusiasm for the move. The joys of an outer-London suburb were the opposite of what he had in mind. He was on the threshold of an exciting life when the closer to the centre of London he was the better. He was already tasting the delights of the big city on his doorstep when he saw his pop idol, Elton John, in concert. It was his first experience of a big pop concert with huge swaying crowds, the loudest of music, smoke and all the usual effects of Elton John's stage act and it left a lasting impression. And at much the same time he made another discovery: sex. Although one account of his childhood suggests that he lost his virginity at just twelve years of age to a much older girl, more plausible perhaps is the version given in his autobiography, in which he confirms that at around this time he started waking up to his first sexual experiences. But there were no girls involved. Instead he confesses that by his thirteenth birthday he had become a 'compulsive wanker'.

There was also a new school to go to. He started at Bushey Meads School on 9 September 1975. It had a good reputation among parents in the neighbourhood for solid, old-fashioned teaching and was a tolerant place, operated along informal and relaxed lines. The house move meant that he started at the school late, but he was considered bright enough to be placed in the top stream of the second year. Like most late-comers in similar situations, he faced the problem of adapting to his new surroundings and catching up with the work covered in the first year.

His first day at the school was to be significant. Georgios Panayiotou – large, awkward and insecure – was self-conscious as he made his way through the school gates. He felt he was bursting out of his smart new Bushey Meads uniform of dark green blazer, green sweater, white shirt, school tie, grey trousers and black shoes. In the first break he made his way out into the playground and caught sight of a chirpy, good-looking boy standing on top of a high wall, loudly challenging other boys to knock him off. The boy's name was Andrew Ridgeley. Georgios had never played King of the Wall before, but he soon got the hang of it and, using his height and his weight, he reached up and yanked the boy down to the ground. As he later recalled, 'I threw him off and he hit his head. He was one of the rowdy ones in the class, so that was a major breakthrough. Everyone respected me after that, until they realized it was a fluke.'

Like the first meeting of Robin Hood and Little John, this bruising encounter in the playground led to a remarkable friendship between the two of them. Ridgeley, who was five months older than Georgios, was quick to take the new boy under his wing and from that moment the two of them sat next to each other in classes, usually nearer the back of the room than at the front, to avoid the teacher's attention.

It was perhaps no accident that the two boys should get on together so well, for they discovered that they had a number of things in common. They were both the sons of immigrants. Ridgeley's father, Albert Mario, was half-Egyptian and half-Italian and had come to England to work. Here he met and married an English schoolteacher, Jennifer, and before long they started a family. Andrew was their second son, born in Windlesham Maternity Home, Surrey, on 26 January 1963. Albert was employed by a film camera company and worked hard to get on in his new country. By the time Andrew was five the Ridgeleys moved to a maisonette in Egham, then to the gentility of Bushey so that Andrew could take advantage of the good education to be had at Bushey Meads School. Georgios and Andrew soon became the best of friends, the young Ridgeley coining the young Panayiotou's nickname, Yog, which came from Georgios's sisters' pronunciation of his name, 'Yorgos'. Before long Ridgeley had lengthened Yog to the name by which everyone would soon know him in the corridors of Bushey Meads School: Yoghurt.

Their friendship continued in the hours after school.

But for some reason Georgios was reluctant to introduce his new friend to his parents and it was a full year before he took Andrew home. Georgios was right to be wary. Lesley found it difficult to hide her indifference to the grinning Ridgeley who by reputation was a lazy boy in constant trouble. She did not want her Georgios to waste his education by hanging around with a ne'er-do-well. By this time Lesley was working part-time for Jack as a secretary, which meant that Georgios came home to an empty house. After meeting Andrew Ridgeley the first time she made it known to Georgios that they were not to return to the house together while she was at work.

Andrew Ridgeley was well aware of how Lesley Pana-yiotou felt about him. As he recalled, 'I don't think his mother particularly cared for me at first. I never understood what it was she didn't like. Maybe she was just frightened for her boy. But she should have known that it was going to turn out all right.'

That was far from clear. Georgios was an intelligent boy with good exam results and university within his grasp. His parents longed for Georgios to study hard and through good education achieve everything that had eluded them in their lives. One look at Andrew Ridgeley and they were alarmed that all their hard work and planning could be put at risk by a silly friendship with a silly boy. What was worse, Andrew Ridgeley appeared to be doing his utmost to lead Georgios astray.

2

Musical Youth

By the time Bushey Meads School broke up for the summer holidays in 1976, Georgios and Andrew Ridgeley were inseparable. At school they had shared the same infantile sense of humour, the same disregard for teachers and indifference to serious study. The long vacation which stretched out ahead of them meant they now had endless time to waste together. They stayed in their bedrooms for hours, listening to music and making humorous tapes, adding their own shaky drums and guitar to snatches of songs and jingles recorded from the radio.

Both dreamt about fame. Andrew Ridgeley, an athletic young man, had once fantasized about becoming a professional footballer, but no longer. Although he was a fearless skateboarder and had injured himself many times, once even breaking his nose, he had left it too late and knew that he did not have the rigorous discipline demanded by life as a professional sportsman. All his football ambitions evaporated. But he still hankered after fame and thought that it could come within his grasp. He was impressed by Georgios's knowledge of pop culture and soon began to share his fascination with music and the notion of pop stardom.

Georgios had just turned thirteen and was besotted with

pop music, pop stars, pop radio and the pop charts. Although he showed little interest in any other subject, when it came to pop music, particularly when watching *Top of the Pops*, BBC television's weekly national chart programme, he became keen and earnest and concentrated hard.

Both boys shared the same likes and dislikes. Their favourite star was undoubtedly the extrovert showman and rocker Elton John, whose first No. 1 hit, 'Don't Go Breaking My Heart', sung with Kiki Dee, stayed at the top of the charts for most of that balmy summer holiday. Another favourite was the ultra-theatrical band Queen, which also boasted an outrageous frontman, Freddie Mercury. Queen were a sensation that year and their orgasmic, pseudo-operatic anthem 'Bohemian Rhapsody' stayed in the charts for seventeen weeks – nine of them at No. 1.

It was significant, perhaps, that Georgios and Andrew Ridgeley preferred such camp and extravagant acts to the more conventional bands. They were not impressed by the Swedish band Abba, with their string of jangling hits that year, such as 'Fernando' and 'Dancing Queen'. And other lightweight chart-toppers of the year, such as The Wurzels, Brotherhood of Man, Showaddywaddy, Demis Roussos and Cliff Richard, left them cold.

It was Ridgeley who first suggested that the two of them form a band. And he persisted in the notion until Georgios finally came round. Neither of them had any idea what the music industry might demand. Their ambition was more simple than that. Having decided against trying to be a top-flight footballer, Ridgeley turned to pop stardom as the quickest way of achieving fame and a fortune. At this time the idea was not a serious ambition, more a summertime fantasy until the drudgery of school and their normal lives resumed.

Georgios was slightly younger than Ridgeley and he was impressed by his older friend's determination to form a band. But while Georgios thought that Ridgeley had the necessary confidence and good looks to be a pop star, he felt that it was way beyond his own capabilities. He lacked Ridgeley's easy confidence and was convinced that he was not good-looking enough. But that summer the seed of ambition was planted in both of them. And when they returned to Bushey Meads school in September, they decided to persist.

That autumn Georgios made the first moves to improve his appearance. He started taking an interest in fashion, in both clothes and how he looked. This determination to smarten up proved George's first tentative steps out from under Ridgeley's shadow. When Georgios had first attended Bushey Meads he wore glasses and appeared awkward, large and clumsy. This disastrous combination was magnified by the fact that he was impossibly self-conscious. But a year on, he started to take more pride in his appearance. And as he started to look better, so his confidence grew. He was still seriously large, but while he couldn't hide his bulk, he made a start on improving the rest. Under his sisters' expert tutelage he learned to hide his sporadic acne eruptions with creams, keep his frizzy hair under better control and even pluck wayward eyebrows.

A full school year later, by the beginning of the summer of 1977, he was ready to change his image more drastically. Frizzy perms for men had been pioneered by the soccer star Kevin Keegan, and in the mid-Seventies many young

British men followed suit. Before long Georgios also got himself a perm, and his uncontrollable curls were transformed.

He swapped his unflattering spectacles for contact lenses. Contacts were expensive, but Georgios persuaded his parents to spend the money. Jack and Lesley agreed, thinking that doing without his glasses would help him come out of himself. Sure enough, the lenses improved Georgios's self-image and his confidence grew. And he was changing physically, too; the overweight, bespectacled, self-conscious schoolboy was giving way to a good-looking, assured young man. The school disco, which once seemed to Georgios a place of potential humiliation and shame, was soon to become a place of endless opportunities.

Not that Georgios was ever first on the floor. Even without glasses, he was still too self-conscious to get up and dance around in front of his highly critical classmates. That sort of courage he left to Andrew Ridgeley, whose confidence and natural exuberance meant that he never spared such things a thought. To encourage Georgios to join him, Ridgeley began rehearsing simple dance routines with him at home, co-ordinating their movements to the disco hits of 1977, of which their favourite was Donna Summer's anthem 'I Feel Love'.

That year Summer was at the height of her success on both sides of the Atlantic and had become a gay icon on the back of her disco music – a lucrative position she lost spectacularly some years later when she made ill-judged remarks about AIDS which offended and alienated her many gay fans. Back in 1977, though, 'Could It Be Magic', a disco reworking of Richard Harris's psychedelic epic

'MacArthur Park', and 'I Feel Love' all found success in first gay clubs, then straight discos and ultimately the national record charts.

The summer of 1977 was one of the hottest since records began and it seemed that the whole country was in party mood, triggered by the national celebration of the Queen's Silver Jubilee. The up-beat atmosphere fuelled the wave of disco sounds in the charts until one honourable exception: on 16 August rock music lost perhaps its greatest legend when Elvis Presley died at his home, Gracelands, in Memphis, Tennessee. Presley's recording of 'Way Down', which was released posthumously, gave him a final No. 1 in Britain.

There were other momentous events during 1977. That autumn Georgios had his first, brief romantic encounter with a girl – who shared his mother's name. He met Lesley Bywaters, a fellow pupil at Bushey Meads School, at a party in October. Georgios was so nervous about what to do that he allowed her to take the initiative and she quickly made her feelings known. When they first met she complimented him on his eyes. He was insecure about his looks and, believing that she must be making fun of him, he took offence. And it was not until her friends reassured him that she was being sincere that he started talking to her.

He remembered: 'She took off my glasses and said, "Haven't you got beautiful eyes?" And I was convinced she was taking the piss out of me, so I just got up and left the party. And that was it. And I was actually in between her legs at the time.'

With a little coaxing from Lesley, Georgios got round to asking her on a date and for six weeks or so they went out together and thought of themselves as boyfriend and girlfriend. They liked to dance and met up with friends at Bogart's Club in Harrow, where the resident disc jockey was Gary Crowley, who was to become a successful Radio One deejay.

Looking back on the relationship with Lesley Bywaters from a distance of twenty years, the singer said: 'We both liked dancing a lot and we often used to go down to a disco in Harrow, which we managed to get into because I looked quite a bit older than I really was. Going out with a girl for the first time in my life made me even more conscious of my appearance than I had been previously and I used to make sure I was always very well-dressed – or, at any rate, what I thought was well-dressed at the time.' He dedicated his 1996 BBC Broadcasting House performance to her.

However, the affair was not made to last. The closest the two of them came to physical intimacy was some clumsy cuddling and some faltering kisses. To mark their first four weeks together, Georgios bought Lesley a copy of one of his favourite disco hits of the time, Chic's 'Dance, Dance, Dance', which was in the Top 10.

By the time the next musical fashion had taken over the discos of Harrow, the love affair was over. Both sides of the Atlantic were set alight by the excitement of the disco film *Saturday Night Fever*, which featured the most spectacular dancing scenes since Fred Astaire and Gene Kelly. It was an enormous box-office success. The film established disco as the dance music of the late Seventies, made swivel-hipped John Travolta the latest sex symbol and propelled the Bee Gees into an unlikely comeback with a string of falsetto hits, all taken from the soundtrack, among them 'How Deep Is Your Love?', 'Stayin' Alive' and 'Night Fever'. The soundtrack song compilation remains the bestselling movie album of all time. Caught up in the global craze, Georgios and Ridgeley practised even fancier footwork in their bedrooms, trying their best to emulate Travolta's steps.

When the summer holidays ended in September 1978, the two boys returned to Bushey Meads School with anything but academic work on their minds. Their teachers were not surprised to find that the two of them had little intention of applying themselves to serious study, even though 'O' level exams loomed at the end of the school year. Instead of knuckling down to some work to make up for the years they had already wasted, Georgios and Ridgeley regularly bunked off classes for days at a time.

Georgios was soon turning a profit from his truancy, taking the Underground into central London to busk in tube stations, where the echo provided an acoustic which disguised the thinness of his voice. A favourite pitch was at Green Park Station on Piccadilly. He was often partnered by David Mortimer, a friend who owned his own twelve-string guitar and, like Georgios, thought of himself as a budding musician. Their repertoire tended to be familiar hits by Elton John, The Beatles or David Bowie. And now and then they slipped in songs they had written together. Although busking was great fun, it was also illegal and Georgios and Mortimer rarely performed for longer than twenty minutes before they were moved on by the police or by Underground staff.

It was a dangerous business for a schoolboy, yet he felt better about himself than ever before. He later recalled:

31

'Looking back on it, the confidence I had there for a short period of time is amazing. Because I still looked absolutely horrendous, I was way overweight, really not attractive at all, and yet I had more confidence when I was sixteen than I have ever had. I looked gross, but when I looked in the mirror I felt great.'

Georgios's parents were devastated to learn of their son's truancy. When Jack Panos heard what was going on he determined to put a stop to it and made clear he disapproved of his son's dreams of becoming a musician. Panos had worked in restaurants long enough to meet those whose ambitions for stardom ended in waiting tables and he did not want to see his son go the same way.

Despite this lack of interest at home, Georgios kept busking. It overcame his crippling shyness – the street performances gave him confidence. Forcing himself to sing and play before an audience of strangers proved to him that he could be an extrovert and the centre of attention. And performing was frightening; it made him feel more alive. Along with stage fright came a sharp surge of adrenalin. And when he made mistakes, which he often did, it didn't seem to matter.

At the end of a day playing to passers-by the two trainee buskers split their takings. This money Georgios added to the odd sums he earned from babysitting and other jobs to pay for nights out in central London. He and Ridgeley and sometimes Mortimer frequented various discos. Their favourite was Le Beat Route in Greek Street, a dance club with more glamour, kudos and street credibility than most, thanks to the pop celebrities, such as Steve Strange or the members of Spandau Ballet, who sometimes dropped by.

Georgios and Ridgeley still talked about starting their

own band, but Georgios said he was in no hurry and he found it increasingly difficult to keep the impatient Ridgeley and his pop ambitions at arm's length. When Ridgeley asked when they would form their band, Georgios said it would have to wait until after they had taken their 'O' levels.

That summer, after the exams, they discovered that neither of them had worked hard enough to do very well. Georgios passed five 'O' levels, but Ridgeley didn't even achieve this. For him the exams marked the beginning of the end of his formal education. Though Ridgeley returned to Bushey Meads briefly in September 1979, within a month he left to attend the more liberal and informal Cassio Sixth Form College in Watford where, it came as no surprise, he also failed to apply himself, admitting to his friends that he was only taking 'A' levels to avoid having to start work. He later boasted, with some pride, that in his two years at Cassio he failed to read a single book.

However, for Georgios, leaving school straight after 'O' levels was never an option. His father had always been keen to push Georgios's academic progress since he had refused to enter the entrance exam for a private school. But despite disappointment Jack and Lesley Panayiotou did exert enough pressure on their son to make him agree to stay on for 'A' levels in English Literature and Art for a further two years. This did not impress the rebellious Ridgeley, who was neither surprised nor persuaded it was a good idea. Ridgeley became angry when Georgios announced that they would now have to wait until he had sat his 'A' levels in the summer of 1981 before they could form their band.

Ridgeley exploded. He insisted they form a band at once. Despite a lack of musical talent which prevented him setting up a band on his own, Ridgeley used his considerable charm to persuade Georgios to start one right away. The result was a half-baked group put together with friends called The Executive. They were joined by Ridgeley's older brother Paul on drums, David Mortimer, who renamed himself David Austin, on guitar, and another friend, Andrew Leaver.

The Executive was a shaky ska band and it was doomed from the start. They were clinging to the coat-tails of a fading ska revival which had been headed by bands like The Specials and Madness. The band regularly met to write and rehearse material, mostly setting up their equipment in the front rooms of the Panayiotou and Ridgeley households. Neither family welcomed the noise, so even deciding where to meet caused endless squabbles. However, from the midst of such chaos some creative energy emerged. The boys worked on the band's ska theme, a song called 'Rude Boy', which Georgios and Andrew Leaver wrote at the first rehearsal. They also came up with a ska cover of a Sixties hit by American crooner Andy Williams, 'Can't Get Used To Losing You', as well as setting the standard schoolboy piano piece by Beethoven, 'Für Elise', to a ska beat.

The Executive played the first of their few public gigs in the Methodist Church Hall in Bushey on 5 November 1979, for the local scout bonfire night event before an audience of loyal friends, well-wishers and local teenagers curious to know what the fuss was about.

Despite the promising debut, the fireworks set off as the evening's finale were nothing compared to the sparks which were soon flying between Georgios and Ridgeley. Ridgeley's new-found freedom as a complacent Cassio College drop-out had made him difficult to deal with. He soon began endlessly hanging out with college friends in a succession of dingy bedsits. He started experimenting with drugs, but, rather than improve any latent creative abilities he may have had, they transformed him into a gibbering, tedious bore. The friendship between the two boys was strained to breaking point and before long they only saw each other when the band met for rehearsals. For the following year or so, The Executive became the only thing keeping their friendship together.

In December 1979 they performed in front of their friends at the Bushey Meads School Christmas party and by the New Year the five-piece band became a four-piece when Andrew Leaver decided to leave. Undaunted, the next move for the remaining members of The Executive was to record their first short demo-tape. Anxious not to venture into the unknown, they chose the three songs they could play best: 'Rude Boy', 'Can't Get Used To Losing You' and 'Für Elise'.

It was only a short time before Georgios started skipping school to meet up with Ridgeley and tout the rough demo-tape around central London to the offices of the biggest names in the music business. They did not bother to make appointments ahead of their visits on the correct assumption that no one would agree to hear their work anyway. But knocking cold on doors of music executives did not get them far and they were repeatedly sent away with a polite but firm refusal. There were numerous false dawns when, after waiting what seemed an eternity, they were ushered before – and were briskly dismissed by –

unimpressed talent scouts who rarely bothered to hide their indifference.

Ridgeley was less affected by the repeated rejections than Georgios, who took badly every standard record company letter of regret. Then Ridgeley tried a different tack. He and his family lived in Chiltern Avenue, Bushey, and in the same road, at No. 25, lived Mark David Dean. Three years older than Ridgeley, Dean was already working in the music industry and his snazzy, garish suits suggested he was a fast rising star making all the right connections. Ridgeley soon made sure he was on nodding acquaintance with Dean, who drank in the same local pub, the Three Crowns.

Dean was indeed doing well. Having joined the music business as a school-leaver, he had served his apprenticeship with Bryan Morrison's publishing company before moving to The Jam's music publishers, And Son, where he began finding talent of his own to exploit. One of his earliest signings was the mod band Secret Affair, who promptly repaid him with a Top 20 hit, 'Time For Action'.

Dean was a busy, hyperactive fellow and he could not resist being flashy with both his clothes and the wads of cash he carried around with him. Ridgeley was awestruck when he saw him in operation at the Three Crowns. Before long Ridgeley plucked up enough courage to approach Dean to tell him about The Executive. He asked whether Dean would listen to their demo, but Dean gave him the cold shoulder. Ridgeley, always a charmer, tried another tack. He turned his attentions to Dean's mother, his neighbour, passing her the demo-tape and pleading with her to persuade her son to listen to it. In order to please his mother, Dean did eventually get round to listening to the tape and promptly declared both it and the band to be dreadful.

Undeterred, Ridgeley kept asking Dean to listen to the band for himself, either in rehearsal or on one of the few occasions they got a booking. Dean's message was clear: he saw no future in the music industry for Ridgeley, his old school friend Georgios or their amateurish four-piece band. Before long, Dean would be eating his words.

One night in January 1981 at the Three Crowns, Ridgeley met Shirlie Holliman, another former pupil at Bushey Meads School who had been in the year above the two boys. She was a pretty blonde girl with a bouncy personality and a Bohemian, independent streak. She had dabbled with the punk scene and was currently working with horses as a trainee instructor. And, most impressive to the boys, she had her own car.

That chance encounter in the pub was the beginning of a two-year romance between Ridgeley and Shirlie Holliman and she was to become an essential part of the boys' success. She would go on to become a star in her own right as half of the pop duo Pepsi and Shirlie before marrying, and starting a family with, Martin Kemp of Spandau Ballet.

Success for Georgios and Ridgeley was still some time off. They took their recordings to a succession of smaller record labels but discovered a total lack of interest in their work. They could not even get bookings to perform locally. Without a glimmer of success of any sort, the four members of The Executive found it difficult to sustain

37

their enthusiasm. And when David Austin and Paul Ridgeley left, disillusioned and bored, The Executive finally folded.

At first Georgios and Ridgeley considered the set-back to be temporary and they tried to team up with a few older local musicians to form a new band, but it too lasted only a short time before it fell apart. Had Ridgeley not been determined to succeed, the collapse of the second band might have put an end to the two boys' ambitions. Instead Ridgeley persuaded Georgios that they must carry on on their own. For Georgios, this meant listening to the constant pessimism of his father who repeatedly told him that he was wasting his time entertaining ideas of pop stardom.

If success in the music business appeared as far away as ever and the prospect of earning his living seemed increasingly remote, this did not spur on Georgios to study at school. He was a persistent truant, often only attending one of his seven scheduled lessons each week. Despite these prolonged absences, however, he coasted easily through his 'A' levels in the summer of 1981, gaining fair passes in both subjects. Considering the lack of attention he had paid the teaching staff and the scant revision he had done, it showed a considerable naked intelligence and one that might flourish given a university education. Yet with these barely adequate qualifications under his belt, he decided, aged eighteen, that he was finished with formal education. His parents were profoundly disappointed. They would certainly have liked him to go on to university and be the first generation in either family to win a degree. But Georgios was adamant. And so, as the long, hot summer of 1981 set in, Georgios Panayiotou took one last holiday before he started looking for a job.

First he embarked on several weeks of lazing around at home with Ridgeley and Shirlie Holliman. Between going swimming in Watford – where former Executive song-writer and guitarist Andrew Leaver was working as a pool attendant for the summer – and hanging out for hours in the local McDonald's, making coffees or milk-shakes last as long as possible, the trio spent their days listening to music in Georgios's bedroom and trying to write songs or practise dance routines. When the weeks of doing nothing came to an end, Georgios found himself a job as a labourer on a building site. It proved to be short-lived. He found the physical exertion too tough and lasted just three days before leaving to find something less strenuous to do.

He was successful in that. He worked by day as a cinema usher and by night as a disc jockey in the Bel Air, a dinner-dance restaurant near Bushey. He loathed most of the music he was expected to play to the middle-aged, middle-class customers at the restaurant, and he hated the banal patter he was expected to provide between records. None the less he stuck it out for nine months. Just like at school, Georgios found it difficult to apply himself and impossible to toe the line. He regularly turned up late for work at the Bel Air and before long he was ignoring the music selection rules, surreptitiously introducing his own taste in records to the play-list.

Ridgeley, too, was finding it difficult to adjust to the world of work. Leaving Cassio College empty-handed, he also drifted in and out of casual part-time work. At college, to supplement the limited pocket money he received from his parents, he had sometimes worked as a cleaner. And when he left college, he briefly went to work for the same company as his father, in the warehouse of the camera firm. Deciding he did not suit a daily working routine, it was not long before he threw in the job and signed on for unemployment benefit. He was to be out of a job for the next eight months.

It was unthinkable that Georgios would take the dole; his parents would never have allowed it. And there were other differences between the two boys which became evident at this time. While Georgios earned £70 a week and would give £25 to his parents, blowing the rest on records, going out or whatever took his fancy, Michael's later autobiography *Bare* suggests that Ridgeley had no qualms about turning to his family and friends for handouts to supplement his dole cheques.

But while they had gone their different ways a little, throughout this time Georgios and Ridgeley met regularly to try to write songs. That arrangement became almost impossible, however, when Ridgeley and Shirlie Holliman began living together in Peckham, south London, twenty miles away from Georgios's home. A few weeks before Christmas they moved to a shabby flat in the basement of her aunt's house. It was in a dreadful state of decoration and the facilities were alarmingly basic, among them an outside lavatory.

The move was highly inconvenient for writing songs together. Some days Shirlie and Ridgeley would drive over to the Panayiotous' house in Bushey; on others Georgios made the long and tedious journey by public transport. But, difficult though it was, they persisted in their determination to become singer-songwriters and the sessions did eventually bear fruit.

Three songs in particular took shape in those early

collaborative sessions. It had long been obvious that the only real songwriting talent between them belonged to Georgios and one of his earliest efforts, a ballad called 'Careless Whisper', was written on the bus on his way to work at the Bel Air. Uncharitably nicknamed 'Tuneless Whisper' by his sister Melanie, the song would prove pivotal to his eventual success. The haunting ballad slowly took shape in his mind over three months; he returned to it and refined it in the most unlikely circumstances – such as whenever he was travelling on buses or trains. Michael clearly remembers it was when paying his fare to a bus conductor that inspiration arrived for the solo saxophone line which perforates the melody and provides the haunting back theme on the record.

When Georgios reached Ridgeley's flat in Peckham, he played the song to Ridgeley, who began adding the guitar chord sequence, and before long 'Careless Whisper', the cornerstone of their eventual success, was finished. And, although it was almost entirely Georgios's work, he was happy that, when it was published two years later, it carried a rare joint songwriting credit – a tribute to Ridgeley's powers of perseverance and encouragement.

Like many other songwriters, Michael from the start drew upon his personal experience, writing largely autobiographical lyrics. And if in this case the emotional context of 'Careless Whisper' wasn't pure autobiography, then the setting and circumstances certainly were. Standing behind the disco console at the Bel Air night after night gave the song its theme and its well-observed emotional angle. 'Careless Whisper' tells of first love and its betrayal. It demonstrated Michael's exceptional economy and poetic skill with lyrics, particularly the haunting refrain: 'I'm never gonna dance again. Guilty feet have got no rhythm'. The song tells of a desperate man, a wayward romantic who gambles and loses, and it is easy enough to envisage scenes being played out nightly on the dancefloor at the Bel Air right in front of the young, observant George Michael (though it could be any of the thousands of other, equally anonymous smoky nightspots the world over). The song closes with a last-minute plea trailing off in darkness and heart-wrenching. And to support the important wailing sax line, the songwriter intertwined a delicate counter melody on acoustic guitar. The finished song was to become an instant classic. But it was evident from the start, too, that 'Careless Whisper' worked best as a solo. That fact hinted at the direction the partnership between George Michael and Ridgeley would eventually take. And it meant, too, that if they were going to perform together they would need some more upbeat material written for the two of them to sing.

The other songs written in those dank bedsit months were 'Wham! Rap' and 'Club Tropicana', which drew upon the boys' limited experience of life. And they also tried to inject some rebel yell into the songs. Though Georgios and Ridgeley were from very stable and comfortable backgrounds, the songs were intended to be taken as edgy, anarchic and challenging.

As the backing vocals chanted the refrain 'D.H.S.S.', the initials of the state benefit agency, the Department of Health and Social Security, 'Wham! Rap (Enjoy What You Do?)' ridiculed young people who chose to work rather than make life one long party. It was a sign that the young Georgios was quietly rebellious and resented his father's heavy-handed admonishments. He found song-writing a good way of expressing his frustration.

According to Ridgeley, the song's catchy main refrain, 'Wham, Bam, I am a Man', was dreamt up as he and Georgios were dancing one night at Le Beat Route. After that, the rest of the song soon fell into place. The song starts with a rhythmic clapping back-track before launching into an appeal to young people to make the most of their lives. To chants of 'Get down' and 'Dig this thing' came the bold ricocheting storyline glamorizing the care-free life of a man without work on the dole.

In stark contrast, 'Club Tropicana' was a breezy song conjuring up a hedonistic pool-side lifestyle way outside the experience and the pocket of a genuinely unemployed young person in Britain. After a bass-led instrumental intro, the song opened with a colourful evocation of a hedonistic disco club in a tropical country. The boys were painting a paradise where visitors could want for nothing.

Although Georgios genuinely found Ridgeley useful as a sounding board when songwriting, the logistics of travelling the long and tedious journey between Bushey and Peckham soon became too tiresome. The cost of the train and bus tickets quickly ate into Georgios's limited funds and after barely a month Ridgeley had tired of the novelty of living away from home. He and Holliman quickly discovered that living together was harder work than they had expected and Ridgeley was missing many of the comforts and luxuries he enjoyed at home. So, while they continued dating, he and his girlfriend moved back to Hertfordshire, to live with their respective families.

For Georgios events were turning in the opposite direction. Having grudgingly stuck it out at his job at the Bel

Air for nine months, he was secretly relieved to be sacked. As time went on he began to drift in late and could no longer bring himself to stick to the restaurant's bland playlist. The sacking caused him some grief at home, where his father was fast running out of patience. Jack Panos dreaded Georgios wasting his life as he drifted in and out of work, so eventually he gave his son a six-month ultimatum: get a recording contract or be kicked out of the family home to fend for himself.

3

Young Guns Go For It

At the end of 1981, the Human League topped the charts for five weeks with their million-selling 'Don't You Want Me'. For Georgios Panayiotou and Andrew Ridgeley the song's lyrics had a special pertinence; it seemed that no one wanted them or their songs. Then, in the space of just a few weeks, everything started going right.

They decided to commit to a demo-tape snippets of their first four songs – 'Careless Whisper', 'Wham! Rap (Enjoy What You Do?)', 'Club Tropicana' and 'Come On!' – with a view to finding a record company who would take a risk on them and their material. Recorded in a makeshift studio in Ridgeley's front room on a modest four-track Portastudio unit hired for a day for £20, the twenty-second snatches of the songs were rough but gave a hint of the duo's potential.

Next they needed to find themselves a name. They tried out dozens on each other, but kept returning to one, using the title of one of their songs for inspiration. They tried 'Wham Bam!' and 'Bam Wham!' but in the end settled on plain 'Wham!'.

Once again the boys began their tour of record company scouts and agents in and around Soho in London. They spent days on end touting their new tape from door to door. Just as their demo-tape for The Executive had met with indifference, so their latest efforts were also dismissed by an endless stream of faceless A&R (artists and repertoire) executives. Ironically, their first real breakthrough was to come from someone much closer to home.

Mark Dean, who had declared Ridgeley, Michael and The Executive to be dreadful two years before, was given a copy of the new demo-tape and discovered, much to his surprise, that he was impressed by their efforts. Dean felt the two boys had improved out of all recognition and now had the makings of something special. Instinct told Dean he should sign them up at once.

Something similar had just happened to Dean himself, who had recently joined CBS Records as a young talent scout with a golden touch. From his company And Son he had moved to the A&R department of Phonogram Records, where his first major signing paid off sensationally in 1981. He signed Marc Almond and Dave Ball, a duo from Leeds calling themselves Soft Cell, and their debut single, 'Tainted Love', quickly climbed to No. 1 in twenty-one countries, including topping the charts in Britain for two weeks in September. Dean also signed what was then a five-piece band from Sheffield, ABC, and within a year they had notched up a No. 1 album in Britain with their debut release *Lexicon of Love*.

On the back of that success, Dean found himself being wooed by Warner Brothers Records. Then CBS started making approaches. Dean played hard to get. He didn't want to be signed to CBS; he wanted his own record label. The CBS managing director, Maurice Oberstein, and the senior management may privately have thought Dean excessively arrogant, but his early successes spoke for themselves, as did the approach by Warner Brothers. At the end of the day both CBS and Dean got what they wanted, with Dean running his own label funded by the American company. The details of the deal, however, were to have long-reaching consequences for Dean and, as it happened, for George Michael.

In the deal CBS agreed to finance Dean's Innervision Records in return for worldwide rights to the label's output, which CBS would manufacture and distribute. Dean signed a five-year contract with CBS, giving him an annual non-returnable advance of £150,000, rising to £199,650 by year five in 1987. CBS would also lend the company an additional £75,000 to £99,825 per year to ease cash-flow and cover capital expenditure, though this was specifically forbidden to be used to pay Innervision artists' advances or to produce master tapes, and would be repaid, with interest, by the end of the fifth year.

By the terms of the contract, Innervision received a royalty rate of 8 per cent for singles sold in North America and 11 per cent for Britain and the rest of the world, from which Dean had to pay his artists and producers. Dean failed to grasp the crucial implications, however, of one part of the contract. Twelve-inch single releases would earn Innervision royalties only when sales exceeded 30,000 in each territory. On albums Innervision fared slightly better, with an escalating scale of royalty rates: for the first three years, Innervision would receive 15 per cent of home sales, 13 per cent on North American, Japanese and German sales and 12 per cent for any other territories. In year four, so long as sales passed 100,000 units, album royalties would increase on a sliding scale by between 1 and 2 per cent in each area. Other clauses were equally likely to minimize royalties to Innervision, including a halved royalty on vinyl pressings in any colour other than black, because black records were the cheapest to produce.

Dean later acknowledged that the CBS deal was horribly stacked against him. 'At twenty-one to twenty-two years of age you don't really care about the deal, you care about getting recognized,' he said. 'You feel you can make money any time. I felt I just wanted to get recognition for my talents and that's what happened.'

Dean signed up with CBS and opened his company on 25 November 1981, in offices on the third floor of 64 South Molton St, in the fashionable Bond St boutique area, aided by his assistant and accountant Shamsi Ahmed. He was eager to get started and sign up the first artists to his fledgling label. Within three months, in February 1982, he approached Georgios and Ridgeley with a contract.

Inspired by the prospect of signing with Dean, Georgios and Ridgeley set about honing and rehearsing their material with renewed energy. Early in March Wham! received a draft of the proposed contract with Innervision and passed it to lawyer Robert Allan of Sims, Muirhead and Allan (a friend of Georgios's father), for perusal. After consideration, Robert Allan replied to Innervision's lawyer, Paul Rodwell at Halliwell Rodwell, that the two young men, to be known as Wham!, were prepared to accept the contract but only with several key changes. For instance, clauses claiming a stake in band merchandising and the right to deduct producers' fees from future Wham! royalties were to be deleted.

Georgios and Ridgeley were rehearsing at Halligan Band Centre in Holloway, working on a new demo version of 'Careless Whisper', when Dean telephoned to say the contracts were ready and he would bring them over for signature without delay. It was 24 March. Dean arrived soon afterwards, waving a contract in the air and asking that they sign at once, calmly blaming his impatience to make a deal on the need for Wham!'s first single to be included in the new CBS release schedules. Although the contract included some amendments it was little more than a draft contract and had not been signed off by lawyers acting for either party.

The young men later admitted they were in complete awe of Dean at that time. They saw him not as the relative newcomer to the music business that he was but as an experienced big shot. They went with Dean to a nearby greasy spoon cafe and gaily signed the five-year contract put in front of them.

It was a contract from hell. No one who had taken legal advice would have signed such a one-sided deal. Like so many young recording artists before them, they had been so eager to strike a deal that they were willing to sign away their earnings to a stranger who gave them their first step upon the ladder of fame. Dean stood to gain the over-whelming share of any money they were to make. Although Michael and Ridgeley would each receive an immediate one-off payment of £500, which sounded good to the young men who had never earned large amounts of money, even that sum was to be repaid from future record earnings.

Thereafter they would receive a royalty of just 8 per cent for single and album sales in Britain, only 6 per cent from albums sold in all other territories and a derisory 4 per cent for singles sales in other territories. What they also failed to notice was that 12-inch-single sales, a burgeoning market in the world of dance music, wouldn't earn the duo anything at all. There was eventually a little relaxation in their terms. After the third year, if they should survive in the business that long, album royalty rates would rise to 9 per cent and 7 per cent, and in year four they would increase to 10 per cent and 9 per cent.

The contract committed the teenagers to at least one album a year for five years, with a second to be delivered each year if demanded by Dean. Most punitive of all, there was a clause that should the band split, Innervision was entitled to a further ten albums from each artist. Georgios and Ridgeley did not read the contract carefully; they were largely innumerate and had little idea what royalty rates were or whether they were fair. They only had one thing on their minds: the lure and excitement of the music business which they were just entering.

Michael has said of this business disaster: 'One of the most incredible moments of my life was hearing "Careless Whisper" demoed properly, with a band and a sax and everything. It was ironic that we signed the contract with Mark that day, the day I finally believed that we had No. 1 material. The same day we signed it all away.' He said he believed that if he didn't sign that day 'it could all slip away'.

However, George Michael has also said that he viewed the contract as being so one-sided that it could be to his advantage if he and Ridgeley did make it big. As he explained: 'I thought it was good we had a lousy contract because it was so bad that, from the day we signed it, we were probably going to get out of it.'

As Dean returned happy from the signing to his plush South Molton St offices, an even more elated Michael and Ridgeley returned to their rehearsals. To celebrate, Michael had both ears pierced; before long he would always wear two hoop earrings.

Even then Dean had not finished with them: barely before the ink was dry on the contract, Dean added a rider in a letter, despatched the following day. The letter gave details of the payment of album advances, starting with £2,000 upon delivery of their first album, £5,000 for the second, thereafter rising by £2,500 increments for the next five albums. The seventh would earn the band £20,000, followed by £5,000 increments up to £35,000 for the tenth.

Then there were some weasel words at the very end of the document, saying: 'In the event of any conflict between the standard artists conditions attached hereto and made part hereto and the provisions of this letter then the provisions of this letter shall prevail. Please confirm you [sic] agreement to and acceptance of this agreement by signing below as indicated.'

Once again, Georgios and Ridgeley happily signed the document and returned it to Dean. Robert Allan, the lawyer who had been advising them, was appalled to discover they had signed the contract before showing it to him and he wrote to Michael in those terms.

Wham!, as they were getting used to calling themselves, set about finding a publishing deal for their music. They approached a new company which boasted two of the most revered behind-the-scenes names in British music. Morrison-Leahy Music Group was a partnership between Bryan Morrison and Dick Leahy. Morrison had once managed the Pretty Things and later became an agent and publisher by founding And Son (which handled The Jam's catalogue, and for which Mark Dean had worked). Leahy had been involved across the board in the industry. He worked for Philips in the sixties, guiding the careers of artists such as the Walker Brothers and Dusty Springfield, followed by a stint as managing director of Bell Records in the early Seventies, handling some of the biggest teen idols of the decade, including David Cassidy, the Bay City Rollers, The Drifters, Gary Glitter and Showaddywaddy. He had also formed his own highly successful label, GTO Records, which made a fortune turning out Donna Summer's disco hits in 1977.

Dick Leahy smoked large expensive cigars and oozed confidence. He was suave and tanned, tall and slender, with grey hair and dark eyebrows, and wore handmade suits from Savile Row. Friends likened him to a healthy version of Soho's boozing columnist, Jeffrey Bernard. Leahy remembered his first meeting with Michael and Ridgeley: 'It was very much a duo that came to see me. It wasn't George Michael with Andrew Ridgeley just sitting there. They walked into the office and almost without hearing the songs you knew they were going to make it. There was something very, very special about them.'

The feeling was mutual. Michael was immediately at ease with Leahy, who would quickly come to be one of the few people Michael would trust and whose opinion on business matters he would seek. Endorsed by Mark Dean, the publishing deal between Wham! and Morrison-Leahy was signed in April 1982.

With a recording contract now in place, the young men began to work on their live act. They were still practising dance routines in the Panayiotous' front room, backed by Shirlie Holliman and a friend of Shirlie's, Amanda Washburn.

Washburn was just sixteen and was soon deemed insuffi-
ciently committed to the band and dropped in favour of
Diane Catherine Sealey, a twenty-year-old from Deptford,
who later became better known as Dee C. Lee.

To prepare the duo for pop stardom, and give them a
chance to hone their routines as well as learn to work an
audience, the troop was taken on the road for a series of
public performances in nightclubs organized by the CBS
Club Promotions department. Escorted by a woman CBS
executive, the quartet would appear in as many as six clubs
a night, invariably before unappreciative drunken audi-
ences. The newly honed Wham!, with female backing,
mostly sang what was planned to be their first release,
'Wham! Rap (Enjoy What You Do?)', the song thought
most likely to do well in the charts.

While Wham! now had a record company and a music
publisher, they were still being managed by themselves,
Georgios taking the lead in making business decisions.
Georgios was set on managing his own affairs. He was
determined to make music on his own terms. The price of
this fierce independence, however, would be the lack of
scrutiny of their recording contract by a business manager
with knowledge about the industry. However, both Georgios and Ridgeley agreed on the approach. But their
existence soon came to the attention of Jazz Summers, a
manager of various music artists, who approached them
through Morrison-Leahy.

Summers was tall and dark-haired. He overcompensated
a receding hair-line at the front by growing it longer at
the back. He had come into the business relatively late in
life, having served nine years of a twelve-year army enlist-
ment before returning to civvy street towards the end of

the Sixties. He tried his hand as a musician, then a manager, first with Richard Digance and in the late Seventies with a few struggling punk bands.

Richard Digance, a folk-singing comedian, who had appeared on television a number of times, remembered: 'Jazz was very personable. He was my best friend for quite a few years. He always used to pull more girls than his artists, which used to annoy everybody, because he had the gift of the gab and was a very likeable bloke.'

Summers first heard Wham! on a demo of 'Wham! Rap' at the offices of Island Records. He approached Mark Dean and a few days later met Georgios and Ridgeley at Innervision's offices. It was a very formal affair which from the start was not likely to reach agreement. Summers explained later he 'couldn't get anywhere near them', 'it was closed ranks'. Dean telephoned him after the meeting to confirm that Wham! were not interested in signing him as their manager. Since Summers's only claim to competence had been managing Digance, a folk singer, they hardly felt him suitable. But more importantly Georgios was confident of his own creativity and did not look for close direction of his musical progress.

The recording of 'Wham! Rap (Enjoy What You Do?)' was arranged by Bob Carter, an experienced producer who had impressed Dean with his work with the group ABC. On the session Georgios sang, Ridgeley was on backing vocals and played guitar and they were backed by session musicians. The single was scheduled for release in the early summer. The only thing to do between the recording and the release was for Georgios to settle on a stage name. It seemed simple. Georgios was shortened to

George and he liked Michael, his uncle's Christian name. So it was 'George Michael'. But Georgios could not make up his mind. He dithered. And while he did so the first 20,000 or so pressings of 'Wham! Rap' carried the credit 'Panayiotou/Ridgeley'.

In June 'Wham! Rap' was released and the verdict of the public was swift. It didn't even pierce the country's Top 100 bestselling single charts. It was time for a rethink. Michael set about writing a follow-up song entirely on his own. Ridgeley was proving to be no help at a time like this. Before long a song was finished and ready to record. Michael was convinced that he knew exactly how the new song, 'Young Guns (Go For It!)', should sound and he insisted that he be the co-producer, with Steve Brown. He knew enough from his home recordings and from watching the early recording sessions to realize that record production was mostly a matter of choice of sounds and that he, not Brown, was this time going to make those choices. The song was an effervescent pop-soul dance song telling of two inseparable pals about to split up as one of them is to be engaged. Michael's economical anti-marriage lyrics homed in on a bleak future for the husband-to-be, up to his neck in debt and nappies.

Michael would return to the theme of the importance of independence to a single man many times in his career. He established for himself a bachelor lifestyle that forwent a wife and family. In private he was coming to terms with his sexuality. In public, for the time being, he would be linked to an occasional girlfriend. One regular female companion for a while was singer Pat Fernandez, a bubbly girl who was one of Malcolm McLaren's Buffalo Girls and a backing singer for Culture Club. She adored the company of gay men and took as a compliment their calling her a 'fag hag'.

The song was more obviously commercial than the first and it contained some wit which young people might relate to, so expectations of the record were high. When 'Young Guns' was released in September, along with a club dance video, sales started off well. It entered the Top 100 at 72, then climbed to 48, before slipping back a little to 52. With the record faltering in the charts, Dick Leahy intervened. Leahy explained: ' "Wham! Rap" had flopped. That was a great disappointment to Michael – not so much to me because I always thought it was a good lesson to learn at that stage. But then "Young Guns" started going down the charts and that was a dangerous time.'

Leahy set about getting all his many contacts in the industry to give the record a quick fix. He wanted Wham! and 'Young Guns' to be the buzz in the business for the next seven days. The full panoply of record promotion was pulled out. The most important thing was to get the song heard. He got record salesmen to pull in favours with managers of stores to get 'Young Guns' played repeatedly in record shops to provoke demand. Sales began to pick up. By the following week it had bounced back up the charts ten places to No. 42. The leap was enough to win them an appearance on the most watched television pop show in Britain, the BBC's flagship *Top of the Pops*, where the song was billed as a climber.

The Thursday night broadcast of *Top of the Pops* had become the engine of the music industry. The enormous national audience ensured that any artist to appear would be granted an avalanche of sales. To this end record companies were happy to do anything to get an artist on the show, even flying over expensive music acts from the United States. For the BBC this free glamour ensured that the show maintained high ratings within an absurdly small budget.

The importance of the appearance on *Top of the Pops* was not lost on George Michael, who like many people of his age had been a fan of the show since an early age. In preparation for the big event, he and Ridgeley worked tirelessly with the two backing girls to perfect their dance routine. On the night the show was to be recorded, they were faultless. Michael and Ridgeley overflowed with sex appeal. They wriggled around, parading their lithe bodies, and flashed their white teeth in broad smiles. They were plainly having a good time and looked like two young men out on the town, looking for dates for the night, flirting with the cameras. The impact on the young female audience in the studio, and their millions of counterparts at home, was electric. The performance was highly charged and extraordinarily confident; in industry terms it was an exceptional debut. The effect on sales was dramatic and immediate. By the following Monday CBS was inundated with more than 30,000 orders for the single. The following weeks 'Young Guns' hit 24, then 10, then 4, and on 4 December it made No. 3. Wham! had arrived. They had hit Top 10 success with their second single. Now all they had to do was sustain the success.

They decided the best way to exploit this sudden explosion of interest was to quickly re-release 'Wham! Rap', a song which was already recorded and pressed. Perhaps it would make some headway if it were given a second chance. However, Leahy said they should forget the original recording of the song and remix it to better effect. So Michael and Ridgeley set about improving the mixture of vocals, backing and beat. When the song was tightened to everyone's satisfaction it was re-released along with a black and white video in which Michael and Ridgeley donned black leather jackets.

It was a different story the second time around. The remixed 'Wham! Rap' entered the charts on 15 January at No. 63. 'Young Guns', though slipping, was still selling well enough to be at No. 18. With the two young men receiving a great deal of personal publicity and with Wham! now almost a national phenomenon, 'Wham! Rap' was almost guaranteed to be a success. It quickly bounced up to 41 in the charts, then reached 34 and 11 before entering the Top 10 at No. 9. On 19 February it reached its peak at No. 8.

People started asking what the lyrics meant. There had been some publicity about how the record was irresponsible in encouraging young people to leave work and live a more hedonistic life. When asked by the *New Musical Express* how he reacted to the charge, Michael said: 'What we are saying in the song is that unemployment is there. And, for all the campaigning that everyone is doing, it's not going to go away. What we should be doing is educating people into how to deal with it, how to use their leisure time. If you're not going to be able to do anything about it, you might as well have a laugh about it. We managed to do that quite well when we were on the dole. It is possible to have a reasonable time without that much money.'

Wham! now set out to find a third hit in a row. It was still possible that they would be dismissed as a two-hit wonder unless the new record also made the grade. They decided the safest thing to do would be to consolidate their reputation with a song as close to 'Young Guns' as possible. The result was 'Bad Boys', which continued to play on the partying soul-boy image. The lyrics were loaded with autobiographical references, as if Michael was purging the years of pressure from his father to do well by including a verse which questioned the right of parents to be judgemental about their children.

Michael has always been dismissive of the song and the single. He explained: '"Bad Boys" isn't a song that I'm particularly proud of as a writer. I feel it's very formularized. It was written in the wake of "Young Guns" and I feel very proud of "Young Guns". To try to emulate it in "Bad Boys", to get that same feel I wrote a formula record, which I've never done before or since, so it's an area that I try to forget about. But it's very hard to forget about because it was a big record for us.'

Michael also deemed the video for 'Bad Boys' his 'all-time career low'. It was directed by Kenneth Anger, the eccentric American film director and film historian whose cult book *Hollywood Babylon* charted every scandal of the early film industry, and it seemed laughably homoerotic, making the duo look like pretty-boy puppets in the music industry. While Michael was fully aware of the benefits of flattering the large numbers of homosexuals who frequented just the sort of dance clubs his music was written for, some years later he said of the video: 'It was just the worst thing in our entire career. We look such a pair of wankers in it. How can anybody look at those two people on screen doing what we are doing in that video, with all those camp dancers prancing around in the background, and think it's good? We lost a lot of ground with that video.'

Whatever Michael's private thoughts about the song and the video, 'Bad Boys' entered the chart at No. 37 on 14 May and four weeks later gave Wham! their highest chart success to date, peaking at No. 2 for a fortnight, and was only kept off the top slot by The Police's four weeks at No. 1 with 'Every Breath You Take'.

Before long Michael was working on the band's debut album, *Fantastic.* Session musicians were drafted in to work with the duo, most notably Deon Estus on bass, Anne Dudley on keyboards (and brass arrangements) and Robert Ahwai on guitar. The album was produced by Michael with Steve Brown.

For the best part of six months Michael had been working hard and playing harder still. On top of the excitement of his success was the pressure to continue writing songs, to perform on them, to make stage or television appearances, to meet the press and attend publicity meetings. And on top of all that he had to tend to the increasingly hectic business side of the band's affairs. Wham! was now in such demand he felt he could no longer cope.

He was drinking and smoking heavily, several packs of twenty cigarettes a day, which began to take its toll on his throat and voice during the recording sessions. And at night he took to escaping from the pressures of work by going out. He spent most nights in a drunken haze at parties or in London clubs, such as the Wag in Wardour Street, or the Camden Palace, a lavishly converted theatre. Unlike Ridgeley, he no longer felt comfortable going to young, lively pubs because he was pestered by people who recognized him. Although on the stage he seemed to be outgoing and confident, this ebullience disguised his shyness, which was as acute as ever, and he was always anxious not to be caught with his defences down. Above all he dreaded the prospect of appearing to others to be out of control. In the crowded clubs he could skulk around in the shadows, lost in the smoky mayhem, and he could drink as much as he needed to lose himself and relax. This unlikely anonymity, lost in a crowd, allowed him respite from his crippling self-consciousness.

The problem with his shyness was that it threatened to inhibit him from going out on his own to hear the music playing in the clubs. The need to know what was going on, to hear what people are dancing to, has remained with him. It is important for his own songwriting to keep abreast of what people like. But clubbing all night and working all day soon proved bad for his career – and bad for business.

Michael realized that the business side of his career was slipping beyond his reach. Too many people wanted to get hold of Wham! for deals and performances. It was time to find a business manager. Between them, Morrison-Leahy and Mark Dean's Innervision Records were fending the enormous number of media approaches and bookings in Britain as well as from other territories such as Germany, Italy, Australia and Japan.

Dick Leahy took Michael aside and told him that he was now putting everything at risk if he did not take managerial advice. With the worries of business being taken care of, Michael could concentrate on what he did best – writing and performing songs. Michael was persuaded and the hunt was on to find a good manager.

First he and Ridgeley approached Andy Stephens of CBS International, but he was not interested. Wham! were still relatively unknown in North America – the largest pop market for an English-speaking act – but they hoped that they had shown enough potential to attract interest from an international manager with strong American connections. They approached Ron Weisner and Freddie De Mann who managed Michael Jackson and Madonna. They agreed to meet and, while declining a long-term arrangement, they agreed to take care of their interests in North America for a short time, with an option of further involvement.

This arrangement was too good to pass up, but it left them looking for a short-term solution for their British interests. Robert Allan of Sims, Muirhead and Allan agreed to act as manager for three months until Michael and Ridgeley had found a more permanent replacement. There were further advances from the unflagging Jazz Summers, but these were met with the same response as before. Summers had made some headway through 1982 by managing a band called Blue Zoo, which notched up some chart success of its own that year, but this achievement did little to impress Wham!. Bryan Morrison told Summers the reason: 'You're not big enough.'

Undaunted, over the next few months Summers set about bringing more experience to his management bid for Wham!. He teamed up with Simon Napier-Bell, who had managed The Yardbirds (which spawned the rock giants Ginger Baker, Jeff Beck and Eric Clapton), Marc Bolan and, more recently, Japan. Napier-Bell first met success in the music industry when he co-wrote the mid-Sixties classic, 'You Don't Have To Say You Love Me', which gave Dusty Springfield her only No. 1 single in

1966. By the time he joined Summers, Napier-Bell was in his forties. He had sun-bleached fair hair and appeared perpetually fit and tanned. He had a lazy left eyelid, which gave him a slightly shifty look, but this did nothing to sap his confidence. He lived in a luxurious apartment in Bryanston Square, near Marble Arch in west London. Napier-Bell had seen Wham!'s confident debut on *Top of the Pops* and was impressed by the duo's likeable chemistry. He and Summers drew up battle plans to win over Wham! and formed Nomis Management exclusively for that purpose.

At the time, as 'Bad Boys' slowly fell from the British charts that summer, Michael and Ridgeley found themselves famous but still not very rich. With three hit singles under their belt but still without money, they began to appreciate just how bad were the terms of the contract they had signed with Innervision Records. They were so short of income that they had to continually ask for small handouts from Dean, who controlled the purse-strings.

Michael and Ridgeley decided to have a crisis meeting with Dean to improve their terms. They were successful now and a great deal of money was being made by everyone except them. They saw him in his South Molton Street office and asked for a review of the suffocating terms of the contract. Dean promised to look into it, but warned that he was in turn linked to tough terms imposed on him by CBS Records. If CBS agreed to renegotiate terms with him, Dean said he would he be able to relax his tight grip on their flow of income. Dean must have known that the likelihood of that happening was zero. CBS was approached but said there was nothing to discuss. Dean told them the bad news: there could be no renegotiation of the contract between Wham! and Innervision.

Until that moment few outside Michael's immediate family had ever witnessed him lose his temper. Now he expressed his utter contempt for Dean and said that there was no future in the relationship. Michael waged a caustic vendetta against Dean. If he saw him in a pub or in a nightclub he would shout abuse at him and Dean repaid like with like. It was, however, necessary quite often for Dean to speak to Michael about business, so Michael adopted another ploy to irritate the man whom he passionately believed was exploiting his talents. It was a ploy he would use time and again in the future. He simply would not respond to any attempt by Dean to get hold of him. Michael decided never to deal directly with Dean again. He would only speak to him, and then only if absolutely necessary, through an intermediary.

When the album was finished, Michael went off the rails. He became obsessed with the contract and the unfairness of it all. He told himself that he was making a fortune for other people. It preyed on his mind. Some of those around him became worried about his health. He seemed on the verge of a nervous breakdown. Even Ridgeley, who left everything musical to his partner, was finding it difficult to carry on partying in the face of what was going on.

Michael made one final, desperate bid to force Dean to renegotiate the contract. He stole his own music from the Innervision office. As he explained later: 'I took the master tapes of the first album and hid them at home. Mark said he was going to send the police round to get them.' Michael was persuaded to acknowledge that what he had done was technically theft, even though he had written the music and performed on the recordings, and he surrendered the tapes to Dean. His fight with Dean would have to continue some other way.

Once more Michael turned to Dick Leahy, who argued again that all this could be best sorted out if he were to find a proper manager. An avalanche of media requests was continuing to go unanswered at a critical time for the new band. Summers and Napier-Bell heard what was happening and saw their chance. They started a charm assault on the two men. Summers started leaving daily messages on their home telephones, asking them to make contact. Eventually they called back, and after several arranged meetings which the young men failed to turn up to, Napier-Bell's Marble Arch flat eventually played host to the first informal meeting between Wham! and Nomis. Napier-Bell did not ask them to sign up right away. Instead he asked for the chance to propose to them a plan of action which Wham! could consider, beginning with Nomis working on a strategy for the group, to be presented over supper. And so, over an Indian dinner at the Bombay Brasserie, an expensive restaurant near Gloucester Road, Kensington, a deal was struck. Wham! agreed to hire Nomis on a short-term contract in return for 12 per cent of their earnings. Nomis was to look after their interests in all territories except North America, where Weisner and De Mann would continue for the time being.

It was a relief to the two men to get their business problems sorted out before the release of Wham!'s debut album, *Fantastic*. But before the album could be signed off, Michael and Ridgeley wanted to make one final addition. They dedicated the album to two childhood friends who had both died young: Andrew Leaver, one-time member of The Executive, had died of cancer; a few months later

Paul Atkins, a school chum of theirs, was killed in a car crash.

Michael hated attending the funerals of such dear friends and not just because he felt a profound loss. He felt that his new-found celebrity disrupted the peace of the occasion. He said later: 'Nearly everyone at both of those funerals was still a teenager. It completely freaked me out and what was really horrible about it was that we came back to these funerals as little pop stars. It was sick because we had that kind of attention. People weren't vulgar about it or anything but we were there to pay our respects to our friends and to their parents, to be part of the mourning, and you can't help noticing when you get that kind of attention.'

The success of *Fantastic* was instantaneous. In the week of release Michael went to Cyprus and it was there he learnt that the album had gone straight to the top of the British charts, where it stayed for two weeks in July. It continued to sell well enough to stay in the Top 100 album charts for 113 weeks.

Although the sales of *Fantastic* were immense, the album was not received well by some critics, who pointed out its most noticeable shortcoming – a lack of new material. The album included the first three single releases as well as 'Club Tropicana', which was about to be released as the band's next single. The other four tracks were 'Come On!', a frothy reworking of the least promising song on the early demo-tape, the bass-line led 'A Ray Of Sunshine', a breathy but minor love song 'Nothing Looks The Same In The Light', and a cover of The Miracles' standard, 'Love Machine'.

By the end of July Wham!'s fourth single, 'Club

Tropicana', was released. It was an intoxicating sex 'n' surf mix, an exotic cocktail evoking a pool-side party, another anthem for hedonistic youth. Exactly a month after its release it reached No. 4. Accompanying the song was a video filmed on location in Ibiza, one of the Balearic Islands off the coast of Spain. The boys wore shorts and sported their now traditional golden tans, but intricate dance routines had been quickly abandoned and the two backing girls merely struck arty poses.

The diminishing contribution of the girl backing singers, along with their relegation to mere modelling assignments on videos, was not going down well with Dee C. Lee. She left the band and began working with the Style Council, where she met her future husband, Paul Weller, before successfully going solo. Her Wham! replacement was Pepsi DeMacque.

It must have seemed a safe bet to industry insiders that within a month or two Wham! would be back with their first No. 1 single. But fate intervened, and it would be almost a full year before Wham! returned to the singles charts.

When Michael and Andrew signed with Nomis Management, cautiously committing them to a trial three-month period only, they instructed their new managers to find a way of resolving their dispute with Mark Dean and Innervision Records as a matter of urgency. Until that had been achieved, Michael refused to hand over any new material to Innervision.

During the impasse, Michael decided to try laying down the definitive version of a song which had been in his mind for a long time, 'Careless Whisper'. He agreed to work with the legendary record producer Jerry Wexler at the Muscle Shoals Studios in Alabama, USA. He arrived in the United States to discover Wham! enjoying their first success in North America. 'Bad Boys' made the Billboard Top 100 singles chart and stayed for nine weeks, peaking at No. 60 for two weeks in September.

Wexler was responsible for turning out hits such as 'I Say A Little Prayer' and 'Son Of A Preacher Man' by Aretha Franklin, and chart-toppers for Ray Charles, Wilson Pickett, Percy Sledge and others. Michael flew to meet Wexler at his home in Texas before heading to the Alabama studios. Although everything appeared to go well, it was clear to Michael during the recording that Wexler had such a smothering style that he would not be able to provide the magic needed for 'Careless Whisper'.

Michael said later: 'Through no fault of Jerry's the record just didn't come up to what I'd wanted. I'd gone to Alabama and literally been so overwhelmed by his track record that I felt that I should just sit back and allow things to happen. Which really was a mistake, because however good it was, it wasn't actually going to be the record that I initially had in my head.'

Michael returned to Britain and thought about the recording. At first he had quite liked it, then he began to feel uncomfortable. He felt it was 'too middle of the road' and 'just didn't have any of my character on it'. Others felt the same way, among them Dick Leahy.

The dispute between Wham! and Mark Dean was heading for a climax. Dean had reluctantly begun talks with Nomis, but then suddenly pulled out without explanation. Dick Leahy said later: 'A deal was almost struck with Innervision. We came to a renegotiation of the contract that Michael and Andrew would have been prepared to accept. And then Mark found he could not accept it [and] changed his mind.'

After a further crisis meeting between Morrison-Leahy and Nomis made no progress, it was agreed that Michael and Ridgeley would hire Dick Leahy's lawyer, Tony Russell, to work at ways of breaking the contract. Jazz Summers explained: 'He was the toughest one around and good at this kind of litigation.' The result was a twenty-four-page letter sent by Tony Russell to Mark Dean in October stipulating in exhaustive detail the extent of his clients' dissatisfaction with Dean and Innervision. It concluded that as their signatures had been obtained by 'fraudulent misrepresentation' the contract was not legally binding – they were thereby free of their contract with Dean and Innervision, and it was the intention of Wham! to sign with another record label.

Incensed, Dean responded with his own legal broadside. He sought an injunction to prevent Wham! from signing with a competitor before the case could come to court the following month. Dean's case was heard when Innervision Limited *v.* Panayiotou and Ridgeley came up before Mr Justice Harman at the Royal Courts of Justice in the Strand, London. The judge granted Innervision an injunction against Wham!, preventing them from signing with another label. However, Mr Justice Harman added that, should the allegations listed in Tony Russell's letter turn out to be true, the contract should be promptly dissolved.

The hearing only served to drive a greater wedge between Dean and the Wham! camp. The saga was further inflamed when Dean scheduled, without George Michael's approval, a Wham! EP for release by the end of the year, the record that became known as the 'Club Fantastic Megamix'. The EP was simply a medley of three tracks taken from the *Fantastic* album – 'Come On!', 'Love Machine' and 'A Ray of Sunshine'. Michael was furious and asked Dick Leahy to see what he could do to stop the record's release, but he was powerless to help. Since the recordings had already been handed over and published, the rights for the recording had already been granted. Wham! publicly denounced the EP in a press statement and on the Channel 4 music show *The Tube*, urging fans not to buy it. It was a remarkable statement declaring: 'We would be very unhappy to think that any of our fans might waste their money on it.'

Michael also said of the EP: 'It's absolutely disgusting. I just hope the radio doesn't play it. It would be so irritating to hear something you think is so bad.' All the same, the EP sat on the charts for eight weeks, peaking at No. 15 just before Christmas. Then Dean, taking advantage of the slowness of the case against him coming to court, tried to get his hands on the Wexler recording of 'Careless Whisper' for immediate release. This time he was outman-oeuvred by Dick Leahy as the recording had not yet been published. Leahy informed Dean that he was withholding 'first licence' permission indefinitely.

Leahy said of the decision: 'We knew how big that song could be, so it was necessary to upset a few people to stop it.' For Leahy, holding up the release of 'Careless Whisper' was more than just a weapon to get at Dean. Leahy's instincts always told him that Michael could record a better version of the ballad.

Since all new recording was on hold until the legal action was settled and there was more revenue coming in,

Michael and Ridgeley agreed to raise some cash by going on their first Wham! tour of Britain. The band would play a gruelling thirty-one dates in a row in different towns and cities around the country. As funds were tight, Nomis sought sponsorship for the tour. Fila sportswear put up £50,000 on condition the boys performed in Fila kit. Before the end of the tour, Fila was reported to have asked to withdraw from their deal with Wham! because their clothes were too expensive for Wham!'s young fans who had taken to stealing it from shops.

Michael and Ridgeley designed their 'Club Fantastic Tour' as an entertainment package for fans in their early teens. As well as backing by Shirlie and Pepsi, the gigs started with a disco warm-up fronted by Michael's mate from Bogart's Club in Harrow and now a rising radio star, deejay Gary Crowley. During the intermission, old home movies of Michael and Ridgeley mixed with early Wham! footage were projected above the stage.

The tour was largely a family affair, with Michael's sisters Melanie and Yioda along for the ride. They did hair and make-up, while Michael's cousin Andros offered friendly support. There were so many of Michael's friends and relations backstage at one point that some crew nicknamed the tour the Greek-Cypriot Charabanc.

The tour started in Scotland and for the first time Michael and Ridgeley realized the full extent of their following. They were besieged by thousands of fans wherever they went. To magnify their manhood, the two stars put shuttlecocks down their trousers, a stunt which was picked up by the tabloid press.

The tour was only marred by the return of Michael's throat trouble. When the tour reached London his throat was very sore and in need of rest, and by the time of the second concert at the Hammersmith Odeon in London he had lost his voice completely. The show was cancelled. His doctors ordered him to rest his voice for a fortnight while Nomis hastily rescheduled dates. It was the first sign that Michael's health might not stand the full rigours of a life in the music business.

- 4 -

A Scream Act

By the time George Michael and Andrew Ridgeley completed their British tour early in 1984, the dispute with Dean's Innervision Records began to show signs of movement. At CBS feelings were running high at the impasse between their sibling label and the hottest property in British pop. Because of the dispute between Wham! and Dean they had nothing to exploit, no new recordings to catch the tide of excitement.

Executives at CBS began pressurizing Dean to find a solution fast and when there was still no settlement by March they ran out of patience and sided with Michael and Ridgeley. The dispute threatened Dean's solvency. Innervision had already run up legal bills of around £80,000. 'They were going to put in the receivers unless I agreed a deal,' Dean explained. 'There was too much power play going on, too many egos, too many reputations to be scored, and not enough peace-makers.'

When a settlement was finally reached, Innervision was bought out of the contract in a deal which saw Dean receive an undisclosed sum and the retention of a small residual royalty on Wham! record sales. The dispute proved the end for Innervision, whose reputation as a poor business partner now spread through the industry. The company ceased trading a year later. Dean left the country shortly after, eventually picking up a job with MCA in the United States.

Released from their Innervision contract Michael and Ridgeley promptly signed on 22 March to Epic, a subsidiary of CBS Records, on greatly improved terms. According to Simon Napier-Bell: 'The new contract with CBS was effectively the same as if we'd never had a contract. It wasn't a restricted settlement, not the kind you'd do out of court. It was what we'd have got if we'd just gone to sign Wham! give or take one per cent.' He added that, had a settlement not been reached with Innervision, 'Wham! would have faded away'.

George Michael learnt a great deal from the affair. 'A business that generally treats artists disgustingly seems to have been quite reasonable to me – probably because I always had what they wanted,' Michael said of the episode in his 1990 autobiography *Bare*. He added: 'In all its history, CBS has never lost a band. Not through a subsidiary or any other way. We would have been a precedent.' He was speaking too soon. A few years after *Bare* was published George Michael would be trying to pull out of his arrangement with CBS and he would discover the full wisdom of his words.

CBS were quickly rewarded for siding with Wham!. The duo's comeback single, written by Michael during the legal deadlock, was inspired by a hastily scribbled note written before going to bed one night by a sleepy Ridgeley to his mother. It read: 'Wake me up up before you go go', adding the second 'go' to echo his mistake in repeating 'up'. Michael read the note and he realized he had the title of his song: 'Wake Me Up Before You Go Go'. Siobhan Bailey, who worked as their personal assistant, later claimed she was the inspiration for the song, as it was often her job to get Michael and Ridgeley up and ready for work. Siobhan, who wore short hair and was dressed casually but immaculately, had extraordinary powers of organization and regularly worked late into the night at the Wham! offices at 17 Gosfield Street.

'Wake Me Up Before You Go Go' opened with a deep refrain, 'Jitterbug', which also peppered the lyric. The song was pure up-tempo spoof Motown, with colourful imagery such as the line that talks about the sun shining 'brighter than Doris Day'. It had a catchy bass line and an equally catchy chorus.

It was around then that Dick Leahy persuaded Michael to take charge of producing his own music. But there was a problem. Michael had dropped out of 'A' level Music at school and, despite years of violin lessons, still could not read and write music without effort. Instead of writing a score and going to the studio, Michael made his own working demo-tape of 'Wake Me Up Before You Go Go' at home, recording bass and vocals. Once he got to the studio he sang the parts to the musicians. He had taken to carrying a small tape-recorder with him at all times, to capture song ideas whenever they struck.

By producing his own records George Michael freed himself from the influences of others. He could now be certain that the sound the public heard was exactly as he wanted it. Simon Napier-Bell gives another interpretation of what was going on. 'I think when you know what you want and it's not coming, you are forced into production.

Michael was really forced into having to learn production and taking the responsibility for it.'

Everyone agreed that George Michael's production of 'Wake Me Up Before You Go Go' was a triumph and that he had instantly established a sound of his own. Bolstered by this confidence, Michael set about tackling his troublesome ballad 'Careless Whisper'. The song was inspired by a memory from his youth, when he had two-timed a girlfriend. 'Careless Whisper' explored the pain she might have suffered, but also reminded him of the excitement of love he had experienced for the first time.

The recording session was quite different from the controversial Wexler session. Michael worked hard in the studio and found a mood which totally matched his intentions for the song. He added synthesized instrumental backing played by Andy Richards. 'What I basically wanted from him [Richards] was a string sound and that's what I got,' explained Michael. 'Also, we programmed my voice into the computer and the very "airy" bits were done with that.' When he finished, Michael knew that he had at last found the definitive sound. He played it to Dick Leahy, the toughest of critics, who liked it a lot.

After the recording Michael flew to Barbados for a short holiday and to top up his now famous suntan before flying on to Miami to make a video for 'Careless Whisper'. There he stayed at the luxurious Mutiny Hotel in its tacky Luna Dreams suite, replete with trashy disco lighting and mirrors on the ceiling. Ridgeley, David Austin and Michael's sister Melanie came along for the ride.

The video was produced by Carina Camamile and

oozed romance. Set against a glowing sunset and bathed in champagne, Michael romped with two scantily clad models. But during filming Michael was beset by persistent bad hair problems. His hair was longer than usual and had gone frizzy in the humid Florida heat and sunshine. Filming stopped and Melanie cut his hair shorter. He insisted that earlier footage be discarded, taking the shoot £17,000 over its £30,000 budget.

As soon as they returned home Michael and Ridgeley went to work on another Wham! video, this time to accompany 'Wake Me Up Before You Go Go'. The overspend on the Miami video had alarmed CBS, so while it was to be produced by Camamile, the video would be directed on a strict budget by Duncan Gibbons. The Brixton Academy in south London was hired and the two young men mimed to their song amid dry ice before a frantic audience of fans, who were asked to arrive in white clothes with fluorescent accessories to facilitate a spectacular visual effect. Michael, now blond, arrived for the shoot in T-shirt and fluorescent gloves.

Referring to the video in *Bare*, Michael said: 'I think "Go Go" is undoubtedly the most remembered Wham! song – because it is that much more stupid than anything else! I still look at that video and think it worked perfectly for that song. Really poppy, really colourful – it totally captures that whole period. But although I see it working as a video, it makes me cringe for myself. Because what I was then and what I am now – one of them has to be a fake! But I was completely into the idea of being screamed at – I was very young and I can't pretend my ego didn't need that. I was so into it that I didn't realize how hard it would be to come out the other side, because it has never been easy to make the transition from being screamed at to being listened to.'

The single was released on 14 May, for the first time carrying a credit for George Michael as producer. By 2 June it had given the band their first No. 1 in Britain. It stayed at the top for a fortnight and remained on the chart for a further thirteen weeks. And the success of 'Wake Me Up Before You Go Go' was repeated around the world. Starting in the UK, the single topped the charts in nine other countries, including the United States in November. It also earned the duo their first gold disc, for exceeding sales of 500,000.

The duo's return to the charts was accompanied by a PR blitz which saw Wham! grabbing tabloid headlines and front pages on a daily basis. They gladly posed for the paparazzi at fashionable London nightclubs. They began to acquire popular newspaper personas. The more handsome Ridgeley was cast as Jack the Lad. His fame for a propensity to drink himself into oblivion was matched only by his ability to bed one-night stands. Such behaviour was too much for his long-time girlfriend Shirlie Holliman. Though she continued working with the band, her relationship with Ridgeley was called off.

There was evidence that all the press attention about his drunkenness and the endless stream of women was going to Ridgeley's head. Michael said of him in *Bare*: 'He would actually go places where he knew that he would be smashed out of his brains by the end of the evening and that they would get their pictures. He thought it was a laugh – it was only later that they tried to make him look like a real idiot. I was going to places where the press wouldn't be.' Michael's idea of a good night out was to shelter in the anonymity to be found in some of London's lesser nightclubs. Not that he wasn't enjoying himself every bit as much as Ridgeley. As Simon Napier-Bell explained, although Ridgeley was always more 'flamboyantly drunk' than his partner, 'Michael was out and about and misbehaving quite often, yet generally didn't get picked up on in the way Andrew did.'

Then came a story about Ridgeley which he did not like quite so much. The tabloids ran stories for four days about him trying to pass off the bandages covering vanity-inspired cosmetic surgery as a laddish mishap. He slipped off to have his Roman nose reshaped and when he next appeared in public he protested that the dressings were the result of a late-night drunken fracas with his drinking mate David Austin. Ridgeley came to realize that his honeymoon with the press was reaching its end.

As soon as 'Wake Me Up Before You Go Go' was released Michael and Ridgeley went to the south of France for six weeks to write and record their second album, *Make It Big*. Recording in France allowed the pair to work in peace, away from the frenzied fans and scandal-seeking press, and it also offered some attractive tax advantages. They were booked into the Château Minerval studios near Brignole in Provence, home of jazz master Jacques Loussier.

In a taxi on the way to the airport, Michael came up with the melody of a song, 'Freedom', which would prove one of the best on the album. The lyrics, added over the next few days, told of a boy's devotion to his promiscuous girlfriend, confronting her over rumours that she had been seen dating someone else. He asks her to be honest, then admits his undying devotion to her and that he would forgive her anything rather than break up.

Once again Michael called on session musicians: keyboard player Tommy Eyre; seasoned drummer Trevor Morais; bass player Deon Estus; Hugh Burns on electric and acoustic guitar; and horn players Paul Spong, Colin Graham and David Baptiste.

For Michael the weeks in France were a time for intense hard work, often ploughing through the night. But as Ridgeley made no contribution to the songwriting, he took himself off for days at a time, invariably ending up incapacitated by drink. Michael tried to ignore Ridgeley's excesses, but it emphasized the imbalance in the effort between them. The reason for the continuing success of Wham! was George Michael – Ridgeley, incapable of writing the sort of music needed, was enjoying a free ride. Michael explained: 'He was getting totally wrecked, he was so lazy and he just couldn't be bothered. I was working my ass off on that album. Andrew would just turn up for a couple of days, do and few things, fall in the pool. That was the only time that I thought, "Oh, for God's sake, *do* something". I was totally responsible for getting the album out for the autumn and Andrew just couldn't give a toss.'

A welcome break from writing and recording came when the two of them agreed to give an interview to *The Tube*, Channel 4's flagship music show. Filming was to take place in the region's vineyards and Ridgeley flew in, as planned, to meet Michael at the studios the night before. He brought with him two drinking friends. Shooting was scheduled to start early the following morning, when

Michael was horrified to find Ridgeley, having been drinking all night, sitting semi-comatose and fully clothed in a bath while his friends tried to sober him up. Michael was astonished and relieved to discover that once the cameras were rolling Ridgeley instantly composed himself and gave a good performance.

It was during a break from the recording of the album, in a few days taken in St Tropez in the south of France, that Michael met Elton John and his new bride Renate Blauel, a recording engineer John met while making an album in London. It was the beginning of what would become one of the most important friendships in George Michael's life. Before long Elton John would be among his closest confidants.

The credits for *Make It Big* make clear the disparity between the workloads of each member of Wham!. Apart from a joint billing with Ridgeley for writing 'Careless Whisper', and a cover of the Isley Brothers' 'If You Were There', all other songwriting credits went to Michael. He was also named as lead and backing vocals, keyboard player and producer and arranger. Ridgeley was billed simply as 'electric guitar'.

Make It Big was mixed in Paris and London, at the Marcadet Studios and Good Earth Studios, during July, August and September with a view to a high pre-Christmas sale. With just eight tracks and running barely forty minutes in total, the album hardly lived up to its title. The album contained 'Wake Me Up Before You Go Go', 'Careless Whisper', and 'Freedom', all good songs. But beyond that the only memorable song among a weak selection is 'Everything She Wants', which tells of a bad marriage. Epic scheduled *Make It Big* for a November release, to coincide with the band's first world tour, the so-called 'Big Tour', which would start on 4 December at the unpromising Whitley Bay Ice Rink in the north-east of England and later take in Ireland, Australia, Japan and North America.

During the summer months while the album was being mixed, Michael's solo career took off with the 4 August release of 'Careless Whisper'. It contained an emotional dedication to his parents: 'To my mother and father, five minutes in return for twenty-one years'. Within two weeks it was at No. 1 in the UK, ousting Frankie Goes To Hollywood's extraordinary nine-week run at the top with 'Two Tribes', which in turn had knocked 'Wake Me Up Before You Go Go' off the top slot.

His success as a solo artist genuinely took George Michael by surprise. 'Careless Whisper' stayed at No. 1 for three weeks and made it to the top in the US and more than ten other countries. The song gave Epic their first million-selling single in the UK and earned Michael his greatest trophy to date, his first platinum disc. It soon became one of the most lucrative songs in the Morrison–Leahy Music catalogue. But it also brought speculation in the press that the band was on the brink of splitting up, rumours that Wham! tried to quash.

Michael insisted that his solo career would not harm Wham!. 'No one credits you with enough suss to develop two careers – one as a solo person and one with Wham!,' he said at the time. 'What's happening is this. As a solo artist, I want to go more towards soul. If I was left to my own devices, I'd probably try and sound like Marvin Gaye for the next five years. But the important thing is that together we make a pop group.' It convinced few in the industry; it was clear that the end of Wham! was now in sight.

Further bad publicity awaited the band in September when Jazz Summers received a call from the National Union of Mineworkers asking Wham! to take part in a fundraising gala for striking coalminers at the Royal Albert Hall. Michael and Ridgeley, who were on record as having voted Labour in the general election a year earlier, agreed. Soon what the two of them thought of as a charitable gesture submerged them in a wave of adverse publicity.

The frothy, hedonistic style of Wham! sat uncomfortably on a bill alongside more politically vocal bands like Paul Weller's Style Council and alternative comedians like Rik Mayall and Alexei Sayle. To make matters worse, in the absence of a backing band, Wham! mimed their four-song set, amid general derision when the backing recording suffered tape problems. The audience made their feelings known and Michael was so embarrassed that he apologized and offered to refund money to any who bought tickets in the belief that Wham! were going to perform live at the gala. The music press universally derided the Wham! performance and wallowed in the climbdown.

A significant change took place in the management of Wham! in the USA after a rancorous meeting between their American management team, Freddie De Mann and Ron Weisner, and Summers, as a result of which De Mann relinquished any professional interest in the band's affairs. Summers then negotiated for Nomis Management to take control of the band's management on both sides of the Atlantic, allowing the company to represent Wham! worldwide.

Nomis devoted most of 1984 to planning how to win the lucrative American market. Summers and Napier-Bell were well aware that Michael would not be prepared to follow the traditional method of conquering the world's biggest music territory – building a fan base with up to five years of stadium tours.

They turned to Gary Farrow, a persuasive, fair-haired PR specialist from Bromley in Kent. He had started out working for Elton John's Rocket Records label as a record plugger before setting up on his own in public relations. Still only in his late twenties, his clients included Elton John, Paul Young, Bob Geldof, David Bowie and, since the early Dean and Innervision days, Wham!. Although Connie Filippello, contracted by Nomis Management, was engaged as the principal Wham! publicist, Farrow made it his business to line up prime time radio airplay for Wham! records.

His personal devotion to Michael rather than the general Wham! team repaid Farrow with a close friendship. He soon gained unrivalled day and night access to Michael. Michael later became godfather to Farrow's baby daughter Lauren.

In *Bare* Farrow described working for Michael: 'Wham! wasn't a scream act when I started working for them. They were initially very hip. My job was to make them a scream act. And then we all waited for the nod from Michael when he made the decision to stop being a scream act. He knew exactly from day one what he wanted to do, the photographers he wanted to use, the radio shows he wanted to do, who he wanted to represent him, who he didn't and why. He knew what he wanted to do all along.'

As 'Careless Whisper' fell from the charts in October, the duo released their first new single taken from *Make It Big*. The neatly crafted 'Freedom' was the song that seemed to Michael of good enough quality to do well as a single and it quickly earned the band its second gold disc. 'Freedom' entered the chart at No. 3 and went to No. 1 the following week, staying there for three weeks until the *Make It Big* album was released. The music press reviews were mixed, but generally credited the album with improving on their debut album.

Make It Big was launched with £10,000 of champagne at a party at the London nightclub Xenon attended by some of the biggest names in pop. There were members of Duran Duran and Spandau Ballet, Bob Geldof, Nick Heyward, David Cassidy, Sandie Shaw, Lulu, Kenny Lynch, Frankie Howerd and John Hurt. The party was something of a double celebration as that same week 'Wake Me Up Before You Go Go' reached No. 1 in the American singles chart.

The album entered the British charts at No. 1 and stayed for two weeks, remaining in the album chart for seventy-two weeks until March 1986. *Make It Big* was released at the same time in the USA and got off to a slow start, inching its way up the chart to eventually reach No. 1, where it stayed for three weeks, ousting Madonna's *Like A Virgin* at the end of February 1985. As in Britain, *Make It Big* stayed on the Billboard Top 100 album chart until March 1986.

The year ended on a highly emotional note in Britain.

Following a visit to famine-hit Ethiopia, where over 3,000 were dying each day from starvation caused by the drought, former Boomtown Rat Bob Geldof started putting together a charity record, 'Do They Know It's Christmas?' Co-written with Midge Ure of Ultravox, Geldof rallied everyone he knew in the music business to help record it. Many of the biggest names in British pop, including George Michael who contributed one of the lead vocals, took part in the marathon recording session at Sarm West Studios in west London on Sunday 25 November. Conspicuous by his absence from the recording session was Ridgeley.

'Do They Know It's Christmas?' by Band Aid quickly became the biggest hit of the Eighties, going straight into the charts at No. 1 and staying there for five weeks. It sold over three million copies in the UK and, of the single's £1.35 price, 96p, an unprecedented sum for a charity record, went to the cause.

Despite the compassionate message of the song, Michael admitted to feeling uncomfortable with the recording session for several reasons. He said in *Bare*: 'I was very aware of the prejudice against Wham! in there. Everybody in there had said things about everyone else in the press and, to a lot of people, Wham! were the laughing stock of the year. Some of it was jealousy and some of it was genuine lack of respect. But the only person who actually came up and had a go at me was Paul Weller, because of something I had said about Arthur Scargill, the leader of the miners.'

At exactly the same time as the Band Aid effort was released, Wham! put out a seasonal single, 'Last Christmas', written ten months earlier in February, during the period of deadlock with Innervision. The song came about after

Michael had been watching football on television one Saturday night with Ridgeley. A melody had been going round in Michael's mind and he stayed up late into the night to develop his thoughts into a song.

It was released as a double A-side single, paired with 'Everything She Wants', and entered the charts immediately behind Band Aid at No. 2 and held the slot until the middle of January. In a much-publicized stunt, Wham! vowed to give all royalties from the single to the Ethiopian Fund, some £250,000 at the end of the day. The single earned Wham! their first platinum disc and it entered the UK record books – as the first single to sell over a million copies and *not* top the charts. It eventually clocked up one and a half million sales.

'Last Christmas'/'Everything She Wants' was not released in America until March. 'Careless Whisper' was released there on 8 December, this time credited not to George Michael but to 'Wham! featuring George Michael'. It climbed steadily, eventually hitting No. 1 for three weeks in mid-February.

'Last Christmas' did suffer one indignity, inflicted by the American songwriter and music publisher Dick James. In a highly successful music career, James had arranged The Beatles' first TV appearance and later formed Northern Music to publish Lennon-McCartney songs. He had also signed the unknown Elton John and his lyricist Bernie Taupin. He instigated legal proceedings against George Michael for copyright infringement, claiming uncanny similarities between 'Last Christmas' and his client Barry Manilow's hit from 1978, 'I Can't Smile Without You'. The effect of the legal wrangle was to freeze further royalty payments on 'Last Christmas' due to Wham!, or in this instance due to the Ethiopian Fund, until the case could be heard in court.

Although Dick James eventually dropped the action and withdrew the allegations, freeing up the royalties at once, George Michael did not easily forgive him and his unchari-table legal action, declaring bitterly: 'If they had won, would they have asked the starving to give back the food?'

The world tour got under way on 4 December, but before long, after just six dates, Michael's health gave way once again. During the opening concert at the Queen's Hall in Leeds, Michael damaged his back during a strenu-ous dance routine. Suffering debilitating pain the following morning, he announced that the next five dates – in Edinburgh, Bournemouth and Birmingham – would be rescheduled. He was well and back on his feet just in time to appear at the Wham! Christmas concerts at Wembley Arena.

Michael spent Christmas with his family. He had left home a podgy boy with a big ambition; he returned a millionaire. More important than anything, he had at last positioned himself perfectly to control every aspect of his career. He told *Time Out*: 'There is not any aspect of our presentation or recording arrangement which is engineered by anyone else.'

The only thing which might have worried him, as he sipped champagne with his family on Christmas Day, was how long he could last in such a cutthroat world. He might never have guessed that of all the major British artists dominating the chart that year – among them Frankie Goes to Hollywood, Duran, Duran and Boy George's Culture Club – only Michael would survive as an enduring recording artist.

5

Chinese Whispers

In 1984 Wham! dominated the music charts; by 1985 they were set to dominate the world. The year started as it would continue: at a frantic pace. First they went on the second leg of their world tour, taking in Japan, Australia and then America. The first dates of the New Year were seven concerts in Japan, including one at Tokyo's 12,000-seat Budokan Theatre, followed by four in Australia, then six in America where they opened in Hollywood on 4 February. As Michael and Ridgeley decided that the trip should be a celebration of their success, they invited their parents to join them. Jack and Lesley Panayiotou and Albert and Jill Ridgeley were to be the VIPs for the duration of the tour.

Touring can be the graveyard of the music business. For those who get into the rhythm of being on the road, there are enormous rewards, but for those who cannot take the endless waiting, the constant imprisonment in hotel rooms, the boredom and the frustration of life on the road, touring can mean trouble. The two young men therefore had a double purpose in taking along their parents: to thank them by giving them a round-the-world trip, staying at expensive hotels, and as a check on their behaviour.

Michael hated touring. He disliked the frantic lifestyle –

the living out of suitcases, the inconvenience of it all, constantly on the move without ever settling in one place for long – and he came to dislike the burgeoning entourage of technicians and roadies which was an essential part of the Wham! road-show. He learnt to deal with his frustrations, however, through a pre-performance routine: he would shut himself in his dressing room for half an hour, tickling up his vocal chords with herbal tea and toning his body with warm-up exercises.

But the wild life of a band on the road cannot be subdued even by the billeting of the stars' parents in the same hotel. As soon as his mother and father had gone to bed, Michael was living the life of a rock star to the full. Most nights he stayed up drinking heavily. Away from Britain it seemed that he was as likely to self-destruct as Ridgeley. He did not expect to sleep alone and many nights he didn't make it back to his own hotel bed.

Saxophonist David Baptiste was with the tour and later told of a typical touring day based on his experience of George Michael in Osaka, Japan. After drinking a great deal of alcohol, Michael set out on the town with a number of women he had recently befriended. On the way out of the hotel he gave Baptiste an address in Osaka where he wanted to be collected at noon the following day. 'The next day one of the security guards and I went down to pick up George,' Baptiste said. 'When he came out his eyes were glazed and he looked totally smashed. He'd been with the three girls all night and there were scratches and love bites all over him. What a mess.'

In February the duo returned to Britain to attend the British Phonographic Industry (BPI) Awards at the Grosvenor House Hotel in London. Set up three years before, the awards had become the British equivalent of America's annual Grammy music awards and this year Wham! took the top prize, Best British Group.

The same month 'Careless Whisper' hit the top of the American singles chart and, in March, *Make It Big* reached No. 1 in the American album charts, staying there for three weeks. And that was not all: in February the song earned Michael an Ivor Novello Award for Songwriter of the Year, the top accolade for a songwriter in Britain, from the British Academy of Songwriters, Composers and Authors, also at the Grosvenor House Hotel. He became the youngest songwriter ever to ever receive it. 'Careless Whisper' also won another award at the ceremony, for Most Performed Work.

It was fitting, too, that the award should be presented to George Michael by his friend Elton John, who welcomed him to the stage by calling him 'the Paul McCartney of his generation'. But for Michael it was all too much, and he started to cry. He tried to make a short acceptance speech, but the tears were swelling in his eyes and he found he could not speak. He paused to compose himself and wiped his eyes with his fingers before carrying on with his short speech.

George Michael's success was well established. He was, at the age of just twenty-one, a successful singer-songwriter and a self-made millionaire. Until now he had still been living at home with his parents. It was time to stand on his own feet and move out. It was anyway impossible for him to introduce his new high-spending and hedonistic lifestyle to his parents' home. So he rented a flat in Knightsbridge, an area of high-class residences and upmarket shopping in west London. But it was not lavish. The rooms were sparsely furnished and he preferred to live alone. Ridgley, too, moved out of his parents' home around this time, to a rented apartment in Kensington, the neighbouring district.

Towards the end of March two final tour dates were announced. The shows would take Wham! into the history books and put them on front pages around the world: they became the first Western band to appear in Communist China. It was a feat Elton John, the Rolling Stones, Rod Stewart and The Police had attempted but never achieved. The effect for Wham! was immediate – it ensured they were considered superstars in every commercial territory in the world. But although the China trip was to be a public relations stunt to beat all stunts, Michael found it a disheartening experience.

Simon Napier-Bell took the credit for the China tour. The invitation came after months of delicate negotiation and planning. Napier-Bell learned that provincial governments in China had been allowed, via their Cultural Exchange Departments, to release recordings by foreign artists so long as a share of profits were given to local charities. Napier-Bell had his eye on reaching China's estimated 200 million young adults. If he pulled it off, Wham! would become the first Western pop group to build a fan-base in China.

Napier-Bell's first approaches to China in 1984 were met with indifference. Eventually he managed to persuade the Chinese Cultural Attaché in London to consider the possibility of Wham! playing some Chinese dates, which was followed up by an invitation to a delegation of embassy employees to watch Wham! in action when they performed in Hong Kong. The night they attended

Napier-Bell was on sparkling form, treating the Chinese like royalty. He threw a private reception and enjoyed the irony of pouring champagne to communists.

By the end of the night Napier-Bell felt optimistic about the prospect of his Chinese plans coming to fruition. To his surprise, the Chinese officials had been relaxed and responsive. Several had studied at Western universities and clearly enjoyed the lifestyle of the West. The Cantonese representatives went one stage further, promising to help release a Wham! record in China. Now all Napier-Bell had to do was get the band invited to China.

After exploring several fruitless avenues, Napier-Bell attracted interest from the All China Youth Federation in Peking. The Federation asked him to submit promotional videos of the band as well as translations of all their lyrics. A carefully edited show-reel of the band at its most inoffensive was compiled including a video of 'Freedom' performed in the *Top of the Pops* studio the previous winter. Napier-Bell thought the tape thoroughly inoffensive, but the Federation saw it and made clear that they did not approve of the sexually provocative performances or the loudness of the music.

Napier-Bell was quick to assure them that both shortcomings could be overcome. Wham! would modify their performance to satisfy the Chinese objections. A deal was eventually struck in which Wham! would give two concerts – one in Peking and another in Canton – so long as they played their music quietly and modified their dance routines by cutting sexually suggestive movements. The band were expected to meet the full cost of everything, including auditorium hire, stage construction costs, lighting rigs, sound equipment and the provision of free programmes. All gate receipts would be 'donated' to the Federation and the Ministry of Culture in Canton.

It is unlikely that Napier-Bell, who travelled to China thirteen times in all to fix the deal, knew the full extent of the financial disaster he was leading Wham! into. CBS put up $500,000 towards the cost of the stunt, but Napier-Bell was aware it would cost far more and he tried to find other ways to offset costs.

Two lucrative warm-up concerts were set up in Hong Kong at the 12,000-seat Coliseum Theatre. Four British tabloid papers were to join the charabanc for a £10,000 fee each. Napier-Bell also hoped to boost profits further with a documentary film to be made of the group's Chinese escapade. But the feeble end result was a disaster which simply sent the losses of the trip spiralling. Though the two concerts were already expected to cost the band between £200,000 and £400,000, the cost of the film project was expected to cost as much again.

A talented group of film-makers had been assembled, headed by Lindsay Anderson, the British film director whose career was founded in documentaries and whose feature credits included *This Sporting Life*, *If . . .* and *O Lucky Man*. Martin Lewis, a maker of pop videos who had been executive producer of the Amnesty International fundraisers *The Secret Policeman's Ball* and *The Secret Policeman's Other Ball*, was drafted to work alongside Anderson. They put together a 35-man Anglo-American film crew, which was soon beset by problems.

From the moment it left Britain the Chinese venture was in trouble. Once again, both the Panayiotou and Ridgeley parents and Michael's two sisters were on the trip, but their presence only added to the worries of those running the show. The cast and crew and administration team numbered about 150 and the stage and film crews were between them carrying more than 30 tons of equipment. The organization was of breathtaking complexity.

And everything that could go wrong did go wrong. One early casualty was keyboard player Mark Fisher, who collapsed from heat exhaustion when the band got to Hong Kong and had to be flown home. Having reporters from four scoop-hungry British tabloid papers watching the duo at close quarters only compounded the problems. George Michael was testy and irritable much of the time. And when they reached China things got worse, starting with the official welcome at the airport on 14 April.

The first minutes in China were weird. They were met by silence. There were no screaming fans to greet them, just a few Chinese officials and an orderly line of cars waiting to take them to their hotel, where they were given the red carpet treatment. Wham!, renamed 'Wei Meing' by locals, meaning 'mighty' and 'vigorous', said they hoped their visit might contribute towards a new relaxed era in China. But within a few days it became clear they had become mere extras in a propaganda exercise masterminded by the Chinese government.

Michael and Ridgeley were soon being whisked away for a succession of photo-opportunities at some of China's great monuments. They were taken to see the 2,000-year-old, 3,000-mile-long Great Wall of China, where they were unsure how to react. Newsreels show them giggling nervously at each other. At the Wall, Lindsay Anderson fell and badly sprained his leg, which meant he was confined to a wheelchair for the remainder of the filming.

The carefully stage-managed tour by Wham!'s Chinese hosts continued with a visit to Peking's Forbidden City, once reserved for China's emperors, the old imperial family and the court. And in cultural diplomacy, no trip to Peking was complete without a visit to the British Ambassador, Sir Richard Evans, for tea in the residence garden.

The two young men also attended a welcoming banquet held in their honour by the Chinese Youth Federation. In a short speech, Michael told the assembled guests, from a carefully prepared script approved by the Chinese: 'Andrew and I are extremely flattered and honoured to be here today. We just hope our performance will represent a cultural introduction between the young people here and in the West and help them to see what goes on in the rest of the world. And I think I speak for everyone when I say that this may be a small step for Wham! but a great step for the youth of the world.'

But what either of them said or did did not matter; what was important to the Chinese was that images of the two of them enjoying themselves in China would be relayed around the world. In the topsy-turvy world of pop music, the facts need never spoil a good story. And, although everyone involved in the tour knew that it had been a fiasco, that is not the way it was understood in the rest of the world. The story of Wham! in China was such a novelty that it made the front pages in every country, and the pictures dominated television news bulletins for the best part of a week. In the United States, there were times when the three main networks, ABC, CBS and NBC, were running the Wham! footage simultaneously. So whatever the financial and physical cost of the China trip, the extraordinary publicity generated meant it was a public relations success for both the Chinese and Wham! in the West and most importantly the United States. As Dick Leahy explained, 'Suddenly in America, Wham! were huge news. It was a major piece of management skill.'

Demand for tickets for the two concerts was unrivalled in a country which rarely mounted pop concerts. Tickets cost about £1.50 each, the equivalent of several days' pay to a Chinese worker. In Peking, at the Workers' Gymnasium Stadium where Wham! were due to play, over 1,000 fans queued through the night to try to secure blocks of ten tickets for their work units. To qualify they had to be vetted by government officials at the box office as well as produce letters of introduction from their employers. The band's visit fuelled a thriving black market in tickets for the shows and in Wham! cassettes. Of the 10,000 cassettes of *Make It Big* set aside to be given free to every member of the audience, half went missing, stolen by corrupt officials. They soon appeared on the black market, along with thousands more which had been quickly copied and bootlegged.

The first concert, on Sunday 7 April 1985, was a night George Michael will never forget. Before the show began the audience was instructed by a faceless announcer to remain seated at all times and 'watch with patience'. The warm-up act was a black dancer, Trevor Duncan, who burst into the spotlight with an energetic routine combining break-dancing and body-popping, throwing himself around the floor and spinning on his head. All around the auditorium the audience, predominantly male, jumped to its feet to imitate Duncan's revolutionary rhythmic routines. The music was immediately drowned out by the sound of officials announcing: 'Dancing is not allowed. All those standing, sit down now!' The crowd, closely observed by ferocious police and security guards, obeyed at once.

When Michael took to the stage, he was immediately struck by the bizarreness of the situation. For the first time in his career he saw an audience staring back at him with what he considered to be an unreachable sadness in their eyes. He had never witnessed such a uniform and uni-formed audience, with most of the 10,000 men and women decked out in identical regulation-issue blue and brown Mao suits. The only colour in the room came from the overseas students and embassy employees.

To further drive a wedge between him and his audience, the first rows of seats were occupied by assorted ageing officials from the Chinese Youth Federation and the Chin-ese government. Others watched from a box, demurely sipping tea throughout the show. The most influential guest at the stadium was the seventy-year-old Central Committee member Hua Xiong, a confidant of the all-powerful Chinese leader Deng Xiaoping. Xiong and his associates looked on with stony indifference, their solemn expressions never changing throughout the ninety-minute show. The only positive response to come from the VIP seats were occasional smiles from Zhou Nan, the country's deputy foreign minister, Sir Richard Evans, and Napier-Bell.

Given the restrictions on the stage show imposed upon them by their hosts, Wham! had to abandon their tra-ditional erotic dancing style in favour of spectacle. Michael wore a white jacket (but no shirt) while Ridgeley dressed in tartan pants. When the show was over, Michael confessed it was the most difficult audience he had ever performed in front of. And when he was told that some of the audience had been hit by security guards during the show simply for dancing, and that a boy had been arrested and beaten by the police for smoking a cigarette, Michael was incensed. His attitude to Chinese officialdom changed and he determined to defy their wishes whenever he could for the rest of the trip.

The concert was later reviewed politely by the New China News Service, which dubbed the band the 'British Wham electronic orchestra' and translated 'Wake Me Up Before You Go Go' as 'Wake Me Up Before You Leave'. The British press, meanwhile, filed a clutch of dreary stories, dotted with polite quotes about the band from the Chinese audience. They would not have to wait long, however, before they had a real scoop on their hands.

While Michael and Ridgeley were scheduled to stay on in Peking to give an interview to an American TV crew, the rest of the party, including their families and the British press corps, set off the day after the concert to Canton in an ancient Boeing 747, complete with wooden seats, which had been chartered locally.

Towards the back of the plane, the Portuguese trumpeter Raul De Oliviera took his aisle seat next to Shirlie Holliman and Pepsi DeMacque. As Flight CAA 1301 headed into the sky, it quickly became apparent to the women that all was not well with De Oliviera. A nervous flier, he had been taking drugs to take his mind off things and to celebrate the first leg of the tour. By the time he reached the plane he felt he was in another world and within a few moments of take-off he was suffering from acute drug-induced paranoia. He began screaming out

'Motherfucker' and writhing around in agony, clutching an open pen-knife.

The pilot was told the plane was being hijacked and sent the plane into a dive which sent bags and luggage flying through the cabin. Amid the turmoil Dave Moulder and Benny Collins, the band's security men, jumped to their feet and overpowered De Oliviera. Minutes later the plane landed back at Peking Airport and De Oliviera was put under sedation and bundled off to the Peking Medical University Hospital nearby. Moulder explained to reporters: 'He was hallucinating and seemed to be in a trance. He thought he was possessed by the devil and was dying.' Raul did not rejoin the Wham! tour and was flown home once he was discharged from the hospital.

The concert in Canton was a more intimate affair than the Peking gig, attracting an audience of just 5,000 at the city's Chung Sahn Memorial Hall. Again a banquet was thrown in honour of the pair and the subsequent concert, on 11 April, was more liberally policed and subsequently less trying than the first. At the end of the show Wham! were given a rousing standing ovation.

Napier-Bell and Jazz Summers staged a press conference in Canton to announce the release in China of two Wham! albums on cassette, making them the first Western pop group to earn regular royalties from sales in communist China. The first was a compilation of their best work from the first two Wham! albums, and the other was a hybrid collection of songs released with one of China's most successful singers, Cheng Fang Yuen. It consisted of five Wham! originals and five covers by Yuen, for which she was to have been paid just £15 for her efforts, until Michael and Ridgeley insisted she should receive royalties from the release, estimated to be worth tens of thousands of pounds. In the end Wham! made very little from the records sold in China, where counterfeiting runs rife, and over the years earnings from Wham! record sales in China barely register on the balance sheet.

George Michael was glad when the whole Chinese experience was over. Despite the gruelling seventeen-hour flight back to London, which left him exhausted, he was relieved to be home. And the sight of the hundred or so fans who had been waiting for hours at Heathrow Airport to greet him was especially welcome.

Michael wasted no time in distancing himself from the China trip. Vowing he would never again set foot in China, he told the style magazine *The Face*: 'Once we got there I just thought the whole thing was a shambles. What was basically going on was that the Chinese government was trying to encourage the Western world to accept Chinese product. They were saying, "Look we have our arms open, we are going to accept Western music." That was total bollocks. They used us. We were a propaganda item.'

The China trip had a profound effect on Michael. It fostered in him a lasting distrust of governments which exploited links with pop music. And it gave him a permanent wariness of the British papers. The trip had thrust him into the arms of the tabloid press and he had quickly tired of their endless demands for trivial stories and nonsensical snippets of news. He pulled up the drawbridge on the press from that time and did not feel obliged to play by their rules.

Filming the China trip had been fraught with problems from the start and all interest in the project was abandoned as soon as Wham! returned to Britain. When the mood took them, Michael and Ridgeley would help Anderson and his crew, but for the most part they kept the film unit at a distance.

Back in China, on top of Anderson's accident, the film crew had encountered problems when dealing with corrupt local bureaucrats. They had demanded an additional $100,000 facility fee on the unusual grounds that Anderson was filming on 35mm stock rather than 16mm. As they refused to pay the officials they were obliged to shoot on 16mm to avoid paying an arbitrary levy.

Anderson realized the film was doomed as soon as he reached China. He was quoted in Johnny Rogan's *Wham! Confidential* as saying: 'George Michael was totally uninterested in what we were doing. He never showed any interest at all in the whole idea of what film-making was. He was extremely bright in his own field, but he didn't want to learn. Of the two, Andrew seemed the most intelligent, but they were both conceited.'

Nor had it taken Anderson long to see what lay behind the brittle Wham! façade. He sensed the drama being played out away from the public: Michael's growing distrust and dislike of Napier-Bell. Anderson said: 'The management were frightened of Michael. They would have put their heads down the lavatory to please him.'

Once the crew returned home the film ground to a halt. Michael demanded that some scenes should be reshot, largely because he didn't like the way his hair looked in the heat. At one point it was decided that instead of a cinema release the film would become a TV special for Channel 4. But even that plan failed. It was ultimately released as a video called *Foreign Skies* a full year after the tour with virtually no publicity, no promotion and no critical acclaim.

In May Michael flew alone to the United States to appear in a gala at the Harlem Apollo in New York. Stevie Wonder had invited him to take part in the event, 'Motown Returns to the Apollo', and Michael had agreed. He sang with Wonder and Smokey Robinson, who also performed a 'Careless Whisper' solo, on a bill also boasting Sammy Davis Jnr, Patti LaBelle, Little Richard, Diana Ross and fellow Brits Rod Stewart and Boy George. And at the end of the month, a full ten weeks after its release, 'Everything She Wants' finally hit the top of the American singles charts and stayed there for a fortnight.

On his return to Britain, Michael agreed to appear in another charity show – the biggest the world had ever seen. He had appeared on the Band Aid single at Christmas and happily agreed to help with the Live Aid concert at Wembley Stadium in Britain for the same cause which was scheduled for Saturday 13 July. Like the single 'Do They Know It's Christmas?', the driving force behind the mammoth music event was Bob Geldof.

The American show would pick up where Wembley left off in Philadelphia's JFK Stadium. The split-venue jamboree was beamed to a global television audience of billions. The biggest names in British rock appeared at Wembley on that blisteringly hot summer's day, including The Who, Queen, Dire Straits, Status Quo, U2, Paul McCartney, David Bowie, Sting, Bryan Ferry and Phil Collins. And as Wembley ended, America began with major stars such as Mick Jagger and Tina Turner, Crosby, Stills and Nash and Led Zeppelin (both re-formed for the occasion), Bob Dylan, Keith Richards and Ronnie Wood and, having jetted in on Concorde direct from London, Phil Collins.

Queen was universally credited with being the band who stole the London show, and George Michael the solo artist who performed the best. He appeared with Elton John, on piano, to perform John's hit from 1974, 'Don't Let The Sun Go Down On Me'. Ridgeley and John's long-time friend Kiki Dee provided backing vocals, but only Michael could be easily heard by the 70,000-strong crowd. He said that nerves caused him to sing the first few verses out of tune, but the crowd did not seem to notice. He was not happy with the worldwide attention the performance attracted and told the *Record Mirror*, 'Sometimes I feel I am in a goldfish bowl with the whole world looking in.'

Long after Live Aid, George Michael and Elton John went on to record 'Don't Let The Sun Go Down On Me' as a charity duet to raise money for the fight against AIDS – an act of generosity and compassion which, ironically, did him no good in the eyes of the bosses of his record company. And it became an incident which led ultimately to the breakdown in relations between Michael and CBS.

That summer the press turned on Andrew Ridgeley. His persistently drunken behaviour meant that be became known by the disgusting sobriquet 'The Vomit Fountain' by the paparazzi photographers and tabloid reporters who stalked him. But details of Ridgeley's latest heterosexual sexual conquest was news no longer; what became far more interesting to the tabloids was the elusive George Michael and his sexual life. Though there was no shortage of leggy Ridgeley girlfriends happy to sell their tales to the papers, Michael's sexual partners were proving harder to track down. Michael had admitted to a blitz of heterosexual activity when Wham! first reached the top, but this very soon gave way to frustration. He said that he soon tired of the young women who fell for his Latin lover creation rather than for the real George Michael.

So, in the absence of any evidence of Michael's sexual behaviour, the papers came up with a story about his taking drugs. It was said Michael had been seen in the London nightclub Taboo sniffing amyl-nitrate, commonly known as poppers. Once used to treat those with weak heart conditions, poppers create a brief euphoric rush by speeding up the heart. The drug's short-term buzz is regularly used on dance floors and was especially popular among gays, who also used them to heighten sexual experiences.

As drug offences go, it was trivial stuff. Poppers were easily bought over the counter at sex shops and amyl-nitrate was not considered to be habit-forming. But the press were quick to use the story to fuel speculation over his sexuality. The AIDS epidemic had broken out and, though later proved incorrect, it was for a time thought that poppers were a contributory factor to the disease. Michael was furious over the stories, which he considered a gross invasion of his privacy. It was important to him that his sexuality remained a private matter. He made a point of being seen and photographed in the company of women, though he did little to dampen the speculation about his sexuality. At this time it was widely assumed that Michael was either homosexual or bisexual. The report that Michael had been seen taking amyl-nitrate, a drug widely used among homosexuals, came as little surprise.

What the press did not discover is that amyl-nitrate was only one of the drugs that Michael was experimenting with at that time. He had started to enjoy other soft drugs, mostly leaf marijuana and cannabis resin, to help bolster his creativity and relieve the pressures of superstardom. It took some years, however, before he was ready to admit to the public that he was a drug user.

In the wake of the China trip, and the publicity it generated in the United States, Jazz Summers was keen to exploit this new American market. For months he pushed Michael to go on a stadium tour of the United States. At first Michael was opposed to the idea, but, after a good deal of persuasion, he agreed.

Summers set up dates for the end of August and the beginning of September, booking the band into cities where album sales and MTV coverage were at their highest. They were to perform nine concerts over twelve days across America, plus one in Toronto, Canada. The tour took in Poplar Creek in Illinois, Hollywood Park in Los Angeles, Alamada County Stadium in Oakland, California, Southern Star Amphitheatre in Houston, Miami Baseball Stadium in Florida, Vets Stadium in Philadelphia and, finally, the Pontiac Silverdome in Detroit. They were to be supported by the Pointer Sisters, Sister Sledge, Chaka Khan and Katrina and the Waves.

Michael developed a new look for the American tour. The pseudo-macho image remained, but out went the blond bouffant hairstyle and in came shorter dark hair and an immaculately cropped stubbly beard. He kept his large earrings, but he switched his stage dress from glitzy figure-hugging short jackets to a no-nonsense studded black leather jacket, a black T-shirt and fingerless gloves.

As soon as he reached the United States, Michael found himself stalked by two very dissimilar hunters: one a famous fan who had become entranced by his records and his videos – the one-time child actress Brooke Shields; the other one of the largest companies in the world, which was keen to harness their product to his sexy, dynamic image. But while Michael was happy to meet up with the delightful Miss Shields and go on a dinner date at the Mayfair Regent Hotel in Detroit, he resisted the charms of Coca-Cola, who wanted to strike an advertising deal with him.

The encounter with Brooke Shields didn't develop into friendship and nor were Coca-Cola any more successful. Diet Coke made Michael seven offers to endorse their product and seven times he said no – even though each time they came back with higher bids. Finally they reached a sum he could not refuse – $3.3 million. But still he was uneasy. In Britain artists who associate themselves with commercials are thought by the fans to have sold out and can suffer as a result. Michael knew that Coke were desperate to cash in on his image and he enjoyed playing hard to get. He also felt taken for granted, as if Coke were so rich that they were capable of buying anyone's involvement. He later revealed his main reason for giving Diet Coke the run-around. 'They had publicized their involvement with me. They had said that this advert was happening before I said yes. They knew that Madonna had just hooked up with Pepsi. They were desperate to do it. They really didn't have much choice.'

Later, Michael told the *Sunday Correspondent*: 'The money kept getting bigger. I kept saying no, and they were saying: You can do this, you can have that. Eventually, on Christmas Day they phoned me up and said, We'll give you this much money. It was a *huge* amount of money. They said, Make the advert. If you don't like it you can give it back to us. Actually they didn't even say I had to give it all back, I could keep a portion of it. Which was still a fair old amount of money. I was thinking, "I can't say no. I can't say no to this." My managers had been working for six months on this and they said, How can you say no? I had this big argument with all the people around the dinner table at Christmas. Eventually I said yes. We ended up doing it with Stephen Frears. I was really pleased with it. And it was the shittiest Diet Coke commercial I've ever seen. I'm sure that's why they didn't show it over here in Europe. They realized it had been a great advert for me and a crap advert for Diet Coke. Ha! While we were making it, they had people putting the product in. I kept taking it out. I had complete control.'

The commercial was shot over two days – one in New York and the other in Spain, earning him $1.65 million a day, or £13,750 per minute, for two twelve-hour shifts. Frears, the perennial English director of commercials of some brilliance, as well as distinguished movies such as *Dangerous Liaisons*, *The Grifters* and *Prick Up Your Ears*, had made a slick, fast-moving commercial for Coke which the company had been pleased with. Michael, however, was too annoyed by the whole affair to acknowledge its competence. The whole episode continued to irritate him and while in *Bare* he mentioned it, in subsequent press reports he was apparently denying that he had made a Coke commercial of any sort.

While Michael, with or without Coke, was making a great deal of money from the American tour, members of his backing band accused him of paying poorly and treating them badly. The band and crew were booked into different hotels from Wham!, which is traditional, but they felt that the quality of their hotels was inadequate. They came to believe that unnecessary economies were being made at the expense of their comfort. The musical director, Tommy Eyre, quit in disgust three days before the tour ended, citing the meanness of George Michael and Andrew Ridgeley as the main reason.

As the tour drew to its close, Michael spent a few days recuperating in Los Angeles and began to think seriously about the future. The first thing he did on his return to London was to call all his business associates together to a lunch at Langan's restaurant in Mayfair. Present were Andrew Ridgeley, Simon Napier-Bell, Jazz Summers, Dick Leahy and Bryan Morrison. He told them that he was tired of being part of Wham! and that he had decided that the band had to fold, explaining, 'This is no longer any good for me.' Ridgeley knew that Michael had been gradually working up to such a decision, so he was not surprised. Yet at the same time he felt apprehensive about the break-up. His life would totally change and he would be left to earn a living from his talent alone. But Michael was determined and there was never an attempt by Ridgeley to persuade him to change his mind. He knew that it would have been useless.

So, over the next few weeks plans were drawn up to

bring Wham! to a carefully co-ordinated demise. While Michael knew his partner had been expecting this, he was anxious to ensure that Ridgeley was not hurt, and so the end of Wham! was planned like a military campaign. Every last drop of interest and money was to be exacted from the break-up and rancour would be kept to a minimum. Until those plans were complete, the splitting up of Wham! was to be hotly denied. Above all, the end of Wham! should be a big affair, a celebration of the end of an era and the beginning of a new one, with George Michael becoming a solo singer at last.

Until then it was to be business as usual. Michael had written most of 'I'm Your Man', Wham!'s next single, on a flight between Los Angeles and Oakland on the American tour. It was quickly recorded and rush-released on both sides of the Atlantic at the end of November. A week later it hit No. 1 in Britain, staying for two weeks; in America it peaked at No. 3. The critics did not consider the song one of Michael's best and in America it hit controversy because of the accompanying video – shot in black and white at the Marquee Club in London – which was so raunchy it was deemed too hot for some television stations to screen.

It was at the time of 'I'm Your Man' that George Michael began to feel penned in by the press. Photographers set up on the doorstep of his Knightsbridge flat, clocking everyone in and out, and he felt persecuted. Instead of taking off out of range of their prying lenses, he stayed put, refusing to leave his home for days on end. He concentrated on the demise of Wham! and the songs with which he would launch his solo career. He blamed Wham! and its pre-pubescent following for the press attention he so disliked and he hoped, by concentrating on his song-writing, to be acknowledged as a substantial singer-songwriter with a more mature audience.

He told the *New Musical Express*: 'Wham! don't need music press publicity any more, but I need something where I'm written about intelligently, even if it's a slag-off. I'm sick of people treating me like I've only got one brain cell and only three lines of conversation. I'm sick of being presented in one-line quotes, and I'm sick of walking into rooms filled with complete strangers who have totally the wrong idea about me.'

Rumours of an imminent split in Wham! began to spill out into the press, but they were dismissed as speculation. In fact, the plans for the break-up were now well advanced. Michael had agreed that the band's final count-down would be made up of one last spectacular concert, to be staged at Wembley, another solo single by Michael and a last release by Wham!. The Wham! swan-song would be an EP, since Michael was not prepared to commit himself to writing and recording enough new material to fill an entire album.

Although everything was done according to Michael's plans, the end of the year was a time of apprehension for him and he became heavily depressed. And yet when he listened to the radio or read the music papers, George Michael was everywhere. By Christmas he featured on no less than four chart singles – 'I'm Your Man', the re-releases of 'Last Christmas' and 'Do They Know It's Christmas?', and he could also be heard singing backing vocals on Elton John's hit single 'Nikita'.

But he was in no mood to enjoy his success. He had hit a sour note in his personal life with the collapse of a rare and short-lived romance with an unnamed woman. Michael claimed he was jilted by her. He took the rejection badly and began to feel insecure. The pressures of the music business, apprehension about the end of Wham!, fears of going it alone, all conspired to preoccupy him. A darker side of the singer's personality became evident and he slipped into depression. Before long he could not keep his mental state a secret and he started losing his temper in public. Above all the constant press attention began to wear him down and he started being aggressive to the very paparazzi who in the past he had been grateful for. Now he found himself out of control in the street, grabbing photographers' cameras and brawling with friends. It was an ugly sight.

Michael, too, knew that he was in severe personal trouble and desperately needed a break. This was the lowest he had ever felt and he struggled to remain in control of his actions. The pressure on him was becoming too much, so he decided to make a run for it. On 28 December he slipped out of the country for a holiday in Australia with Andrew Ridgeley and two friends, David Ridler and Jon Fowler.

6

Planning on Going Solo

The holiday in Australia gave George Michael and Andrew Ridgeley the space they needed to escape from the pressures of London life and gradually they were able to relax. They spent their time swimming, drinking too much and generally lounging about. Then from Australia they flew across the Pacific to Los Angeles where, in January 1987, they were to receive the Favourite Rock or Pop Video award at the thirteenth American Music Awards ceremony staged at the Shrine Auditorium. For Michael, Los Angeles was a city which granted him the anonymity he craved and that year he was to spend a great deal of his time there.

With the end of Wham! looming, Ridgeley was also having to make decisions about how he would spend the rest of his life. He too had instantly benefited from the renegotiation of Wham!'s contract. Unlike the deals with Mark Dean, Epic records paid promptly. The problem for Ridgeley was knowing what to do with it. He had never been well off, let alone rich. But now he was earning so much he felt obliged to move to Monte Carlo, a tax haven, to avoid a thumping £600,000 tax bill. Then he set his heart on motor racing. He decided to leave Britain in the spring to live with his American model girlfriend

Diona Fiorentino in Monaco and pursue his dreams of becoming a racing driver. Although still only twenty-two, it was too late for him to think about breaking into Formula One. However, he hoped to be able to race in Formula Three events, having already driven in a series of celebrity races in Renault cars.

While Ridgeley was flying to Monte Carlo, looking for a suitable apartment to buy, Michael was in Los Angeles relaxing and working on solo projects as well as the all-important final new Wham! material.

Michael had a new woman friend, with whom he spent much of his time. He had met her a few months earlier during a trip to Los Angeles. Kathy Jeung was a Chinese-American model and make-up artist who at their first meeting took little notice of him. Michael persevered and the two slowly got to know each other. Michael found her down to earth and he trusted her. Although, like Michael, only in her mid-twenties, she seemed wise beyond her years and he felt he could open his heart to her more readily than with anyone else. They spent their days listening to music and chilling out around the pool and their nights were spent clubbing. For once everything seemed calm and in order and George Michael found the first equilibrium he had enjoyed since the Wham! phenomenon had taken off.

This equanimity came to an abrupt end when his American promoter, Rob Kahane, showed him an article in the *Hollywood Reporter* declaring that Nomis Management, the company formed solely to represent George Michael and Wham!, had been sold behind his back by Simon Napier-Bell and Jazz Summers to a firm with controversial ties to South Africa, at that time still under apartheid. Kahane said later: 'He went bananas. This was the first time I saw George Michael lose it – because he is pretty together. He was so angry and pissed off and he kept saying, "How could they do this? How could they sell me to something they know I don't believe in?"'

Michael read there were plans for Nomis Management to join forces with a bigger organization which included the legendary rock promoter Harvey Goldsmith. But Napier-Bell and Summers did not check into the background of the other parties involved in the deal. It was an error which would cost them a hugely profitable business and cause the abrupt end of all links with Michael.

In 1984, Harvey Goldsmith Enterprises had merged with Hotel Television Network to form Allied Entertainments. A year later, Allied Entertainments floated on the stock exchange, only to be taken over in August 1985 by Kunick Leisure, an enormous entertainments organization, in a deal which earned Goldsmith £6.7 million. Harvey Goldsmith later told Napier-Bell that he had sold his company and now had £15 million with which to expand a new global entertainment operation for Kunick Leisure.

Napier-Bell was before long in touch with Kunick, who offered to buy Nomis for £5 million to be paid over five years. Napier-Bell and Summers would be retained as consultants and awarded large salaries, and extensive funds would be made available to enlarge the business. A provisional contract was agreed towards the end of January 1986 but the deal awaited formal approval by Kunick Leisure's annual general meeting on 10 March.

The undeclared business connection which was to prove

so catastrophic for Napier-Bell and Summers was the identity of Kunick Leisure's biggest shareholder, the South African Sol Kerzner, who owned a stake of around 30 per cent. He also owned over a third of Sun Hotels International, the British subsidiary of his South African company Kersef Investments. He was known around the world as Mr Sun City after the luxurious gambling resort in Bophuthatswana which Kerzner had built and from which his fortunes had been made. Sun City catered almost exclusively for rich white South Africans and Kerzner came to epitomize the flagrant exploitation of cheap black hotel labour by hedonistic whites looking for sun, sex and a flutter on the gambling tables. Like many in the entertainment industry, including the Musicians' Union in Britain, George Michael had become politicized, particularly on global issues. He joined the anti-apartheid movement and co-wrote an anti-apartheid protest song with the black American star Stevie Wonder.

Napier-Bell and Summers were not interested in Kerzner's politics, but as Kunick Leisure's AGM neared and plans of a takeover of Nomis Management were made public, the business press wasted no time in pointing out the apparent clash between George Michael's anti-apartheid stance and Kunick's South African investments. In Los Angeles the story was splashed over *Variety* and the *Hollywood Reporter* under the unambiguous headline 'Wham! Sold To Sun City'. In Los Angeles, Michael could not believe his eyes. He had intended to end Wham! then renegotiate his contract with CBS records ahead of a new solo career. The sale of Nomis to Kunick not only offended him politically but, he believed, might jeopardize his carefully laid business plans.

As Michael exploded with anger in Los Angeles, so tempers were also running high back in London. On seeing the story in the newspapers, it finally dawned on Summers that he had been most foolhardy. He knew he had to act quickly if he was to salvage any kind of working relationship with Michael, and that Nomis must be kept out of the clutches of Kunick Leisure. But it was already too late.

Michael returned hurriedly to London where a lunch meeting was hastily arranged with Napier-Bell and Summers at the San Lorenzo restaurant in Knightsbridge. According to Summers, the only question Michael asked was: 'Why are you doing this? I've got ten more years of career at least.' The rest of the time he moodily avoided eye contact. He listened patiently as his managers pleaded for time to unpick the Kunick deal. By the end of lunch, Summers still thought there was hope that all might turn out well, but Michael had already made up his mind. From that moment, Michael would refuse to take telephone calls from either Napier-Bell or Summers. Their only means of communication would be through Dick Leahy or Michael's solicitor, Tony Russell. Michael had shut out his new management just as he had abruptly cut off his relationship with Mark Dean at the start of the Innervision troubles.

Relations were visibly strained the following month when Wham! appeared in public alongside their managers, sharing the stage at the British Phonograph Industry awards in London. All four went up to collect the trophy, awarded to Wham! for their Outstanding Contribution to British Music stemming from their two-date visit to China. Elton John received a similar award, for Outstanding

Contribution, for concerts in Russia back in 1979. The awards were presented by the lugubrious Conservative trade minister, Norman Tebbit, whose incongruous presence at the occasion became the joke of the evening. Michael was sporting a newly grown beard and a stetson hat. Under other circumstances the four men might have gone on to dinner and a well-deserved celebration, but as soon as the ceremony came to an end, so did the socializing. The end of Wham! was becoming painful.

Michael and Ridgeley began falling out again. Nightclub owner Peter Stringfellow remembered how the two men had grown so frustrated with their partnership that they came to blows. He recalled: 'George and Andy came in and stayed with me for a private party. Some arguments started between them. Suddenly they were rolling on the floor fighting. They always used to horseplay but this was serious. The band were splitting up and they looked like they were really going for each other. At one stage, George had Andy pinned to the floor and was letting him have it. We had to split them up. George never came in again.'

Michael formally broke off his working relationship with Nomis Management on 21 February. Lawyer Tony Russell telephoned Ridgeley at the Loews Hotel in Monte Carlo to explain the details. He and Michael expected Ridgeley to put his name to the statement Michael intended to release to the press. But, taken by surprise, Ridgeley said he did not want to be rushed into any hasty decision and asked for more time. Russell reported back to Michael, who made it clear he was not prepared to wait. Four hours later the statement was released declaring that Michael had ended all relations with Nomis.

The news sent the press in search of the full story. They interpreted it as a much bigger entertainment story – final confirmation of the rumour that Wham! was splitting up. Reporters and photographers were dispatched to door-step the offices of Nomis Management at 17 Gosfield Street, but Summers and Napier-Bell had already slipped into hiding.

According to Napier-Bell in *Bare*: 'Michael put out a press release saying that he was no longer associated with Nomis. So Jazz and I put out a press release saying that for the moment we were still continuing to manage Andrew. That was interpreted by the press as meaning that the group had split. So the press ran headlines saying "Wham! Split!" and didn't mention us, which was what we also intended. Bigger story. And we weren't splattered all over the papers. Tough manipulation, but there you are, you see. If I'm working for Michael, I do it for him. The minute he tells me I'm not, I do it for myself.'

When the press tracked down Ridgeley in Monte Carlo, he was caught off-guard. Asked why Wham! were splitting, he responded angrily: 'Nobody told me anything. Why don't you fuck off? The whole business makes me effing sick.' Before long Ridgeley too broke with Nomis Management.

In the termination agreement Napier-Bell and Summers received a sum based on the band's earnings, both in the past and future. Without the major talent of George Michael on its books, the proposed merger deal with Kunick Leisure evaporated overnight. And it was only a matter of time before Napier-Bell and Summers also parted company. As Summers, who went on to run Big Life

Records in London, remembered in *Bare*: 'One minute we were managing the biggest act since The Beatles. Within ten days we'd lost the biggest pop band in the world and the £5 million deal.' Napier-Bell was more bitter, being quoted in *Bare* as saying: 'We'd been fabulous managers and done everything he wanted. Yet he knew in three months' time that what he wanted more than anything was to run his life and not be managed.' It was a lesson that all who dealt with Michael would sooner or later discover.

By comparison, Harvey Goldsmith got off lightly. He skilfully plucked himself out of Kunick Leisure, effectively selling his shares in the company to buy back Allied Entertainment. But Goldsmith's fancy footwork did not convince Michael, who withdrew from him the chance to stage the 'Wham! – The Final' concert at Wembley, transferring it to a rival promoter, Mel Bush. Bush had promoted some of the biggest names ever to appear at Wembley, such as Crosby, Stills, Nash and Young, Joni Mitchell, the Beach Boys, The Eagles and Elton John.

In *Bare*, Michael said the Nomis Management fiasco was caused by a combination of greed and stupidity. 'I always thought that the smart people are the ones who don't piss me off, because I intend to be around for a long time. However mercenary they are, these people would make a lot more money by sticking with me rather than by doing something to make a fast buck or a fast £5 million. But I was disgusted I had been roped into something that was so bad, ethically and morally, and totally surprised by the assumption that I wouldn't feel so personally involved, even though I was most of Nomis's income and every

George Michael and Andrew Ridgeley – Wham! – after their earliest chart successes. Soon smiles gave way to bitter behind-the-scenes rows with Mark Dean, the man who had signed them. *Copyright © Dave Hogan. Unless otherwise stated, all pictures are the copyright of News Group Newspapers.*

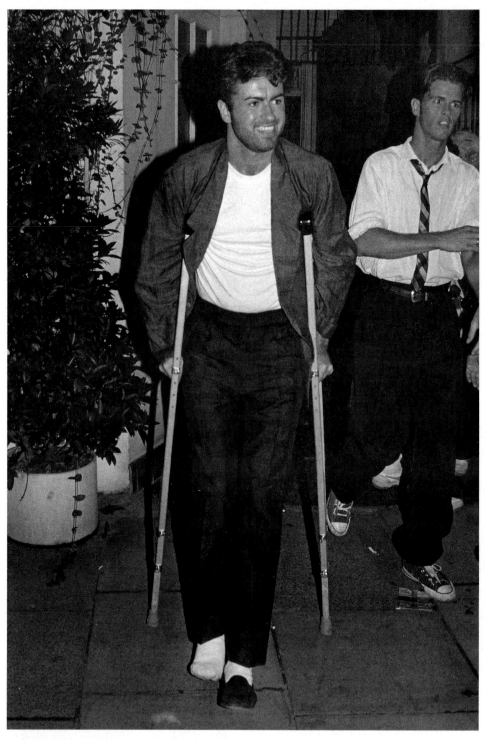

At 'Wham! – The Final' George sprained his leg but it was ousted partner Andrew Ridgeley who was to become the singer's emotional crutch when his world caved in.

Above: George and Diona Fiorentino, with whom Andrew Ridgeley set up home in Monte Carlo after the Wham! partnership, at Michael's insistence, was dissolved.

Right: With Brooke Shields, whom George was said to have dated. In fact, they dined together but no hot-blooded romance followed.

George has always found it difficult
to hide his loathing of the pressures of
mega-stardom in public, as these pictures
at Fashion Aid, in 1985, show.

George and his sister Melanie, who
has always helped her brother backstage
whenever he has performed.

The gold earrings were invariably fake when he performed, but among
George's own modest jewellery collection is the gold ring carrying
his childhood nickname Yog – short for Yoghurt.

record I made would benefit the shareholders of that company.'

Few names from the Nomis Management days stayed with Michael as he prepared to end Wham! and embark on a solo career. The services of publicist Connie Filippello were retained, though she also continued working on other projects for Simon Napier-Bell. Recording engineer Chris Porter, who worked on the *Make It Big* album, also cut his ties with Nomis to continue working with Michael. And Michael offered one Nomis employee a job, as his personal assistant: Siobhan Bailey, whom he felt he could trust.

Michael now dealt directly with Ridgeley, Dick Leahy and Mel Bush on the final arrangements for the demise of Wham!. Before that, however, he released on 5 April his next solo single, 'A Different Corner', a sultry ballad similar to 'Careless Whisper'. He had written some of it in 1985 when he recorded a demo of the song, and completed it in Los Angeles in the early months of 1986. The 'Different Corner' video was moody and emotional, with Michael, now wearing his hair long and dressed in white, crouched in the corner of a room drained of colour.

'A Different Corner' had a lilting melody and a melancholic style and some critics hailed it as 'melodically one of the greatest songs ever written'. His voice sounded more mature than before, laced with a pain which seemed genuine. It opens with slow, purposeful bass and keyboards before Michael bursts into breathy song, giving way to some of his most powerful and autobiographical lyrics to date. Singing to a lover, he tells her that she was the first to truly understand him. The title of the song referred to their chance meeting and how different it would be had they taken a 'different corner'.

Although earlier songs had appeared to be autobiographical and must have drawn upon his life experiences, Michael said 'A Different Corner' was the first time he had intentionally written an autobiographical song. The lyrics, he said, were inspired by a romance which lasted little more than a fortnight. Despite his devotion to and infatuation with his partner, he had been dumped. 'This was the first time I had ever really fallen in love and it seemed that it couldn't work because of everything I already had,' he explained. 'It was like someone saying, "You don't think you can have it all do you?"'

'A Different Corner' entered the British singles chart at No. 4 and a fortnight later began a three-week stint at No. 1. Released in America on 26 April, it entered at 57 and peaked eight weeks later at No. 7, a position it held for three weeks.

As the record made its way up the charts around the world, Michael flew back to Los Angeles where he threw himself into finishing songs for the Wham! EP. Work became the best way of fighting the depression and the growing sense of loneliness that had begun to haunt him, even though he found solace from time to time in the company of Kathy Jeung.

He also set under way a second solo project, a song which would once again portray him to the public as the one thing he believed he could never be – the Rudolf Valentino of his generation. Michael was approached via Dick Leahy by the legendary soul singer Aretha Franklin's management in America and asked whether he would record a duet with her. It was suggested that the unlikely partnership would offer considerable benefits to each singer. It would help give Michael a solid soul following in America and it would introduce Franklin, who had never had a No. 1 hit in Britain, to a much younger record-buying public. The song chosen for their duet was 'I Knew You Were Waiting (For Me)', written by Simon Climie, a little-known British songwriter, and veteran Nashville country and western writer Dennis Morgan. Michael agreed in principle, although the project would have to wait until both artists found time in their busy schedules.

When the time came to make a recording, the song provided a welcome relief for Michael from the mental strains of ending Wham!. 'I Knew You Were Waiting (For Me)' was the first song for years that he had not written and arranged himself. He found that that lack of responsibility had distinct merits. All he had to do was turn up at a studio and sing. The track was produced by Narada Michael Waldon, who two years later co-wrote the biggest hit of Gladys Knight's career after she broke with The Pips, the theme song from the James Bond movie *Licence to Kill*.

Michael and Aretha Franklin met up in a studio in Detroit, where Franklin lived. Michael considered it something of an adventure to work in the city which founded the Motown sound. But nothing prepared him for what he found. As Kahane said in *Bare*: 'We pulled up outside this building in the ghetto and Michael and I looked at each other and said, "This is a recording studio?"' Franklin was already at work inside, rehearsing the song. Michael and Kahane strolled in to the smoky, incense-filled control room and all eyes turned on them, like greenhorn cowboys entering a western saloon. They were the only two white people in the room.

But the ice melted immediately. Waldon was in the gallery and he quickly introduced himself. Although Michael later confessed to being a little nervous, he soon got used to the company and before long he felt the studio had a good atmosphere. He got on well with Aretha Franklin, who said that she liked the quality of his voice. He came to the conclusion that he had been chosen for the project as the 'acceptable honkey'.

'We recorded the song together and then did our ad libs separately,' he explained. 'I just tried to stay in character, keep it simple – it was very understated in comparison to what she did.' The video, made over two days that November, was also filmed in Detroit. Directed by Andy Morahan at a cost of £150,000, it featured Michael and Franklin standing dwarfed in front of a massive video screen.

On his return to Los Angeles Michael resumed work on the swansong 'Wham! EP', which was to be made up of four tracks: 'The Edge Of Heaven', 'Battlestations', a cover of a Was (Not Was) song, 'Where Did Your Heart Go?', and a remix, 'Wham! Rap 86', to feature Elton John on piano. 'The Edge Of Heaven', which had been in the band's live repertoire for many months, was by far the strongest song and contained the most sexually suggestive lyrics of any Wham! song to date, including the sado-masochistic lyrics about hurting a lover – unless they specifically wanted to be hurt.

At the beginning of June, just before the EP was released, Michael returned to Britain to take his driving test. Success had come so quickly for him that many of the rites of passage which ordinary young men pass through had been ignored, overtaken by events. The most frustrating thing was that he had failed to obtain a driving licence. Having spent much of his young adult life being chauffeured about in luxury cars, he yearned for the independence and serendipity that driving himself might bring. So he started to learn to drive. Whenever he was in Britain he practised, driving around London's back streets with his learner plates on, jerkily reversing around corners and stalling the engine during emergency stops, and he dreaded the thought of failing the Ministry of Transport examination. But when the day of the test came, he got into the Ford Escort and passed without difficulty, marking his success by buying his first car, a Mercedes.

His driving test out of the way, he met up with Andrew Ridgeley to make a video to accompany 'The Edge of Heaven' and embark on one last publicity push before Wham! was broken up for good. The video was again filmed at the Marquee Club in Wardour Street, Soho, where he had once mimed to 'I'm Your Man' before invited fans. Wham! were now so popular that the logistics of employing genuine young fans was quickly dismissed as too dangerous and likely to waste time. Instead, several hundred art students were employed to pretend to be the audience for £30 each. Behind Michael and Ridgeley, miming guitar alongside David Austin, snatches of earlier Wham! videos were projected on to large screens, then at the end of the video two giant words appeared: 'Good Bye'.

In a television interview at the time, Michael explained why he understood Wham! to be splitting: 'Most of the

opportunities which would excite people have been presented to us within four years. So the thrill of the chase is
not really there for us any more. Andrew's racing driving
is a totally new chase for him and I have some challenges
in going solo.' He also gave an interview to the *Sunday
Times,* in which he appeared to express his doubts about
being able to reach superstardom as a solo performer. He
told Julie Burchill: 'I'm not what stars are made of. I'm
not Prince and I'm not Madonna.' In fact it turned out he
meant something quite different.

Much later he qualified those remarks and told a television interviewer what he really meant: 'I don't think I
really understood it when I was speaking to Julie Burchill,
but all I knew at the time was that I just didn't see myself
as someone living twenty-four hours a day as a star.' He
added: 'I never wanted to be someone else. I wanted to
be a star and I wanted people to love me and recognize
me in the street. As a child that was what I wanted. But I
never really wanted to be someone else and I think the
people that are the most vivid and colourful, fascinating
stars are always people who basically want to be someone
else. I believe that of Madonna, I believe that of Prince, I
believe that of Michael Jackson. I'm not saying there's this
terrible flaw in it. It actually makes them very, very
interesting people. But I've never seen myself in that light.'

The timing of the EP release was perfect. The sleeve
carried a short, emotional message from the duo: 'We
would like to thank everyone who has helped us to come
through the last four years with our careers, our sanity and
our friendship intact. Special thanks, as always, go to our
families, our close friends and, of course, Siobhan.' The
record came out on 21 June, entered the charts at No. 2

and jumped to No. 1 a week later, the day the band finally disbanded.

In the last week the band was together they staged two warm-up gigs at the Brixton Academy in south London, on 23 and 24 June. The following day, on Michael's twenty-third birthday, he and Ridgeley arrived at BBC Television Centre for the last time to make their final appearance as Wham! on *Top of the Pops*. Three days later, on 28 June, the 'Wham! – The Final' concert was held at Wembley Stadium, before a sell-out crowd of 72,000. It was the hottest day of the year. In a bid to prevent a black market in tickets, several thousand were held back for sale on the day. The scheme, to protect Wham! fans from exploitative touts, worked, and the touts discovered to their cost that they were the ones being exploited, with some obliged to sell tickets they bought at £13.50 a time for just £10.

Wham! were driven at speed across London to Wembley escorted by four police motorcycle outriders. Backstage there was an atmosphere of high jinx tinged with an undercurrent of sadness. Elton John, who was to appear in the concert, had already set up camp and was doing his best to relieve the strain of the event on his friends. He had his own trailer for a dressing room and the hospitality inside was typically lavish, with endless beer matched by an endless supply of the best champagne. His final touch, perfect on a day when temperatures soared into the nineties, was to create his own absurd oasis. Green plastic turf was rolled out and a small children's paddling pool was set up and filled with water. To commemorate the occasion, Elton John gave the two men a Reliant Robin with 137,000 miles on the clock and furry dice hanging in front of the windscreen. Among those turning up to wish Wham! good luck, to drink champagne and even to take off their shoes and paddle, were Rod Stewart, Ronnie Lane, Martin and Gary Kemp from Spandau Ballet, Patsy Kensit and designer Jasper Conran.

The rest of the bill included Gary Glitter, Nick Heyward and Simon Le Bon. But the show belonged to Michael and Ridgeley. Michael dressed from head to toe in black – black leather jacket, black T-shirt and black jeans and sporting short black hair and stubble. And when he performed his tear-jerker 'A Different Corner' he dedicated it 'to one special friend' in the audience, adding 'they know who they are'. (It is generally thought that this referred to his old friend Lesley Bywaters.) Although both Michael's and Ridgeley's parents were in the audience, it was not intended for them.

Although few in the audience suspected it, the show did not pass without incident. Michael was suffering from the pain of a torn tendon as the show neared the finale and he later confessed that he felt he had not quite managed to rise to the occasion. Despite his personal reservations, 'Wham! – The Final' was universally deemed an unequivocal success by all those who saw it and performed in it.

The after-show party, held at the Hippodrome night-club in Leicester Square, was a magnificent wake and cost £65,000. Although it was the middle of July, the club was decked out with artificial snow and thousands of balloons, and the very last hours of Wham! were played out to music of the band's seasonal hit 'Last Christmas'.

Kathy Jeung flew over from Los Angeles to accompany Michael to the bash, which created a stir, since this was the first time she had been seen at his side in public. Ridgeley arrived with Diona Fiorentino. At the climax of the party, Michael and Ridgeley stared sadly into each other's eyes and hugged on the dancefloor in a public display of friendship and affection, defying anyone to suggest that Wham! was breaking up in acrimony.

After 'The Final', Wham! made one extra-time assault on the album charts with a double-LP compilation of Wham! 12-inch mixes. It was released on 19 July as *The Final* in Britain and *Music From the Edge of Heaven* in America. In the UK it went straight to No. 2 and held the slot for three weeks, staying on in the charts for almost a year – which was considered an extraordinary achievement for a record which, by definition, received no promotion from the artists. In America, the album had a shorter life, peaking at No. 10.

And there is a Wham! postscript. That summer the video of their China tour, *Foreign Skies: Wham! in China* was released. The film, which started out with the best of intentions and star director Lindsay Anderson, was little better than a hugely expensive home movie – and was as tedious to watch. Anderson, who died in 1994, said: 'The film I made was rather good. They [the producers Martin Lewis and Jazz Summers] took it over and fucked it up. It was a lack of intelligence on Michael's part that he didn't learn from it. It ended up awful and badly edited. They had made an absurd amount of money and didn't seem bothered about wasting it. Michael even seemed pleased to hear it had cost £1million. He just shrugged his shoulders and said, "So what?" Poor little rich girl.'

George Michael was twenty-three when he laid Wham! to rest. He was worth between £15 million and £28 million. But success had already taken its toll. With Wham! behind him he decided that he should take a holiday and consider the future. But what started as a few weeks on holiday quickly drifted into aimlessness. Having achieved so much in so little time, he suddenly lost confidence in himself and could not muster much enthusiasm for the solo career he said he longed for. He began to suffer heavy depression and loneliness again and took to drinking heavily. He could be found reeling night after night around hotels and rented villas in Los Angeles and Florida, in Portugal and St Tropez, even in Australia, or staggering aimlessly around nightclubs in New York.

Whenever he could, Michael persuaded Kathy Jeung to join him. Kathy was a confident young woman who did not suffer problems over her identity and Michael admired this strength of character. She did not care what strangers thought of her, nor did she ever have any intention of doing anything other than what she wanted to do.

Life was not so simple for Michael. He had created two of the most successful names in popular music – Wham! and George Michael – yet he was already tired of what he had achieved. Despite his success, he remained very much the young man he was when he was at school, vulnerable and lacking in confidence, hounded by insecurities about his future. Success had come so fast for him that he had never really achieved equilibrium. He was now only happy with himself when he was alone or with Kathy.

He later confessed: 'For a time I really didn't want to get back into the music business when we finished Wham!. The problem was just that I had developed a character for the outside world that wasn't me, and I was having to deal with people all the time who thought I was.' He was reminded of a strong childhood memory: 'I was basically bunking off school and I was terribly depressed at school, I can't remember what about. But I remember I was just riding around on buses all day thinking that I would get caught if I was out somewhere, that someone would spot me, and that the safest place to be was on a bus. And I remember thinking to myself, "One day no one will be able to touch you. You'll somehow get away from everyone else in some respect."'

Having achieved his ambition to be a successful pop star, he discovered that more than anything now he wanted to live an ordinary life. He wanted to be able to walk the streets without being stared out or have people scream their undying love or sing Wham! lyrics at him. At least in Los Angeles, where so many celebrities lived, it seemed a little easier for Michael to blend in. And he believed he was not being stalked by press photographers as much as in Britain. In fact his actions were eventually meticulously recorded.

But even in Los Angeles there were problems. Kathy, who provided such solace, was not always free to drop everything for him. She had her own life to lead, her own work commitments in Los Angeles. So Michael found himself alone, drifting through weeks of mounting depression. Soon he was drinking so heavily each night that the only thing that stopped him was passing out. He would then sleep for days to recover from the effects. He liked swigging Californian wine, which he thought was less damaging to his vocal chords than hard liquor, but he would sometimes turn to whisky or tequila. But drinking heavily was not only bad for his liver, it began to dramatically change his appearance. He had always had to work hard, with diets and regular work-outs, to keep his weight in check. Now the alcohol abuse started to show, putting fat on his face and belly.

Alcohol was not the only drug he took. Before long he was experimenting with other drugs, his favourite being the designer drug Ecstasy. Although he claims never to have taken heroin and that he has snorted coke only once or twice and even then he had not enjoyed it, his preference for Ecstasy was partly because it was convenient to take, without any ritual or paraphernalia.

He confessed in *Bare*: 'For the main part it was booze, but I was doing a fair bit of drugs as well. For a while I took Ecstasy when it was not very available over here. I took it simply because it made me feel that everything was wonderful. And I went through that and came out the other end realizing that there was no point to it because I'm not the kind of person who can actually escape through anything like that. I get a terrible down from that stuff and it hits me at three in the morning. All these things I'm trying to escape from, all the nasty things, suddenly become very clear, and all my more pessimistic views suddenly become very clear.'

Ecstasy was certainly no cure for his repeated fits of depression. After a buzz which can last several hours, users are left drained of energy and suffering gruelling after-effects, include acute dehydration and debilitating exhaustion. Because of these after-effects, Michael cut down on his use of the drug. But this was not the last time he took drugs. Later he spoke frankly of his enjoyment of marijuana and cannabis, which he claimed helped him overcome many of his personal problems.

While Michael was getting wasted in Los Angeles, or

rambling, incoherent, around the world, his family back in Britain were getting increasingly worried about him. He regularly spoke to his mother on the telephone but he kept the calls short if he thought he might sound unhappy. On the few occasions he visited his family, he always put on a brave face and gave nothing away. But his parents and sisters knew him too well to be fooled. They knew he was unhappy, but they found themselves unable to do anything to help him. While they suspected something was seriously wrong, they did not know that he was now on the brink of collapse and self-destruction.

7

Born Again in the USA

It was, perhaps surprisingly, Andrew Ridgeley who eventually put George Michael back on his feet. He flew out to Los Angeles for what was intended to be one last drunken night of self-indulgence. But when Ridgeley saw Michael, he found himself unprepared for the difference in him. His friend, once handsome and usually the picture of health, now looked drawn in the face, noticeably overweight, out of condition and fragile both mentally and physically. Ridgeley, never one to mince his words, could not hide his concern over the state his friend was in and the depths of unhappiness to which he had sunk.

Ridgeley remembered: 'I had no idea that he felt so bad emotionally. What was troubling him seemed to be a combination of things. He was doubting everything and, more than anything, I think he just needed to get all the tears out.'

Michael did not look to Ridgeley for advice; he simply needed someone to talk to, who would listen to him without interruption. No one was better qualified to do that job than Ridgeley. As they cracked open a case of wine, then moved on to spirits, Michael rambled through a catalogue of problems which he felt had all but submerged him. And at the top of the list was self-doubt.

Eventually, through the drunken haze, as his oldest friend reached out to him, Michael started slowly to regain some confidence.

When Michael woke up the next day he said he did not have the hangover he expected but was perfectly clear-headed. He came to compare the marathon tearful drinking binge with Ridgeley to a purging of some devil inside. He said: 'Until that moment, the way I felt and what I was really thinking hadn't crystallized. When I heard it actually come out of my mouth it was like an exorcism.' He was at last ready to pursue his solo career with all the energy he could muster. He said: 'I gave myself a quick kick and said, "You know there's not really anything else you want to do." I decided just to come back and do it again, but maybe on different terms.'

When Ridgeley flew back to Europe, Michael got back to writing the songs he needed for his debut album. He only broke off briefly, to renegotiate the terms of his five-album contract with Epic Records. Epic was happy to sign on almost any terms, as Michael had become their biggest single asset, the most lucrative name on their roster. With Dick Leahy guiding him, Michael was an astute negotiator. He would listen politely during meetings and then explain his career plans with enormous confidence. In four years he had changed beyond recognition as a businessman. Now he never allowed himself to be put on the spot to make a take-it-or-leave-it decision. If he sometimes made a quick decision at a meeting, it was not because he was being rushed, but simply because someone had proposed the deal he already had in mind.

Michael came back to London for Christmas 1986. It was a quiet time. He had put drink and drug binges behind him and settled for more traditional pursuits. He was feeling so benign that he even considered going carol singing with a group of friends around local pubs and went so far as to consider a suitable disguise, a long-haired wig. Friends found him more relaxed than he had been for years. And he seemed more sure of his future; sure of what he wanted and sure of what he could achieve. His family were among the first to notice the difference in his outlook when he visited to wish them a happy Christmas and exchange gifts.

His first single release since the end of Wham! was the track he laid down in Detroit with Aretha Franklin, 'I Knew You Were Waiting (For Me)'. When it was finally released on both sides of the Atlantic in January 1987, it gave Michael his next No. 1 in both America and the UK. And it was Aretha Franklin's first No. 1 in America for twenty years, since the soul standard 'Respect' hit the top in 1967. In Britain 'I Knew You Were Waiting (For Me)' became, remarkably, Aretha's first No. 1 single ever. Although released in the UK on the Epic label, in America it was issued by the label to which Franklin was signed, Arista.

The success of the single in America gave Michael a new burst of enthusiasm for conquering the territory and the first indication that he was capable of joining the ranks of rock's other megastars. He said in *Bare*: 'The success of the Aretha thing, especially in America, made me realize that there was something for me to sink my teeth into over there. I knew I had to get into line with Madonna, Prince, Jackson, and some of that came from the fact that a lot of people I'd been competing with in England – the

Frankies, Spandau Ballet, Boy George, Duran Duran – had either cooled off or fallen away.'

Having renewed his relationship with Epic, Michael was soon to agree a new management deal, with Rob Kahane and his lawyer partner Michael Lippman. An agent with ten years experience, Kahane had started out in the mail-room of a music company and worked his way up in the industry, along the way serving an apprenticeship of coffee-making for luminaries like Barbra Streisand and Anthony Perkins. Kahane's partner Lippman had started out working for the celebrity divorce lawyer Marvin Mitchelson before becoming David Bowie's lawyer for many years.

When Michael sacked Nomis Management at the beginning of 1986, Kahane, the producer of Wham!'s American tour, quickly set his sights on taking over the job. Michael explained: 'He came up to me and said, "I'm going to be your manager!" and I just laughed at him. He used the Aretha Franklin single as an example of what he could do. It was always going to be a big record, but the way Rob Kahane and his partner, Michael Lippman, worked the record company and the radio stations made it obvious they could deliver.' As before, Michael, ever-cautious, agreed first to hire Kahane and Lippman as his managers in North America only. Later, when he was more confident in their efforts, he made them his managers for all territories worldwide.

The same month as the single with Aretha was released, January 1987, the two former backing singers from Wham! emerged as pop stars in their own right. Pepsi DeMacque and Shirlie Holliman became Pepsi and Shirlie and in the course of the year notched up two Top 10 hits. Their debut single, 'Heartbeat', was their highest performer, making it to No. 2 for two weeks and, ironically, was only kept off the top slot by George Michael's duet with Aretha Franklin.

The first half of 1987 saw Michael working flat-out on his album. He was now dividing his time between the two studios where the solo album was to be recorded, Sarm Studios West, in Notting Hill, west London, and the PUK Studios, in Denmark.

He was still capable of mood swings and some days suffered from sudden bouts of insecurity causing him to cancel studio sessions or simply not turn up. When he was in the studio, he liked to be surrounded only by the members of his small personal team headed by Siobhan Bailey and recording engineer Chris Porter. Michael arranged and produced all the tracks. If things were not going the right way Porter's opinion was one of the few he respected. It was a fruitful collaboration. With so many Wham! tracks already to their credit, each knew the other's strengths and weaknesses. More importantly, they found they could work long hours in close proximity without falling out with each other.

The tracks emerging for the new album revealed a new style for Michael. Harnessing the potential of digital equipment and computers to the full, he could bend his notes electronically, allowing him sing in any pitch and in any key to extend his range. He first laid down many of the instrument tracks himself, then added the vocals. Other musicians brought in to work at various times on the album included Michael's long-standing bass player Deon Estus (who wore his hair Rastafarian style complete with coloured beads in his dreadlocks), seasoned guitarists Hugh Burns and Robert Ahwai and keyboard player Betsy Cook. But Michael provided all lead and backing vocals himself, played many of the instruments and was also credited as writer, arranger and producer. It was a happy album to record and the result was evident in the music emerging; it was turning out to be upbeat and energetic, with a raw, spiky edge.

On 1 April – deemed International AIDS Day – Michael took a break from the recording schedule to make a rare public appearance at Wembley Arena at an AIDS benefit gala called The Party, to raise funds for the London AIDS charity, the Terrence Higgins Trust. The line-up included Elton John, Meat Loaf, Boy George, the Communards, Bob Geldof, Andy Summers of The Police, Sandie Shaw, Aswad, the Frankie Goes to Hollywood frontman Holly Johnson, The Who's John Entwhistle and Kim Wilde. Andrew Ridgeley also agreed to appear on guitar and backing vocals when Michael performed the Wham! hit 'Everything She Wants'. Ridgeley was relieved that Michael was now fully confident and content and quite recovered from his crisis of confidence in Los Angeles the year before. Ridgeley slipped back into the wings after one song, leaving Michael to perform two more alone – the Len Barry Sixties hit '1-2-3', and Stevie Wonder's 'Love's In Need Of Love Today'.

Two months later, in June, Michael bought his first house, a sprawling mansion in Hampstead, north London. He paid nearly £2 million for the property, and he was said to have paid in cash. Modern and spacious, the house had large windows which allowed daylight to flood into the big living rooms. He fitted white carpet throughout and apart from some large sofas, the rooms were sparsely furnished. It had the aura of an airport lounge. There were stacks of CDs and an elaborate sound system. Each of the five bedrooms, as well as the kitchen and the living rooms, had televisions. There was a three-acre garden, tended by a number of gardeners, and a Range Rover and a Mercedes parked in the garage.

June also saw the release of Michael's first record as a post-Wham! solo performer, his most daring and controversial single to date, 'I Want Your Sex'. It soon became notorious for its potent refrain, declaring sex to be natural and sex to be good, and while not everybody does have sex, 'everybody should'.

The steamy video to accompany the single, directed by Michael and Andy Morahan, featured Michael cavorting with Kathy Jeung, on whose body he wrote in lipstick the words 'Explore' on her thigh and 'Monogamy' across her back. Michael, who had reverted once again to blond hair, wore a small crucifix earring in his left ear. But he was still overweight and did not feel comfortable about his figure. A body double, Chris Beedie, took his place for some of the close-ups.

The single was received with outrage on both sides of the Atlantic and it is not hard to see why. The release of a flagrantly sexual song, titled 'I Want Your Sex', with its erotic incitements appeared spectacularly ill-timed. Both Britain and the United States were at the height of the hysteria surrounding the AIDS epidemic and the media were quick to attack the record as irresponsible, suggesting that it encouraged indiscriminate sex and discouraged confining sex to one partner. In Britain commercial television, through the demands of the Independent Broadcasting

Authority, commercial radio and the BBC banned it. The BBC's pop network, Radio One, was allowed to play the song only after nine in the evening. In America MTV refused to show the video until it had been edited, at their insistence, three times to remove what they considered to be its pornographic content. And the station also demanded that Michael record a pro-monogamy prologue making clear that wanting too much sex could have 'deadly consequences'.

The ruckus refused to die down and Michael was obliged to defend the song and the video in public. He said that the message of the song was being misread and he in turn criticized the media for being so ready to approve censorship. Above all he denied that the song encouraged people to be promiscuous or indulge in irresponsible unprotected sex. 'It wasn't just about fucking – it was about fucking within a relationship,' he explained. 'I wanted to reach a new bunch of fans with a single, and it worked well in the States. But I couldn't attract new fans in Britain – because of the IBA ban nobody heard it.'

In the face of hostility to the video from the broadcasters, the Michael camp had to quickly start distributing the video by other means. It was important to build up a head of steam behind the record, for without radio or television play it would not sell. Copies were shipped out in vast quantities to bars and video cafes around the country. Michael agreed to a cut in his royalties to subsidize the video so it could be sold cheaply to fans. He is also reported to have retaliated against the BBC by instructing that no further versions of the song or the video should be dispatched to any of the corporation's television and radio departments.

Later Michael insisted that the ban was silly and hypocritical. 'I just thought it was so pathetic. American rap music and heavy metal are so aggressively sexual in a completely distasteful way – and I didn't think "I Want Your Sex" was at all,' Michael said. And the British attitude was put into perspective by a final twist of the story when in Belgium 'I Want Your Sex' was used to help teach safe-sex education to children and teenagers.

During the fuss, Michael was asked what he deemed pornography to be. He answered: 'Sex detached from feeling. People fucking for the sake of fucking is fine. People fucking for the sake of other people is pornography. In terms of casual sex there are great lovers and lousy lovers. I think I'm pretty good, probably.' It was a good commercial answer. Caught up in controversy, Michael needed to defend himself while not diminishing his sexual image. He wanted to confirm that he was still in favour of sex while not seeming unaware of the dangers of rampant sexual activity. And, as his whole act was based upon his sex appeal, it was impossible to deny that sex was important to him. It was typical of his vanity, his immodesty and his lack of sophistication, however, that he could not resist the assertion that he was himself a good lover.

Despite the widespread air-play problems 'I Want Your Sex' encountered in Britain, it still made No. 3 in August. In America it performed even better, reaching No. 2 in the same month, thanks in part to its inclusion in the soundtrack for the Eddie Murphy film sequel *Beverly Hills Cop II*. And the commercial success of the single repaid the guile of Michael's methods. He was not surprised that the single attracted controversy because it was intended to do just that, to shock and therefore attract publicity. But part of this gambit was then to act as if it was he who was outraged.

Record plugger Gary Farrow, one of the Michael entourage to survive the purge of Nomis Management personnel, revealed in *Bare*: 'I remember he sang "I Want Your Sex" to me in the back of a car and I knew we would have trouble with it. We decided that if it was going to be banned, then we would throw the shit against the wall and really make a big fuss.'

Trevor Dann, who worked on Radio One, described how records came to be banned in those days. 'Of course, records are never banned, even in the bad old days of the Eighties. Even "Relax" by Frankie Goes To Hollywood, was not actually banned, although that is the phrase that careless journalists like to use. I would imagine that what will have happened is a bit like when I was at Radio One, when we had "Sexual Healing" by Marvin Gaye. Everyone says we've got to play this record, but we clearly can't play it at prime time because, well, you can't. Because, family audience, and so on. So they will have found ways to stick it out with kind of flags and claxons when they felt they needed to, like in the chart show. But otherwise not play it.

'I remember in the press George got terribly heated about it because it was stopping his marvellous song reaching the public. But you've got to be a tosser not to know that that's going to happen. Write a lyric like that, it's not going to get played on Radio One. Oddly enough it would stand much more chance now because now Radio One has almost half the listeners it had ten years ago and it would be a little bit easier for them to play it. I think if I was running the play-list and it came out now I think I would play it.'

Michael said of 'I Want Your Sex': 'It was just huge in America. It basically launched my career with such a bang – no pun intended – that I couldn't have wished for anything better to happen in the sense that my career needed to go somewhere. I needed to do an about-turn.'

Although he profited from it, Michael felt wounded by some of the hostile treatment he received from the British tabloid press. As ever, they profited daily from their hypocritical attitude to sex, using fake indignation as a means of telling all the details of a sex scandal. And it wasn't long before they started making tenuous links between AIDS – which some misinformed papers described as a purely homosexual problem – and George Michael's own possible sexuality.

By 1987 the tabloids in Britain had written numerous sensational stories at the expense of a number of artists who had conceded that they may not be heterosexual, among them Boy George and Holly Johnson. Column miles were devoted to first reporting in detail their – in the parlance of the day – 'gender-bender' antics, then they wallowed in the inevitable fall from grace. Boy George's own family told the press about his heroin addiction, while the tabloids had a field-day when Johnson, who sang the controversial 'Relax', later fell victim to HIV, the precursor to AIDS.

And no personality, however successful, was safe from the prying of prurient reporters. Elton John, a pillar of the British rock establishment, had admitted to being bisexual in an interview with *Rolling Stone* magazine in the Seventies. But such honesty had only whetted the appetites of the British tabloid editors who always wanted to know more. The climax to Elton John's persecution came in 1987, the year of 'I Want Your Sex', when the *Sun* splashed a story about Elton John and homosexual prostitutes on its front page, written by Craig 'The Bouncing Bogbrush' MacKenzie (younger brother of the legendary *Sun* editor Kelvin MacKenzie). But the *Sun*'s glee was short-lived. Within a year a jubilant Elton John picked up a record £1 million libel damages from the paper, but a close friend admitted the stress of the action had brought the singer close to a breakdown.

George Michael's own sexuality aside, as a result of 'I Want Your Sex' he emerged, albeit reluctantly, as a spokesman on sexual attitudes for an entire generation of young people. 'I wasn't at all comfortable with being a sex spokesman,' he confided. 'I didn't see why anyone should ask me. The song anyway wasn't just about fucking – it was about fucking within a relationship. My whole point was that there should be an attack on promiscuity, but you could do it without making kids frightened of sex.' But the controversy surrounding 'I Want Your Sex' ensured that George Michael and the serious business of sexually transmitted diseases were permanently linked in the public mind.

Three years later, in 1990, Michael was more comfortable as a sex spokesman and his words revealed a greater wisdom on the subject of AIDS. He said in *Bare*: 'I still don't know anyone who has died of AIDS. There will be a period when I'm going to know people; there will be people I know from London who will die. But I think the generation of gay people which follows them is not going to fall in the same way because I don't think they're going

145

to be anything like as promiscuous. Yes, there are still loads of gay clubs that are full every night, but I'm sure the fear is there and that it's changing the way a lot of people are acting if they've just come on the scene.'

Michael learned a number of lessons from the avalanche of publicity surrounding 'I Want Your Sex'. First he was aware that it was his first single in over four years not to reach the top of the British charts (with the exception of 'Last Christmas' which was held off by Band Aid's 'Do They Know It's Christmas?'). His immediate response was to head in a quite different direction and plan his return with a very different image.

In the meantime he devoted his energies to completing work on his solo album, provisionally entitled *Faith* after the strongest song yet recorded on it. It was evident to those close to him that he had discovered a new and potent source of creativity in the studio and that he was about to emerge with a new batch of songs which would show sustained lyrical and musical depth.

George Michael's new image was launched alongside his new songs when the album's title track was released in October. Out went the last vestiges of the shiny-faced boy pop star; in came a broody but carefully manicured hunky style. A larger crucifix than before now dangled from his left ear and Michael hid his brooding sexuality behind mirrored Ray-Ban sunglasses. His hair was jet-black again and he returned to his uniform of black leather jacket, black jeans and black T-shirt and black pointed, metal-tipped leather boots. And overnight he launched what would quickly become the world's most famous five o'clock shadow. Sales of beard trimmers rocketed in Britain and America.

The makeover worked wonders and established Michael as the King of Cool. At times, however, it seemed he was trying a bit too hard. His new image was tough, mean and arrogant. But those who really knew him barely recognized the macho, rugged, rough and ready James Dean persona he now displayed on stage. Having denounced the cute boy-next-door image he enjoyed in his Wham! days as nothing more than a sham, in time he would say the same of his butch Faith front. He had created another monstrous image and he would use it to remarkable effect.

The *Faith* album was written with the American market in mind, and he played the full rock star part to give the Americans a clearly identifiable character to grasp. Michael thought he might have overdone the manliness of his new persona. 'I wasn't comfortable with how strong that image became,' he later admitted. 'I never considered it a particularly macho look, but I tried to soften it just a bit by having a string of pearls on one of the shoulders of the leather jacket.'

The single 'Faith' entered the British chart at No. 10 on 24 October. A week later it reached No. 2, remaining for two weeks, held off the top spot by the Bee Gees' four-week run with 'You Win Again'. In America it was a different story. Michael reached the top of the Billboard Hot 100 chart on 12 December and held the slot for four weeks over the most lucrative Christmas holiday season in the richest territory in the world.

Michael explained that the song was autobiographical: '"Faith" was inspired by a couple of relationships that didn't happen. Very soon after the break-up of the group and before I started seeing Kathy, there were people who

I played around with the idea of starting relationships with and eventually decided against them.'

In November the album was released and surged to the top of the sales charts. The album opened with thunderous chords played, on what sounded like a cathedral organ by Chris Cameron which gradually melted away into the title track. Of the eight further songs, 'I Want Your Sex' had been released as a single and eventually four more, 'Father Figure', 'One More Try', 'Monkey' and 'Kissing A Fool', would be released as singles and dominate the charts on both sides of the Atlantic. Of the remaining songs on the album – 'Hard Day', 'Hand To Mouth' and 'Look At Your Hands' – the last was the weakest. Perhaps tellingly, it was co-written with his friend David Austin and was the only track on the album which was not entirely Michael's work.

The launch party for *Faith* was at the Savoy Hotel on the Strand and the champagne and dining bill came to £100,000. It was the traditional music industry mix of real stars and second-rank, faded pop names and lesser television celebrities. Among those at the bash were Elton John and wife Renate, Bob Geldof, Curiosity Killed the Cat, Jonathan Ross, Mandy Smith, Anne Diamond, *EastEnders* star Anita Dobson, former *Coronation Street* star Chris Quentin and one-time suburban brothel-keeper Cynthia Payne. *Faith* did not need such a tacky send-off, but Michael liked a cheesy party as much as anyone and he enjoyed being the centre of attention at an event he controlled.

Faith was soon proving to be an extraordinary success. CBS found itself in the odd position of allowing some of its biggest names to be eclipsed by the brightness of the talent on its small and hitherto undistinguished subsidiary Epic. But despite albums from some of the biggest names in American music, Michael Jackson, Bruce Springsteen, Pink Floyd and Mick Jagger, George Michael outsold them all. In Britain, the album went straight to No. 1 on 14 November and continued selling well for the next two years. In America, no sooner had *Faith*'s four-week run on the singles chart ended than his album took over at the top of the Billboard album chart. The following week it was briefly dislodged, by a singer called Tiffany, but two weeks later *Faith* returned to the top and held off all comers for the next five weeks. Two months later, in May, it topped the album chart for the third time and remained there for another six weeks. It went on to spend a full year in America's album Top 10, not finally falling out of the Top 100 until May 1989.

There were numerous religious symbols on the album's packaging other than the title. The cover featured George Michael wearing his large crucifix earring. And on the inner sleeve were printed five icons symbolizing Faith, Music, Money, Religion and Love. But although some songs appeared to be inspired by gospel music, that was as close as it came to genuine religious content. Michael went out of his way to say the project had boosted his faith in himself, but he avoided commenting on his feelings about religion.

He did explain the significance of the album title, saying: 'To me the album was about an affirmation of faith – because before that period of my life there had been a lack of it. What "Faith" meant – the album, the campaign, all of it – was that I had faith life was going to deliver, that I was going to get the things I wanted, that my life would bring me the things that are important to me.' And a sleeve note carried the following words: 'These songs are the results of the last two years of my life. They are dedicated to my family and friends, whose loyalty and time are more important to me than ever before. Love as always.'

While the press in Britain continued to hound Michael, looking for scandals to bring about his downfall, in America he was winning praise from all quarters. Even *Playboy* gave a glowing review for Michael and his music. The magazine's reviewer, Nelson George, wrote of the *Faith* album: 'It's arranged with wit, intelligently written and beautifully sung.' The review concluded: 'It's Michael's superb feel for R&B/funk that makes *Faith* so imposing.' He picked 'Hand To Mouth' as the album's 'most brilliant song', noting it was 'a seductive R&B groove that underscores Michael's sardonic view of America's appeal to foreigners'. And Nelson George reported that the singer had given off an unlikely sexual message. 'Michael is, of course, more than just musically gifted,' he wrote. 'He's sexy in a fey way, but with enough believable machismo not to offend straight-arrow types.'

Faith was well received by critics around the world. *Rolling Stone* hailed the album as the work in which, finally, 'the pop star grows up'. Michael told the magazine: 'If you can listen to this album and not like anything on it, then you do not like pop music.'

Of the album's few critics, the American writer David Hiltbrand made one of the fiercest attacks in a piece for *People Weekly*, a celebrity magazine, declaring: 'Michael has meticulously crafted the sound of the LP, but the record is marred by his weakness for mawkish material.

He carried the torch enough on "Faith" to qualify for the Olympic opening ritual. Other selections such as "Hard Day" are clearly just half-baked song fragments endlessly repeated. Michael's voice can be quite appealing when he puts some muscle into it. Most of the time, however, he's trying to inject it with overwrought drama. There seem to be only two shades on his emotional palette. Michael's voice either gets all soft and breathy (signifies he's being sensitive or seductive) or distraught (signifies he's heart-broken, angry or horny).'

Even if the material may have been too mawkish for some, Michael was not much interested in what the critics wrote about it. He only measured the album's success by the business it did around the world. A carefully planned timetable of single releases from the album, backed up with impeccable marketing campaigns, ensured that the success easily drowned out dissident voices.

By the end of 1987, Michael was a fast-rising star in Britain's wealthiest people polls. According to a report in the *Sun*, by the end of 1987 Michael had spent over £6 million on gifts for his family and friends. In particular he enjoyed giving away cars. He had given his mother a £14,000 BMW, his father a Rolls-Royce, his sister Melanie a BMW and Kathy Jeung a £17,000 Toyota sports car.

Yet despite his wealth he remained a man of modest tastes who lived alone and found the scale of his success something of an embarrassment. He did not want servants waiting on him, not because he would feel uncomfortable with them, but because they would intrude upon his privacy.

151

8

Caged

The *Faith* album thrust Michael to the top of the music industry and, throughout 1988, it went on to sell in record numbers. The 'Faith' single had received saturation airplay on radio stations ensuring that it, then the album, then the other singles from the album came to conquer the sales charts on every continent. *Time* magazine was in awe, concluding: 'No one is playing the pop game as cannily as George Michael.'

Realizing the extent of Michael's exceptional worth, CBS set about trying to extend their remunerative relationship. The company was under pressure. Through a series of decisions taken way above them in the entertainment industry, Sony had bought CBS and with it Epic records and George Michael's contract. During the Eighties, the music industry was gradually taken over by a few gargantuan, mainly Japanese, electronic equipment manufacturing companies, who discovered that the success of hardware sales was directly linked to the quality of creative product available. The first round of the battle between the companies took place in the early Eighties, when Philips, the Dutch owners of Polygram Records, locked horns with Sony over videotaping systems. Philips' system was VHS; Sony made Betamax, a slightly more compact format.

The battle was decided not on the relative quality of the engineering but on what was made available to play on the respective systems. After a long struggle, Philips, with its access to product through its ownership of music companies, established VHS as the market leader and Sony's Betamax died, except in the professional television field. Humbled by defeat, the mighty Sony vowed it would never again let its lack of access to music and film rights stand in the way of future innovations. Sony determined to buy into the American music and film industries to ensure that it had a repertory of big-name recording artists at its disposal. They were determined that history would not be allowed to repeat itself. What was at stake was dominance of the two next important domestic equipment market break-throughs, the US introduction of digital audio tape, or DAT, and the mini-disc.

They therefore set out in the late Eighties on a stampede to buy up all providers of available creative product. And so Sony, through spending £2 billion to buy CBS Records and its record labels Columbia and Epic, came to own a seven-album agreement with George Michael. He was just one of hundreds of bestselling recording artists in the deal, among them Michael Jackson, Bob Dylan, Bruce Springsteen and Barbra Streisand. Its corporate rivals rapidly followed suit: Philips, the Dutch company who had led the fashion in acquiring exclusive recording rights, added Island Records to its Polydor, Phonogram and A&M labels; the British group Thorn EMI snapped up Virgin and Chrysalis; while the Japanese company Matsushita bought MCA and Geffen Records; and Bertelsmann of West Germany bought RCA. It was the right business decision for Sony, for the world of talent was being bought up around them, but the scale of the ownership battle going on above their heads disturbed some of their newly acquired artists, among them George Michael.

He was among a number of CBS names who became anxious at the prospect of their output being managed by a Japanese company with no experience of handling creative artists. Sony went out of its way to reassure them that nothing would change. They first confirmed that the main CBS executives would be retained. Walter Yetnikoff, the CBS Records group president, and the other senior CBS executives who had worked so closely with the artists were not only retained but awarded a $50 million goodwill bonus. Yetnikoff's presence was vital in the new organization because he and he alone was able to handle some of the more demanding names on the rosta. It was said that Barbra Streisand wouldn't talk to anyone else at CBS. And Yetnikoff reassured the artists that Sony would treat them with great respect. 'They like the artists and the business,' he said. 'They understand it's more important for me to take Bruce Springsteen's call than Norio Ohga's [world president of Sony].' But Michael, at the time the biggest name in Sony's repertory, did not share Yetnikoff's faith in Sony.

When Sony bought CBS Records in January 1988, the cherry on top of the cake was George Michael. His debut solo album had taken Michael right to the top of the global music industry and throughout 1988 the album went on to break a succession of sales records. The new Sony management wanted CBS to keep control of all its successful product, so an offer was made to Michael that he would deliver seven albums over the next fifteen years. There would be a massive cash advance of $11 million.

There was financial advantage to George Michael if a deal could be made quickly as he was preparing to set off on a gruelling world tour to boost sales of *Faith*. As he would be out of Britain for most of the year, any income that year would be tax-free, so it was worth taking as large an advance from the new CBS contract as possible.

For months Michael attended intense tour planning meetings to maximize the impact of his personal appearances in sports stadiums and enormous theatres on every continent. Advising him were his artistic mentor, the British music publisher Dick Leahy, his recently appointed American managers, Rob Kahane and Michael Lippman, and Jake Duncan the tour manager who had ensured that all previous public appearances had been trouble-free.

For a long time George Michael had wavered about whether to mount such a long tour. His previous experiences had been mixed. His tour of China with Wham! had been a publicity success, even if it had proved unexpectedly expensive. But he was worried now about the strain of holding up a whole show on his own. And he was concerned, too, that he might suffer the voice trouble which had caused concerts to be scrapped in the past.

He came to the conclusion that, having sold enormous numbers of albums around the world, he needed to consolidate his network of fans with a live tour. In the past he had denied that he deserved to be ranked alongside pop music's greatest performers – Michael Jackson, Madonna and Prince – but the runaway success of *Faith* meant that he could come clean. He thought he was every bit as good as they were. The tour would be a way of proving to himself, as much as to his fans, that he was in the same league as the others. He believed he could entertain fans in their hundreds of thousands, but the only way he would know for certain would be if he went on the road.

Above all he knew that if he was to conquer the American market once and for all and win over a massive permanent fan-base there, he would have to do it in person. He did not want to be dismissed as a transitory talent who could not perform consistently and who could only make music in a recording studio, backed by session musicians and protected by the wonders of recording technology. Neither did he wish to remain principally a British success. But he did not need to take on the scale of tour that was being planned.

It would last an exhausting ten months, starting in Japan in February 1988. It would then take in Australia, move on to Europe, then arrive for the final forty-six concerts in America at the end of the year. Only hardened rock stars volunteered for such a tour – and even by the standards of gluttons for punishment like the Rolling Stones, the tour being planned for George Michael was a monster. He agreed to play over 160 dates in all, which would reach a total audience of more than 20 million. If it was mad to agree to such a punishing schedule, it would demand a kind of madness to survive it. His new tough-guy stage persona was a good start, for it allowed him to hide behind a mask of confidence and cool. But even as he agreed to the tour dates, Michael began doubting whether he could fulfil the obligations he was now entering into.

The dangers were evident from his earlier experience of continual performing. There was the isolation from real life and the false remedies for it. He already knew himself to be vulnerable to drink and drugs. On tour both would appear like an oasis in the desert. There was also the threat to his voice, which might leave his throat permanently damaged. Then there were the mental pressures. He was already prone to loneliness and the tour would emphasize the fact that he was on his own and that he alone could satisfy his millions of fans.

Moreover, he knew that he was at heart a recluse, happiest when hiding out in the comfort of his Hampstead home, in control of those who came and went. On tour, he knew he would lose control of his domain. He knew himself to be a private person, yet he was about to invite the world to invade his privacy every night for ten months.

He had made some effort to prepare himself for the onslaught. The release of the single 'Faith' and its video in October 1987 had seen Michael reinvent himself as a more robust character. His uniform now was a thick-skinned black leather jacket worn over tough skin-tight jeans. His boyish face was hidden behind thick dark Greek-Cypriot stubble, his most famous feature. To show that, despite his sweet songs, he held traditional notions of gentleness in contempt, he wore a crucifix as an earring. And to complete the camouflage, he hid himself behind impenetrable mirrored Ray-Ban sunglasses.

In case anyone had failed to understand the extent of the transformation from cute Wham! singer to George Michael solo star, the video to accompany the release of the single 'Father Figure', directed by Tony Scott in January 1988, would run the message home. No longer the boy next door, he was now an unattainable, forbidding superstar.

In the video Michael posed as an American taxi driver cruising deserted downtown streets late at night looking for a fare. With a cigarette hanging from the corner of his mouth, he stops to pick up a stylish leggy blonde. The video was shot in black and white to suggest that Michael wanted to shun the limelight and take refuge in the shadows. To that extent the image was true, because the real George Michael wished to keep away from prying eyes.

In Britain, there was resistance to Michael's new look. Former Wham! fans did not instantly take to the new, brooding George Michael. 'Father Figure' performed disappointingly in the UK singles charts, peaking just a week after its release at No. 11, the worst performance for a Michael single since the early days of Wham!.

By contrast, in America the lush soul sound of 'Father Figure' instantly found a massive following and huge sales. Within a month of release it topped the singles chart and stayed there for two weeks. Americans took Michael's change of image in their stride.

Just as he was about to set out on the world tour he received another clutch of music industry tributes. In February, at the British Phonographic Industry awards ceremony, he scooped the Best British Male Artist title. The timing of the award was perfect for Michael as it coincided with the final stage of negotiations between CBS Records and Michael's management. The negotiations were up against a deadline, the start of the tour, after which talks would be put on hold. At the last minute CBS secured the contract they were seeking: a seven-album deal over fifteen years.

And there was one final piece of personal investment business for Michael to settle before embarking on his tour. He had learnt that some of his vast fortune was held in shares in an American arms company which supplied weapons to the Contra rebels in Nicaragua, who with American backing were attempting to overthrow the elected Sandinista communist regime. He instructed his accountant to dispose of the stock at once. He expressed his anger at his financial advisers, making it clear that he expected them to be more sensitive to his personal feelings in the future and that they should have noted his aversion to politically reactionary business ventures when he sacked his former managers for attempting to sell him into the hands of Sun City in South Africa behind his back. This was the second incident to suggest that George Michael was firmly of the liberal left and that he would have no links, however invisible, with those on the political right.

Before setting off on his marathon tour, Michael began to get himself in good physical shape. He arranged that his touring entourage include a chef to keep an eye on his diet and a personal trainer to keep him trim. He still fought a constant battle against gaining weight, trying to resist his fondness for Galaxy chocolate bars and seafood doused in mayonnaise. He had already tried a number of different slimming diets, including a period as a vegetarian. Like many stars he had become obsessed with his weight. For the tour he instructed his chef to prepare salads, to use white meats such as chicken, and to roast, not fry, the vegetables. His personal trainer, Paul Corkhill, set up a strict daily routine of physical work-outs which could sometimes last as long as four hours.

Superstardom also brought a new danger to his health. Like many celebrities it was possible he would become the target of a deranged fan. The lessons of John Lennon's death and the stalking of stars like Jodie Foster were clear. So from the beginning of the tour Michael was protected by a small army of vigilant, zealous bodyguards to save him from over-eager fans, obsessive people or any kind of trouble which might gain bad publicity.

Other important preparations were set in train for the journey around the world. The abiding symbol of the 'Faith' tour was to be Michael's crucifix earring. The original was an inexpensive ring bought by one of his sisters, both still living at the family home in Bushey. But to be on the safe side, in case of incident or loss, seven identical rings were bought. Michael's greatest fear was that an over-enthusiastic fan at the front of the stage would reach out and grab the ring from his ear as a souvenir, perhaps ripping his ear-lobe in the process. So each night before he took to the stage his dresser was instructed to ensure that the earring was not securely fastened.

The 'Faith' tour opened in Japan on 19 February 1988, at Tokyo's 12,000-seat Budokan Theatre. Although the *Faith* album had only been released in Japan shortly before Christmas 1987, it sold so many copies by the end of the year that it had quickly become the country's bestselling album of 1987.

The first concert was a gruelling three-hour set featuring tracks from his *Faith* album, supplemented by a few favourite songs from the Wham! days – most importantly the successful solo single 'Careless Whisper' – and a handful of soul covers, such as Stevie Wonder's 'Love's In Need Of Love Today', a firm favourite with the fans, and Labelle's hit 'Lady Marmalade', with which he closed the show.

Although Michael was comfortable with his own songs, he enjoyed performing other singers' material. He found it relaxing in a way that performing his own work was not.

'I used to love sound checks because that's when you get a chance to play those kind of numbers,' he said in *Bare*. 'I'd get such a lot of pleasure to go out and do that for a couple of hours, but as a singer and a media artist you never get the chance to enjoy yourself, you never get to just go out and sing some songs you love. You always have to play your own material, which you're sick of, or you're recording or promoting.'

The need to constantly restrict himself to his own repertory of songs was demanded by his record company, who needed to sell the latest album and held no commercial interest in the other songs. His frequent flouting of that restriction would eventually get him into trouble with Sony, who began to insist that he stick to material from which the company could profit, rather than lend his talent to the work of others (whose rights were probably held by competitors).

The 'Faith' tour offered him total control over the choice of material and the way it was presented, but still Michael was unhappy. On leaving Japan he realized with a jolt that touring was not a musical experience and that the hard work was upon him. 'I can remember the exact moment that I decided I must change my life,' he said. 'We opened the "Faith" tour in Japan, which was fine because they are reasonably quiet and they listen to the music. But then we went to Australia, and the roof came off the first place we came to. The screaming. I thought, "God, it's happening all over again. I'm not going to have the chance to really sing." And I realized I had to do it for ten months.'

He responded by cutting himself off as much as possible, keeping his privacy and shutting down on those who wanted to befriend him. Like The Beatles before him, he felt unhappy that no one was listening to him any more, they simply wanted the experience of seeing him perform. But to Michael the song was everything.

He soon discovered that there were drawbacks to being the centre of an audience's attention. This was his first time on stage as a solo performer and he soon found that he missed the camaraderie of the Wham! years. On previous tours he counted on Ridgeley to make him smile or take the attention away from him and share the burden of the show. Now, alone on stage and behind the scenes, he found himself surrounded entirely by paid employees. He felt like a lonely inmate in a prison of his own making.

Partly at the insistence of his managers, Kahane and Lippman, Michael kept himself distant from those he worked with. He erected a wall around himself when he was in public and few got past his security guards. On stage he was accompanied by a large backing band made up mostly of session musicians, except for Deon Estus, his regular bass guitarist, but he rarely socialized with them. He saw them at the on-stage sound-checks before the show, then during the show but rarely in between. Nor did he care to relax with his road crew.

A rare exception to this carefully constructed isolation was when one of the band, a reformed heroin user, lapsed back into the habit when the tour reached New York. Michael was sympathetic and asked him to promise it would never happen again. But this was a rare involvement in the day-to-day experiences of the band. For most of the time he felt the band performed better and the road crew harder when he kept them at a distance.

As he explained in *Bare*: 'The only time they'll do their

best is if there's some kind of barrier between you and them and they genuinely believe that, if they don't do their best, they're out. I never impressed that upon anyone. I didn't have to.'

In Australia a new stage prop joined the tour, a vast white cage in which Michael was to make his spectacular entrance. Like many extravagant stage ideas, the cage soon became a liability because it was so large, and Michael came to dread climbing into it. It added to the general air of jitters backstage because Michael became so anxious about whether it would work or not. But the logistics of erecting and rigging the massive steel structure soon seemed insignificant compared to the problem of George Michael's health.

By the time the tour reached Australia, Michael was complaining of acute problems with his larynx. Each concert was putting such a strain on his throat that it was causing him great pain. Throat lozenges and antiseptic throat sprays proved to have little effect. Some nights he battled to hit notes which he had always before reached effortlessly. And even mirrored sunglasses couldn't conceal from the audience the obvious pain he was suffering. Before long, concerts had to be cancelled to ease the strain on his throat, which added to his troubles, for few critics or fans believed he was ill; too often a cancellation was blamed on his temperament.

When the tour reached Europe in April, Michael's deteriorating health took a dramatic turn. He had seen a number of doctors about his throat and each offered the same diagnosis: there was nothing wrong with him. Michael knew otherwise, but he realized, too, that if his health problems were caused by fatigue or were psychosomatic then his whole career could be put in jeopardy. He became haunted by the prospect of a forced retirement from performing in public, which added anxiety to the strain he was already suffering.

He tried to ease his voice by minimizing the pressures of being on tour. In Japan and Australia he was forced to stick it out on the road, bouncing from anonymous hotel to anonymous hotel, sometimes interspersed with rented houses and hide-outs. He found it a horribly lonely business. The constant movement and disorientation began to take its toll on his mental health after a while, so, in an attempt to keep his sanity, he invited friends to join him for a few days or even a few weeks if they could find the time. Most discovered that on tour he was a very different George Michael from the man they thought they knew. Michael the stadium rock star was irritable and bossy and often moody and irrational, and they found that some of the employees around him were aggressive, hectoring bullies.

Michael said he 'developed this kind of shield from the majority of people on the tour and it's very hard to let down for ten seconds when you're with your friends. So I was in this kind of halfway house all the time. I had to keep trying to reassure them – look, I know I'm being a bit weird, but this whole thing is very hard to deal with. And I'm dealing with it the only way I know how, which is just to keep emotionally removed from everything – by being in my own world'.

Among those who joined Michael on tour were David Austin and, for almost a third of the tour dates, his cousin Andros Georgiou. But although both of them were old mates and reliable friends in London, Michael admitted that on tour he 'really couldn't communicate with them'.

Michael recalled in *Bare*: 'They were told by my minders what they should and shouldn't do with me and how I had to be at this place at a certain time or they were blamed if I went out with them after a gig and my voice was fucked up the next day. I had to sit down with everyone and say – look, stop having a go at my mates for things you want to say to me.'

When the tour reached Europe, he found a way of relieving the pressures and the tedium of being on the road by basing himself in a villa in St Tropez in the south of France. From there he was ferried by private helicopter to Nice airport, then on by plane to the next venue. In this way, instead of being on tour, he could consider himself to be on a series of day-trips, leaving St Tropez around lunchtime, flying to a European city to perform in the evening, then flying back to his villa the same night. The system helped him regain some sanity and it seemed to have some effect on minimizing the damage done to his throat.

On 16 April 'One More Try', the latest single lifted from the *Faith* album, was released in America. It was also the first single to be released in America before Britain, a pattern to be followed with every subsequent single release from the album. In the States the single reached the top on 28 May in just six weeks and stayed there for three weeks. In the UK, the song entered at No. 14, peaking the following week at No. 8.

In May Michael's decision to adopt a new soul style paid off handsomely when he won the ultimate accolade –

'One More Try' topped the American black album chart, the first album by a white solo artist ever to do so. In the music industry on both sides of the Atlantic he was deemed to have pulled off the impossible, the equivalent of selling ice-cream to Eskimos.

By the time the European leg of the tour opened in Rotterdam, Michael's health had become the story of the tour and the main subject of the opening press conference. To try to rest and hide from the press, he stayed in a hotel in Amsterdam. But he soon found himself having to deny a report in a British tabloid that the reason for the cancelled concerts and the repeated health scares was that he was suffering from AIDS. At a press conference staged in Rotterdam on the day of the first concert, Michael confidently told the assembled journalists, 'What I'm not here to do is make a series of denials into speculations about my private life.' However, when a *Daily Mirror* reporter asked Michael if he had taken an AIDS test, he was obliged to reply: 'No' and he refused to be further drawn on the question. However, the *Mirror* took Michael's denial as evidence that it was his fear of AIDS which prevented him from being tested.

In fact Michael was constantly being tested by doctors, but not for the AIDS virus. They were still puzzled by the pain he was experiencing in his throat. He explained in *Bare*: 'In five months I went to eight doctors, but none of them diagnosed the problem. They kept telling me it was just tour fatigue.' It was widely believed among the tour's personnel that any illness Michael was suffering from was merely a figment of his imagination. So Michael returned to London to be diagnosed by one of Britain's leading throat specialists, who immediately pinpointed the cause of the problem.

'He told me I actually did have a very large cyst at the bottom of my throat and that I should have it operated on as soon as possible,' explained Michael. He was booked in for an operation, to be done after he had completed five concerts, all sold out, at the Earls Court Exhibition Centre in London in June.

Between the concerts at Earls Court, Michael took part in a seventieth birthday benefit concert at Wembley for the freed South African ANC leader Nelson Mandela. The bill included many of the top rock acts, among them Dire Straits, the Eurythmics, Simple Minds, Whitney Houston, Natalie Cole, Sting, Joe Cocker and Al Green. Michael performed three soul covers by celebrated black musicians: Marvin Gaye's 'Sexual Healing', 'Village Ghetto Land' by Stevie Wonder and a subtle reworking of the Gladys Knight hit 'If I Were Your Woman'. But Michael was uneasy about the show and felt that many of the audience were simply there to see the white acts, not to celebrate the freedom of a great man.

As soon as the Earls Court concerts were over, the 'Faith' tour was temporarily halted while Michael under-went surgery to his throat. The operation to remove the cyst was straightforward, but had its surreal moments. A clause in the contract with the tour's insurers, liable for compensating any stadium owners for loss of income if the operation were not a success, insisted that Kahane, Michael's manager, should personally oversee any treat-ment Michael was to be given. So, while Michael lay unconscious on the operating table and went under the knife, Kahane stood by his bed, scrubbed up and sterilized and dressed in a surgical mask, watching every move. 'I looked at George and I felt completely sick,' he recalled.

The operation was deemed a complete success by the surgeons and Michael's throat consultant and the singer soon slipped out of Britain to quietly recuperate for four weeks in the south of France. The American leg of the 'Faith' tour would have to wait. He returned to the villa in St Tropez he had taken as a hideaway during the European leg of the tour. His doctors had told him that if he was to save his voice for the remaining forty or so American dates, it was best for him not to speak at all during his convalescence, but Michael found the instruction too much to bear. He talked and talked. And with the cyst removed, his throat felt better by the day.

While in St Tropez, Michael gave an interview to *Life* magazine, published in the September issue. The title's London bureau chief, Liz Nickson, asked Michael why he had decided to make himself look so hard and tough. Why should he make out by his looks that he was the sort of guy who broke hearts when his lyrics displayed quite the opposite emotion – vulnerability? Michael replied: 'It's a defence, isn't it? The way you look isn't necessarily the way you are. I'm easily hurt in some ways, and I suppose my appearance wards it off.'

Nickson asked what it was that the English press seemed to have against him, and Michael replied: 'They wish I didn't know I was capable of certain things. They want me to be a lot more humble. I won't be humble about songwriting and things I know I'm good at. It's a very jealous country. I love my country, but my father is Greek, so I don't think I have a totally English outlook. One thing about the people that drives me to distraction is their desire to keep everyone in their place.'

Michael laughed off Nickson's suggestion that he might feel a connection with Elvis Presley. 'I've never even dared to think of any comparison,' he said. And he put his success down to his devotion to music. 'I've only met a handful of people who are as committed to this business as I am, who believe in what they do,' he said. 'Especially at a time when music is so processed, when there is very little soul at the centre of it, to be singled out for being calculated, apart from being wrong, is incredibly hurtful.'

Nickson asked Michael whether he was religious, and he replied: 'No, religion has its structures, its rules and explanations for everything. I'm not really keen on explanations. I'm developing my own theory on the way to live life.'

But when asked about the powerful religious iconography on the cover of the *Faith* album, he confessed to being in awe of God. 'The imagery of Christianity is very powerful,' he remarked. 'Anything which gives people that much hope is a good thing. When I was a child I was an atheist; when I was a teenager I was an agnostic; now I know there's got to be a force far greater than we can imagine to believe in. As for the cross, it's an attractive symbol. My mum hated me wearing it originally. It was too strong for someone whose beliefs were as vague as mine.'

The next cull from *Faith* was 'Monkey', another slow-burning ballad. The song was remixed for its American release by two former musicians from Prince's backing band, Jimmy Tam and Terry Lewis, with a strict brief to give the song a flavour which would appeal to black urban Americans.

'Monkey' was released in America on 9 July and by the end of the following month gave Michael his third consecutive No. 1 of the year. In Britain the song entered the chart at No. 19, but a week later it had done its best business, reaching a peak of No. 13. For Michael, now used to automatic No. 1s, it was a disappointment, but considering that it was released from a bestselling album the sales were respectable.

Just four weeks after the operation on his throat, Michael returned to America to continue the remaining forty-six dates of his world tour, which was to include playing more than forty nights in a row of sell-out concerts. It was an extraordinary show business achievement which earned him the admiration of his fellow singers. With his ill-health behind him, he showed a renewed burst of energy. But he still found the strain of life on the road was getting him down.

As before, he shipped in friends when he could to alleviate the boredom, but for many nights he returned after the show to the loneliness of life in hotel rooms, which all came to look the same. Still, he preferred to return alone to his suite and surf the television channels than to 'relax' in the company of his entourage or employees. And he had felt no desire to meet new people or make friends as he travelled. The artificial life of a rock star on the road made him incapable of reaching the real lives of those around him. He found that he became easily bored with the sycophantic enthusiasm he received from his employees and he deeply missed his more down-to-earth friends in London.

He later spelt out his loathing for life on the road: 'You put yourself emotionally on ice. You have to. You put all your relationships on ice. You spend ten months in the company of people who work for you and so you don't get any honesty. You get it to a degree but there aren't enough people around to tell you you're being a wanker.'

When Michael reached preparations for the concert at the Forum in Los Angeles he partied hard, since the sprawling city had become his second home, and it is little surprise that there he gave some of the best performances of the entire tour. These were witnessed by three of the most successful female singers in America: Madonna, Janet Jackson and Whitney Houston, who turned out to see him on successive nights. The triumphant, back-breaking ten-month tour came to a halt in Pensacola, Florida, on 31 October.

Michael said later the tour was 'devastating', admitting that during it he had become 'hugely temperamental'. He explained: 'It was a combination of things, including being on the road for that long. I'm someone who needs a centre. I was very close to what I could call a breakdown until I finally took a month off, because of surgery, and sorted it out.' He determined never to do anything as long and unmanageable again and that he would avoid all unnecessary promotional work. He felt he had already endured a lifetime's promotional activity spending ten months and most of his patience on relentless touring.

Michael's final single release of the year was timed to

coincide with the last few weeks of his American tour. 'Kissing A Fool' was a smouldering and breathy ballad in the 'Careless Whisper' mould. It was released on 8 October in America and by the end of November, just after the tour ended, it reached No. 5. In Britain the release of the single was held back until December but then only managed to make No. 18.

The 'Faith' tour was, in retrospect, a triumph. He built upon the success of his record sales to become the world's most popular performer. And he proved to the music industry that he was capable of immense hard work and that the public seemed to adore him. The tour boosted the sales of *Faith* which that year became the biggest selling album worldwide. Over half the tracks also topped the singles charts in America. And even today it remains one of the most successful rock albums of all time, with sales in excess of 15 million.

And then, without warning, Michael's public appearances melted away. With the exception of the delayed UK release of 'Kissing A Fool' on 3 December, he disappeared. He did not release another single for two years.

This silence marked the end of an extraordinary period in his life. In the Eighties Michael clocked up an astonishing eight American No. 1 singles. To put that achievement in context, the artist then known as Prince had only one chart-topping single in America, while Madonna came close to Michael with seven. Only Michael Jackson outdid George Michael's success by reaching the top nine times.

Michael happily returned to the seclusion of his life at home in north London. There, as he began to relax, he decided that he would never again tour on such an exhausting scale. Instead he decided to save his strength for more important battles. In the process he determined to master the business implications of the new digital age.

The 'Faith' tour and the sales of the album gave him an extraordinarily powerful position from which to do business. The first thing he did as 1988 neared its end was to once again amend his contract with CBS. And before long he set out to establish himself as the undoubted master of his own destiny in the complex age of rights deals and the explosion in back-lists reissued on CD and other new electronic media and formats.

Michael could barely bank the multimillion-pound royalty cheques quickly enough. Yet he said he wasn't really driven by making money. 'I'm not a possession-orientated person,' he said, 'but I swear if I lost every penny tomorrow I'd be rich again within two years. Even if I couldn't do it for myself. Writing songs is my bank.' Being poor was no longer something he needed to think about. By the end of 1988 his impressive back-catalogue of songs was already earning enough to ensure that he would always be comfortably well-off – unless he did something foolish to lose it all. Which, within a few years, he very nearly did.

In the meantime, as 1989 began, at the age of twenty-five George Michael had reached the pinnacle of megastardom. The global reach of the rock music industry meant he was as famous in Africa and Asia as anywhere in America, Europe or Japan. It all seemed a far cry from the overweight boy lacking in confidence who dreamt of success as a pop singer in the tiny bedroom of his parents' modest house in north London.

9

Heard and Not Seen

With the 'Faith' tour behind him, in early 1989 George Michael took some well-deserved rest before thinking about his next album, the first of seven he was expected to produce in his new contract with CBS. George Michael decided to shut himself away to restore his creative talents. He adopted the life of a recluse and would only be tempted into the public eye when accepting music awards.

Michael's only contribution to the 1989 pop charts in America and Britain was a single, 'Heaven Help Me', co-written and produced by Michael and issued by his regular bass player, Deon Estus. Released in America at the end of February, over the next ten weeks it climbed steadily from No. 67, reaching No. 5 by the end of April. In Britain the record did very little business and failed to pierce the Top 40 list when it was released at the end of April.

April also marked the start of the annual round of music awards in London, which Michael would dominate. The night he picked up an Ivor Novello Music Award as Songwriter of the Year, his second, he found himself ill prepared. When he came to walk to the podium to accept the award he was slightly drunk. He had set off clutching a bottle of wine in his hand until Gary Farrow, his record-plugger, suggested he leave it behind at the table. According to Farrow, Michael replied: 'Fuck it, I've won, I don't give a toss.'

The honours also kept pouring in in America, where, at the sixteenth American Music Awards at the Shrine in Los Angeles, he scooped three of the biggest in a single night. He walked off with Favourite Male Artist (Rock and Pop), Favourite Album (Soul/R&B) and Favourite Male Artist (Soul/R&B). But while the soul awards showed that he had penetrated the large black record-buying market, they also engulfed Michael in controversy. The two soul awards had traditionally gone to black artists and the fact that a white artist had won them sparked outcry – from Gladys Knight, Dionne Warwick, Spike Lee and the militant black group Public Enemy, among others, who thought the category should remain a redoubt of solely black performers.

As Gladys Knight later explained, black artists had traditionally been excluded from all the main prizes, such as Pop Male Vocalist, which had always gone to white stars. The soul awards were designed to give black artists an award of their own and that for George Michael to be included was an intrusion. 'The black male artist works very hard to get his due in that area – to say, you're the best,' she said. 'So when you have an outsider to come into that, that has all of these other opportunities to be something different. If Bobby Brown had across-the-board play and he could compete in the same categories George Michael competes in, that would be a whole 'nother thing. But to get to be Pop Male Vocalist of the year – he's just not going to be considered.'

Michael was unhappy to suddenly find himself caught up in an American racial controversy. His own views on race were well known to be tolerant and he had not canvassed for the award – it had been given to him. And he saw the argument in a particularly English light. Surely the problem was that black artists should be in the running for mainstream awards? But to be caught in a running story in America concerning black people taking offence at a white singer winning an award was terrible publicity and demanded a response. To emerge with a tarnished image because of a misunderstood quote would be severely damaging to his future record sales, so he decided to keep quiet, refusing to be drawn on the issue.

Some time later, when the storm had cleared, he explained what he had been feeling at the time. He said: 'I can understand people who have a very strong objection to me being quoted as a soul singer or being on top of the black charts. But I think that white and black people making similar music and crossing over that way can't be anything but a good thing.

'I beat Michael Jackson and Bobby Brown and a couple of other people in different categories. And I totally agree with the criticism that as they are public awards, a lot of white people are going to vote for a white guy before they vote for a black guy. I didn't ask to be given those awards; I'm not going to pretend I wasn't happy to get them. But I do understand the argument that says that this guy is just an acceptable version of black music for white America.' In fact the contrary was true, it was a mark of Michael's success that he was able to bring out a version of white music acceptable to black Americans.

'I am very pleased that a lot of black people appreciate my music,' he said. 'Winning those awards or getting those chart positions are largely attributable to black people that like my music. And that means that somehow I'm doing something right as a vocalist. I don't think I sound black; I've never thought I sounded black; I don't think there is any attempt to steal black heritage in what I'm doing. All I think is happening is I'm trying to make good music.'

The awards kept coming. At the thirty-first annual Grammy Awards *Faith* won Album of the Year; Madonna presented him with a Silver Clef at the fourteenth Nordoff/Robbins benefit lunch; and in September he received the Video Vanguard Award at the MTV Music Awards in California.

In between attending awards ceremonies, Michael relaxed. At the beginning of 1989 he took a long break in Miami and at the end of the year went skiing with friends in Colorado. And he bought himself a second home in Santa Barbara, the Californian seaside playground for the super-rich who prefer seclusion. It was a most unusual property, hexagonal and built on the hillside, with orange and lemon groves looking out over the azure blue of the Pacific. Costing about £3 million, it was a space-age home nestling in the mountains, with a 'starship console' which meant everything, from drawing the curtains to answering the door, could be done at the touch of a button.

Michael liked to describe the house as his 'vacation/investment' home and he revelled in its sumptuous comfort. It was quite a contrast to his home in Hampstead, which was comfortable only on a British scale. He said of his new American home that it was 'very big and very showbiz. It cost me an arm and a leg'.

The house was perfect for relaxation. Whereas his London home in the middle of busy Hampstead offered seclusion only so long as he remained inside the house, his

West Coast home allowed him to feel more liberated and at ease. He could go cycling for hours in the densely wooded countryside, exploring the mountains and creeks above Santa Barbara. Mostly he just hung out at the pool.

A year later he confessed that the good life was all right for a while, but it had its limitations. 'I used to just sit in the sun all the time,' he said. 'But now I get bored doing that. I start getting restless – and, besides, I'm starting to burn. That's something that never used to happen.'

Through the whole of 1989 and the best part of 1990, Michael bounced between London, which he still considered his main home, and his house in Santa Barbara, writing songs for his next album, which was to be called *Listen Without Prejudice, Vol 1*.

And when he had finished writing he returned to London to record at Sarm Studios West and the Metropolis Studios, teaming up again with engineer Chris Porter. Apart from Stevie Wonder's 'They Won't Go When I Go', all the songs on the album were as before written, performed and produced by Michael, with Deon Estus and Chris Cameron drafted in to play bass and keyboards. Michael was so prolific that he had enough material to make two different albums, which he considered putting out together.

George Michael was in an extraordinarily powerful position. He had conquered the music charts, had swept the music awards and was on the verge of releasing two dozen new tracks to a keen new fan-base. Sitting in the sun in Santa Barbara, he could look back on his short life with astonishment. And he must have spared a thought for his old Wham! partner Andrew Ridgeley, whose story was very different.

Since the abrupt break-up of Wham! at the band's peak in 1986, Ridgeley had tried in vain to pick up the pieces of his career. By 1990 he had made very little headway. A comeback single, 'Shake', was released in Britain on 31 March and appeared in the charts for three short weeks, hovering in the upper fifties before vanishing. Ridgeley's debut solo album, *Son of Albert*, didn't even feature in Britain's Top 100 album charts. It entered at No. 130 and disappeared two weeks later.

Ridgeley began living mostly in Cornwall, in the south-west of Britain. The disarming good looks he boasted as a teenager quickly faded and his once crowning glory of thick dark hair began to thin at the front. He started to put on weight. But he continued to live comfortably, bolstered by his stake in the royalties earned from the back-catalogue of Wham!. As half of one of the most lucrative bands of the Eighties, unless he did something very stupid, he could be comfortably well off without working again. At first he spent a good deal of money on reviving his failed ambition to be a racing driver. Now he spent the money on travelling and skiing.

While recording *Listen Without Prejudice*, Michael was tempted into a concert. He agreed to appear alongside Paul McCartney, Elton John, Eric Clapton, Phil Collins and other rock luminaries at a summer charity event at Knebworth Park in Hertfordshire. It was an enormous event, in front of a massive crowd of 120,000, as well as a global audience of millions through MTV.

A fortnight before the show, Michael withdrew from the concert because of recording pressures. Within a few days, the *Sun* pop columnist Piers Morgan claimed the cancellation had nothing to do with recording and everything to do with vanity. According to Morgan, Michael pulled out over a clash over his billing. He had wanted to appear between Collins and McCartney in the evening, but had only been offered a 'warm-up' slot earlier in the day.

It appears the recording pressure was genuine. He had worked hard to complete the new album and before long he delivered the finished tapes to his CBS executives. When they first listened to the completed demo of *Listen Without Prejudice, Vol 1* in July 1990 they were so delighted with what they heard that they promptly set about renegotiating their contract with him yet again. George Michael was going to be a lasting talent and their seven-record deal now seemed too conservative. He should be brought on board permanently.

On other floors of the CBS building in Manhattan other deals were going on, unrelated to George Michael but which would embroil him before long. CBS was gradually being absorbed into the huge Sony empire. The company was suffering immense personnel changes, each of which rocked those who had come to prosper under the old CBS hierarchy. Morale among the old CBS hands came to a new low with the departure of Walter Yetnikoff, the chief executive, who eventually resigned along with a whole raft of other long-standing executives. Michael kept up with the corporate game play and became depressed at what he heard. All those he knew and trusted appeared to be disappearing. Soon he came to feel his only friend at Sony was Paul Russell, the president of Sony Music Europe.

As *Listen Without Prejudice, Vol 1* was being prepared for release, Michael began to differ with his record company over publicity for the album. Even the title, with its legal term 'without prejudice', seemed ironic, warning Sony's lawyers that here was a document which should be considered for its content and worth, rather than another piece of evidence in the battle. But there is little suggestion that Michael was intending to be ambiguous. He explained in *Bare* that the title merely reflected his decision to keep a distance from promotion and that 'prejudice' to him simply meant without preconceptions: 'If a by-product of stepping back is that people who have had difficulty with my image can start listening to my music without all the old prejudices, then that's great. But that's not why I'm doing it. I'm doing it because I want to keep my life together.'

Michael infuriated his new CBS bosses by refusing to take part in any of the promotional chores expected of an artist in selling a new album. His sole contribution to publicizing *Listen Without Prejudice* was to be interviewed for a British television documentary devoted to him, ITV's *South Bank Show*. He refused a launch party and all but a very few press interviews, to the *Los Angeles Times*, the *New York Times* and *USA Today*. And furthermore he refused to make videos for single releases taken from the album.

In September Robert Hilburn of the Calendar section of the *Los Angeles Times* interviewed Michael on the beachfront patio of Rob Kahane's home in Marina del Rey. He wrote: 'The former Wham! star thought he'd walked away from teen adulation with his *Faith* album, but his sexy image became a nightmare. Now he's trying to make sure it doesn't happen again.'

Hilburn explained that Michael had been on the verge

of a nervous breakdown at the beginning of the 'Faith' tour and so was taking the 'potentially revolutionary steps' of cutting out most of the usual work of a recording artist such as making videos and going on tours. 'It's quite simple really,' Michael told Hilburn. 'The thing I really needed was my songwriting. I didn't need the celebrity.'

Hilburn commented: 'To a cynical pop world that has heard everyone from Frank Sinatra to David Bowie threaten to say goodbye to the microphone, the latest vows of George Michael may seem like little more than a calculated publicity move. After all, he's obviously still doing interviews.' Michael responded: 'I'm sure a lot of people are going to believe all this is just some sort of gimmick, just another way to stir interest. But I'm also sure that most people find it hard to believe that stardom can make you miserable. After all, everybody wants to be a star. I certainly did, and I worked hard to get it. But I was miserable, and I don't want to feel that way again.'

Michael went on: 'The truth is, it all got much bigger than I ever imagined – and much harder to control. Ultimately, I wasn't comfortable with that kind of visibility and power. Once I became more confident as a writer, I realized I didn't need all that other bolstering.'

Michael explained why he wouldn't make videos: he didn't like the interpretational confines of videos as they could do disservice to the metaphors and subtlety of his lyrics. 'If my life goes the way I want it to, I would like to never step in front of a camera again,' he said.

Michael's remarks were played straight back to CBS president Tommy Mottola, who appeared to back the singer's decision to stick to songwriting and recording: 'I think you'll have a lot of disappointed fans because there is no video, but when they get to understand his point of view and hear the record, I don't really think there will be any problem. He explained that he wants to do more work, more songs, more albums rather than have his time diffused with touring and doing videos and things that really rub him the wrong way. And if doing those things are going to cause that kind of reaction in an artist, then what's the point of doing them?' But Mottola was privately far from happy, as Michael knew.

Michael confessed: 'I'm sure everyone [at CBS] is terrified that all this is going to sabotage the album. But I honestly feel I am in a very privileged position because I have the luxury of knowing that simply because of the size of my last album, this album will be heard regardless of whether I make videos or not.

'I also have enough faith in the songs to believe that if people hear the album, enough will like it. I don't necessarily believe it will sell fourteen million copies. I'd be very surprised if it does. But I do believe it is a much better album, and I think that in itself will compensate for part of the lack of presence.

'I can't lose because I know what the alternative is. I'm not stupid enough to think that I can deal with another ten or fifteen years of major exposure. I think that is the ultimate tragedy of fame, people who are simply out of control, who are lost. I've seen so many of them, and I don't want to be another cliché.'

Michael's frank attitude to the trials of fame earned him, oddly, a public rebuttal from Frank Sinatra. On reading Hilburn's profile, Sinatra fired off an angry letter to the editor of the *Los Angeles Times* which suggested that Michael should smarten up. Sinatra wrote: 'When I saw your Calendar cover today about George Michael "the reluctant pop star" my first reaction was he should thank the good Lord every morning when he wakes up to have all that he has. And that'll make two of us thanking God every morning for all we have.

'I don't understand a guy who lives "in hopes of reducing the strain of his celebrity status". Here's a kid who "wanted to be a pop star since I was about seven years old". And now that he's a smash performer and songwriter at twenty-seven he wants to quit doing what tons of gifted youngsters all over the world would shoot Grandma for – just one crack at what he's complaining about.

'Come on, George. Loosen up. Swing, man. Dust off those gossamer wings and fly yourself to the moon of your choice and be grateful to carry the baggage we've all had to carry since those lean nights of sleeping on buses and helping the driver unload the instruments. And no more of that talk about "the tragedy of fame". The tragedy of fame is when no one shows up and you're singing to the cleaning lady in some empty joint that hasn't seen a paying customer since Saint Swithin's day. And you're nowhere near that; you're top dog on the top rung of a tall ladder called Stardom, which in Latin means thanks-to-the-fans who were there when it was lonely.

'Talent must not be wasted. Those who have it – and you obviously do or today's Calendar cover would have been about Rudy Vallee – those who have talent must hug it, embrace it, nurture it and share it lest it be taken away from you as fast as it was loaned to you. Trust me. I've been there. Frank Sinatra.'

The original article, and Sinatra's attack, became a

subject of heated debate in the paper's letters page which lasted several weeks. Some complained that the paper had devoted a total of 'ninety-six column inches' pandering to Michael; others admired the singer's bravery. 'So Frank Sinatra doesn't think that stardom is something that carried the potential for destruction,' said another, citing Elvis Presley, Marilyn Monroe and Janis Joplin as examples of lives botched by the pressures of superstardom. Michael was appalled by Sinatra's attentions. He wanted to maintain his personal anonymity above all and he was always anxious that rumours would start circulating about homosexuality and promiscuity. Sinatra had come to terms with total intrusion of his private affairs and had paid the price of super-celebrity. Michael was determined that such a fate should not face him.

In early August news broke that Michael's American managers, Rob Kahane and Michael Lippman, also representing Neneh Cherry, had decided to split. Lippman had suggested dissolving the partnership in order to form a completely new company. It was unfortunate timing. Michael once again found himself without good management advice at an important phase of his career. He had come to depend upon Lippman's advice as a lawyer with enormous experience in the music industry, and he trusted Kahane, who had been so successfully devoting himself solely to managing Michael.

CBS planned to lift 'Praying For Time' from *Listen Without Prejudice* and release it as a single in August, to excite interest in the imminent album. They were desperate for a video to accompany the single, but Michael was still in dispute with them about promotional commitment and flatly refused to take part in one. He refused to grant his permission for anything other than a video which contained no images of him. He said that the video should be very simple: the lyrics of the song should appear in white against a black backdrop while the music played.

The song was released and received enormous press attention. *USA Today* compared it to John Lennon's peace anthem 'Imagine'. Michael did not see any similarities. He said of the remark: 'It's not like "Imagine" at all. It's much more negative. I'd like to say things are bound to get better, but I don't really believe it. The song is my own way of trying to justify people's actions and their selfishness.'

The song entered the British charts at No. 8 and a week later peaked at No. 6. In America, it attracted more radio air-play than any record since 'We Are The World' in 1985. 'Praying For Time' entered the America charts at No. 41 and six weeks later it reached the top to become Michael's ninth American No. 1.

But success was not everything. Michael was deeply upset when he heard that Nigel Browne, who worked as one of his inner circle of personal bodyguards on the American leg of the 'Faith' tour, had been killed in a helicopter accident. Michael issued a statement: 'He is very sad and sends his deepest sympathies to Nigel's wife Sonia and daughter Michaela.'

On a lighter note, Michael was included in a book of celebrity insults published in America. Called *Bitch, Bitch, Bitch*, his entry was a crack about Bruce Springsteen. 'What annoys me is that he gets to wiggle his bum and no one slags him off,' said a peeved Michael one day. 'What's so incredible about his bottom compared to mine?'

When it came to the London Weekend Television

documentary Michael had reluctantly agreed to to publicize the release of *Listen Without Prejudice*, no such flippancy was evident. Amidst the dreary television coverage of the arts in Britain, the LWT's *South Bank Show* had achieved a reputation for bowing to its subjects' co-operation in exchange for some exclusive access. Michael had agreed to be interviewed by the programme because he was allowed a final say over what was broadcast.

Michael came across as articulate but earnest and used the programme as a personal manifesto, explaining he would rather be remembered as a songwriter than as a performer. 'I don't believe that I am important as a pop star,' he said. 'At the end of the day I want to leave something as a writer. I believe I can leave songs that will mean something to other generations.'

With the ground well prepared by 'Praying For Time', *Listen Without Prejudice, Vol 1* was released. Even the cover was a surprise to fans, since it didn't feature a picture of Michael but a single black and white photograph, taken in 1940 by the American socio-realist photographer Weegee, of a massively overcrowded scene of youthful sun-bathers.

It was never going to be easy for Michael to top the success of *Faith*. Michael Jackson, who was older by five years than Michael and had been making solo records for twelve years longer, had also found it impossible to top the success of his bestselling album *Thriller* which with forty-eight million copies sold worldwide achieved the highest sales in the history of recording. Although Jackson's follow-up album, *Bad*, was a great success, it did not do well by comparison.

CBS grumbled about Michael's refusal to do helpful promotion work, but the new album seemed to sell perfectly well without it. It went straight to No. 1 in the British album charts on 15 September, selling 300,000 the first week alone and stayed on the chart for fifty-five weeks. In America the album was released on 29 September and entered the chart at No. 22. The following week it leapt to No. 5 and a fortnight later peaked at No. 2, staying on the Billboard Top 100 for thirty-four weeks.

It was an impressive performance, but compared to the *Faith* album – especially in the eyes of company executives – it was selling badly. The perceived failure of the album became a story in the music industry and the press on both sides of the Atlantic. Everyone asked the same question: was the lack of promotion by Michael or by CBS the key to the album's slow sales?

In November the *LA Times* published a story, written by Steve Hochman, which explored why the album was failing to sell. The headline said it all: 'Why Isn't This Man's Album Selling? Maybe It's Because George Michael Has Taken Himself Out Of The Picture'.

Ron Weisner, who had managed Wham! in America before Jazz Summers and Simon Napier-Bell, was drawn into the story. 'It always comes down to music,' Weisner said. 'I respect him for taking the stand, and he can afford to because he's a powerful songwriter. But is this a wrong move or a right move? Only time will tell. I hope it's right. Major artists have to be careful of overkill.' Around the world, newspapers and radio stations were speculating on the poor sales and linking it to Michael's Greta Garbo stance.

But Michael was about to spectacularly break his silence. In the autumn of 1990 Michael released his autobiography, *Bare*, co-written by Tony Parsons, in a publishing deal which netted the singer a reported £430,000 – £200,000 for newspaper serialization rights alone – and which he split equally with Parsons. In the book the singer confirmed his vehement dislike of the promotional aspects of his career and laid down his future plans on the subject: he announced he would do very little touring, that he would not appear in videos any more, and that he would not be giving any further interviews to the press.

And there was someone new in his life – Hippy, a young golden labrador bitch, given to him by Gary Farrow. Although he would not dare to walk around central London for fear of being mobbed, he would happily stroll around Hampstead Heath and the parks of Highgate exercising Hippy. In public, Michael declared that the only thing he felt to be missing from his life was a stable relationship with a partner he loved.

As the title suggests, Michael used the book to reveal some of his soul. The preface did most, perhaps, to expose how much the public image of George Michael was no more than a skilfully conceived façade by an astute operator. He wrote: 'My name is Georgios Kyriacos Panayiotou. To the outside world I am and always will be known as something else, but it's not my name. As a boy, my biggest fear was that my huge ambitions would stay just out of reach of the child I saw in the mirror. So I created a man (in the image of a great friend), that the world could love if they chose to, someone who could realize my dreams, and make me a star. I called him George Michael, and for almost a decade, he worked his arse off for me, and did as he was told. He was very good at his job, perhaps a little *too* good. Anyway, shortly before I was approached with the idea of this book, I decided that his services were no longer required. He went quietly, didn't make a fuss. I know many of you will think that it was a strange thing for me to do, but believe me, he really had to go.'

Despite the certainty with which he wrote that in 1990, it did not prove easy for Michael to shed his larger-than-life alter-ego. Six years later he admitted in an interview on Radio One that he still hides behind his stage persona. His fans, he said then, had come to expect it of him.

He said in *Bare* that he would not, like David Bowie, dream up new stage personas, though a few years later he did just that. He said: 'I'm just not going to make that effort to go out looking different any more. It's okay if you're interested in that chameleon business and you want to do, for instance, what Madonna or Prince do – and they do it very well. But it's not for me.' He added: 'I just don't have the kind of face that can withstand lots of different looks. Some people have that kind of bone structure. Not me, I've spent years just trying to make the best of it.'

The next single from the album, 'Freedom 90' (to differentiate it from the earlier Wham! hit, 'Freedom') came out in America on 27 October. The video reaffirmed Michael's remoteness. It cost around £300,000 to make, yet Michael was not the star. His presence could be detected only fleetingly, with the symbolic torching of his leather jacket as if to lay the ghost of the 'Faith' image. The stars of the video were the world's top five models – Naomi Campbell, Cindy Crawford, Linda Evangelista, Tatjana Patitz and Christy Turlington. In Britain the same month a different track was taken from the album for a single release, 'Waiting For That Day'. It reached a peak at No. 23 half-way through its five-week appearance in the charts.

While the release of a song called 'Freedom 90' suggested that Michael wanted to stay uncluttered and unburdened by the tedious duties of his career, it was soon reported that he had agreed to go on a seven-city, small-venue charity concert tour of the United States and elsewhere in the New Year as part of a world tour to raise money for AIDS research. The tour would start in Canada in February 1992 and take in America, Japan and Britain. A little later it was reported that Michael had scrapped plans for the charity mini-tour of America in favour of a major arena tour later, after the release of the album he was working on, *Listen Without Prejudice, Vol 2*. In the event, the album would never be released.

Michael believed he was helping record sales by performing in important territories, but CBS executives were not happy with his association with an AIDS charity. Michael, in turn, thought them homophobic. Although he kept his homosexuality a secret, Michael was confident about his own behaviour and took great offence at those prejudiced against gays. Rather than ignore the remarks Michael decided to take offence.

Disagreements between Michael and CBS remained private for a while, but before long they spilled into the press. And the press coverage in turn did not help his relations with his record company. He further irritated CBS by announcing to the press that he was not happy to discover that American troops had adopted his song 'Praying For Time' as their anthem at the time of the Gulf War. Michael was unhappy to be linked to anything military. 'I'm very uncomfortable with any connection,' said

Michael in October. CBS came to think of Michael as unhelpful and unpatriotic. But whether Michael liked it or not, the lyrics of 'Praying For Time' struck a chord among soldiers preparing to be sent off for war.

'Freedom 90' was released in Britain on 15 December. A week later, it peaked at No. 28. By then the album from which it had been taken had notched up worldwide sales of seven million, going multi-platinum. But at CBS, it remained a disappointment. They still maintained it would have sold more had Michael got behind it.

In 1988 Michael was reported to have earned £19.4 million in America alone, which made him the fifth largest entertainment earner of the year – behind Michael Jackson, Mike Tyson, Sylvester Stallone and Steven Spielberg. By the end of 1990, Michael was hovering just outside a list of Britain's richest 100 men. The *Sunday Times* placed him 128th, with an estimated fortune of £65 million. The only music industry stars ahead of him were Paul McCartney, Mick Jagger and Elton John – who had each been selling records for at least a decade longer than him. McCartney and Jagger began recording hit singles in 1963, before Michael was born. With a fortune growing at £66,000 a day, it was only a matter of time before Michael would catch up with the others.

10

New Friends, Old Enemies

In the New Year, trouble was brewing with the men in suits. Michael's first single release of 1991 in America was 'Waiting For The Day'. It had been released in Britain the previous October and struggled to make No. 23 in the charts. In America sales were even worse; in seven weeks it did no better than reach No. 27.

Disagreements between Michael, CBS and Sony came to a head when it emerged that *Listen Without Prejudice, Vol 1* had ultimately sold only half as well as *Faith*, which sold fourteen million copies. Each side blamed the other for the failure: Michael blamed Sony for providing inadequate marketing funds; Sony said the album failed because Michael did not back it with a tour, as he had for *Faith*.

Michael further showed his contempt for CBS by announcing that the brief twelve-date international tour he was undertaking early in 1991 would be called 'Cover to Cover', and that he would ignore the songs from *Listen Without Prejudice* in favour of songs by other artists. CBS executives were outraged.

The tour opened in the middle of January at the NEC Arena in Birmingham. He performed with a nine-piece soul backing band and a gospel choir. The set included just one of his own songs from his latest album – 'Freedom

90'. 'They Won't Go When I Go' was on the album but was a Stevie Wonder cover. He sang 'Father Figure' from *Faith*, and three Wham! hits – 'Freedom', 'Everything She Wants' and 'Careless Whisper'. The other fifteen or so songs in the concert were covers, taken from a list of his favourites. It was a diverse selection including The Temptations' 'Papa Was A Rolling Stone', Adamski's 'Killer', David Bowie's 'Fame' and 'Desperado' by The Eagles. He also sang a number of songs by Aretha Franklin and Elton John and others by Stevie Wonder.

The thirty-strong London Community Gospel Choir backed Michael on two of his own songs – 'Father Figure' and 'Freedom 90'. The choir, which was paid about £10,000 to appear, were not Michael's first choice. He had preferred the London Community Gospel's chief rival, the International Choir of London, and he approached them first but they refused to sing with him because of 'Father Figure''s steamy lyrics. The Reverend John Francis, leader of the choir, told the *Sun*: 'I am very angry and disappointed. The lyrics to "Father Figure" were just too explicit for us.'

While many in the audience at the first night of the 'Cover to Cover' tour were surprised at the extent to which Michael was ignoring his own material, the British critics wrote rave reviews. A notice in *The Times* concluded, '. . . the readings by Michael and his three backing singers were little short of immaculate.'

Three days later Michael flew to Rio de Janeiro to make two appearances at the world's biggest rock festival. The month-long event called 'Rock In Rio II' was staged at Rio's Maracana, the world's biggest football stadium, with a seating and standing capacity for over a hundred thousand (and much more for a concert). The festival included a string of concerts by Prince, Guns 'N' Roses, Robert Plant, Judas Priest, New Kids on the Block, Run DMC, Billy Idol and Lisa Stansfield. Michael staged his first solo concert in the last week of the festival, returning two days later to top the bill on the closing night gala concert – with a carefully planned 'spontaneous' stage reunion with his old Wham! partner, Andrew Ridgeley. The gig would earn the duo £500,000.

At first the Rio visit seemed doomed. Musical instruments and sound equipment were impounded by Customs officers at Heathrow Airport as part of an increase in security surrounding the Gulf War. Officials held Michael's equipment to be checked over by the bomb squad. After a delay it was released and sent on its way.

Michael used the opening concert of 'Rock in Rio II' to display his latest public image. He sported a newly cropped hairstyle and a Sixties Beatnik look, and wore a Beatles jacket. He was not pleased to discover that he had drawn a relatively poor crowd of less than 30,000 and he was startled when some of them were quick to voice their disapproval at his performance. They had hoped for a night of George Michael singing his greatest hits; instead they were treated to his contentious 'Cover to Cover' running order of old songs by other artists.

But all was forgotten a few nights later when Michael, reunited with Ridgeley, closed the festival in front of a sell-out crowd of 170,000. The reunion of Wham! was seen as the undoubted highlight of the festival and it was a big night for Michael and Ridgeley, too. Michael ensured that it was an especially memorable occasion by taking over an entire floor in his hotel to accommodate over two dozen of the band's close relatives and friends. None of them could resist the chance to see the Wham! magic one last time.

At the Maracana Stadium that night, Michael came on to the stage on his own. Then, after singing the opening strains of 'Careless Whisper', he stopped to introduce the 'great friend' who had helped him write the song. Ridgeley walked out to share a brief few minutes of superstardom with his old friend. The reunited duo performed a slick set of Wham! favourites – 'Careless Whisper', 'I'm Your Man' and 'Freedom' – before the night reached its climax with a £30,000 firework display above the stadium.

Michael told reporters after the show: 'It was something we wanted to do just once, to show people we were proud of what we did. It was an incredible night. I've never known an atmosphere like it. It was very emotional when Andrew came on. We are still the greatest of friends.' Ridgeley enjoyed the evening every bit as much and said, 'We had a great time. After a few bars of "I'm Your Man" I looked over to George and it was like nothing had changed. We were two mates enjoying ourselves again.'

At his party after the show, Michael was in good spirits. He was surrounded by good friends. Work over, he was about to embark on a luxury holiday with Ridgeley and some friends and relations, along the coast from Rio at beautiful Armacao dos Buzios. But among the many familiar faces at the party there was one who Michael had only recently met: Anselmo Feleppa, a gay Brazilian two years older than him. In a very short space of time Feleppa had become a most unlikely close companion and lover.

Feleppa was the son of a relatively wealthy clothing

manufacturer from a town about fifty miles away from Rio de Janeiro, who was expected to follow his father into the family business. Feleppa had sat in the front row for both of Michael's Rio shows and they later met at Michael's hotel, the Copacabana Palace. In Feleppa Michael found both a lover and a friend, which contrasted sharply with the impermanence of a brief encounter. He felt quite at ease with Feleppa. As he later explained, 'He broke down my reserve. Anyone who knew me before I met Anselmo would tell you that he opened me up completely – just in allowing myself to trust my intuition.' Michael explained that Anselmo had shown him how to relax. 'I didn't really know how to enjoy myself before I met Anselmo. I learnt to travel more, to experience new things – and not only with him. I went scuba-diving, hang-gliding – I jumped off Sugar Loaf Mountain a couple of years ago. He made me realize how English I was. After I met him, I became much more tactile with people.'

In private, there was a flirtatious chemistry between Michael and Feleppa which Michael rarely enjoyed with anyone. From the beginning they were attentive to one another, taking a close interest in anything the other said or did, constantly shooting glances at each other to judge reactions or to elicit comments. Even in the company of others they kept closely in touch, enjoying private jokes behind the others' backs.

When Michael left South America to continue on tour alone, he promised Feleppa that they would meet up again before long. In America, CBS began blaming Michael's long absence from the territory for his poor record sales. Different tracks from the *Listen Without Prejudice, Vol 1* album were released in America and Britain. On 2 February 'Mother's Pride' was released in America where it barely made any impact on the charts. It entered at No. 87, peaking four weeks later at No. 46. Meanwhile in Britain Michael released 'Heal The Pain' on 16 February. It stayed on the chart for only four weeks and the highest position it reached was No. 31. The following month 'Cowboys And Angels' was released in Britain and also slipped off the charts after just four weeks, reaching No. 45. It was the last track Michael would allow to be released from the album. He then set forth on a very strange period: eight months without a chart hit.

Despite poor singles chart performances for the tracks taken from it, *Listen Without Prejudice, Vol 1* still scooped a number of important music industry awards. At the BRIT Awards in London it was named Best British Album. At the ceremony Michael dedicated the award to Ronnie Fischer, Epic's product manager who had died a few months before. Michael was also scheduled to perform at the awards ceremony, but he cancelled a few days before, saying he was suffering from throat problems. Michael was also voted Best Male Singer and Sexiest Male Artist by the readers of *Rolling Stone* magazine.

Michael performed his final 'Cover to Cover' dates at Wembley Arena in March. On the last night he was joined on stage by a surprise guest, Elton John. They sang together on John's Seventies hit 'Don't Let The Sun Go Down On Me' and it was a brilliant performance.

Although John appeared with Michael at the concert, he did not go on to the end-of-tour party. It was held at Smith's Gallery in Covent Garden and £80,000 of champagne and food was served. Among those who did turn up were Andrew Ridgeley, Paul Young, Patsy Kensit, Betty Boo, Neneh Cherry, Yazz, Bananarama and the beefcake actor Dolph Lundgren, passing through on a visit to Britain. Boy George turned up ahead of Michael but did not go into the party. His friend, Eve Gallagher, did not have an invitation and was refused admittance, so Boy George left with her. According to Piers Morgan in the *Sun*, Michael invited Boy George to the party to put behind them a four-year rift in their friendship, caused when Boy George said that Michael was 'a closet gay'. Michael was still eager to keep his homosexuality from his fans, and he considered George's outburst an assault.

To the outside world, the two singers had finally made up, but the rift never healed. There was always a friction between the two performers. A few years later, when Boy George published his autobiography *Take It Like A Man* in 1995, he took several swipes at Michael. He wrote: 'The mere mention of George Michael was enough to start me off. I'd known him for years, but he was always so snotty. I cracked jokes like, "George Michael's got no sense of humour." It was true: the more successful and rich he became the more seriously he took himself. Of course, I was jealous. I hated the way he was portrayed as a serious songwriter while I was treated like a pop joker.'

'I called George a "closet" on Radio One. He was touring Australia and he said he was going to kick my arse. I retorted, "Don't you mean fondle?"' And George went out of his way to irritate Michael. At the recording of the Live Aid single 'Do They Know It's Christmas?', Boy George made Bob Geldof and Midge Ure laugh at the mixing desk when, on hearing Michael's vocal track, he loftily declared: 'My God, he sounds camp. But then he is.' When George saw Michael with Brooke Shields at a birthday party for Grace Jones held at The Palladium in New York he whispered in Shields's ear, 'He's a poof, he's a poof.' When Michael passed George one day in his car in Oxford Street, in Boy George's words 'posing at the wheel of a convertible, wearing dark shades and blaring his own music' he shouted out 'Hairdresser!'

With the 'Cover to Cover' tour behind him, Michael once again set about renegotiating his recording contract with CBS. In a deal totalling $60 million, he was signed as a singer and producer and given his own fledgling record label, funded to the tune of £100,000 by Epic. It was to be called Hard Rock Records and Michael would invest a further £250,000 of his own money in the venture. The chairman would be his cousin and long-standing close friend Andros Georgiou. As well as looking out for raw musical talent to nurture and record, Hard Rock Records was designed to allow Michael to record and release cover versions of songs without upsetting CBS, which would continue to release his original material on Epic.

Despite the revised deal CBS persisted in pressing him to do some live concerts in their major territory, the United States, to give *Listen Without Prejudice* one last boost. Michael refused.

It seemed that his new constant companion, Feleppa, was becoming a distraction. Michael was for once happy in his private life and was reluctant to accede to his record company bosses' requests. With the 'Cover to Cover' tour concluded, the two men were free to holiday together. According to a report in the Brazilian magazine, *Interview*, Michael and Feleppa went cruising on a private yacht off

Fabulous wealth has brought George Michael fabulous homes in the most expensive parts of the world. His sprawling hillside villa in St Tropez leads down to the swimming pool, affording sensational views.

Reflecting unlikely flippancy, he decided his multi-million pound investment in St Tropez should be called Chez Nobby, a reference to another lasting childhood nickname.

When he eventually left home for the first time, George rented an apartment
in Adam and Eve Mews, Kensington, but he was not happy there. With the
press camped outside he refused to leave for days on end as he struggled
to write Wham!'s swansongs.

George hides behind heavy iron railings and security cameras, like these at the rear of his London home in Hampstead. With such security he has been able to keep unwanted visitors and prying eyes out of his life – but there have been breaches.

Above: With parents Jack and Lesley, at Newmarket Races for the start of carefully orchestrated celebrations to mark George's 30th birthday. *Copyright © David Koppel.*

Opposite page: George in pensive mood arriving for his acrimonious action against Sony at the High Court in London.

The aloof businessman may pay tax as Georgios Kyriacos Panayiotou, but he signs autographs for fans as George Michael, sometimes adding a kiss.

Main picture: Long-standing bass player Deon Estus with George, who is looking fit and trim. In reality, Michael has had to battle to keep his weight from dramatically ballooning – as it did in his childhood.

George Michael with Diana, Princess of Wales, at the World AIDS Day concert, Wembley Arena, in 1994. The singer's open support for AIDS causes brought rebuke from – and lasting problems with – his bosses at Sony.
Copyright © Dave Hogan.

George broke down in tears during the funeral service for Diana, Princess of Wales, which he attended with Elton John.

the coast of Rio. During the holiday they entertained Lucia Sednaoui, a Brazilian socialite, and her husband.

Michael was well known for buying expensive presents for his close friends and Feleppa was soon showered with gifts. In the course of the cruise, stopping off at some of the world's most exclusive restaurants, Feleppa was given a gold Rolex watch and a Mercedes car. Over the next two years Michael and Feleppa went everywhere together, dividing their time between Brazil, which Feleppa knew well, and Michael's homes in London and Santa Barbara. Michael is also reported to have bought a remote farm in Brazil where he and Feleppa spent their time, out of the prying gaze of the world's press. The only time Michael appeared in public at this time was at a low-key wedding in Los Angeles when he was best man to his cousin Andros Georgiou at the marriage to his long-time partner Jackie Crevitas.

Michael returned to London in April and went straight back into the studio to continue work on his next album, still provisionally called *Listen Without Prejudice, Vol 2* and which was due to be released at the end of the summer.

Then, for little good reason, Michael's dispute with the top management at CBS and Sony over the failure of his last album flared up again. Statements by both sides became increasingly acrimonious and gained escalating amounts of publicity. Angry telephone calls and faxes were fired between the two camps as a matter of routine. CBS executives could not resist a smile when *Punch* magazine voted Michael the most miserable man in Britain, for 'doing interviews about how he'd given up interviews, being depressed by his millions and by female fans who lust after his body'.

In the summer, when Michael should have been putting the final touches to his next album, he stopped work in protest at his treatment by CBS. He blamed the break-down in the relationship to the insensitivity of the Sony management who were directing the CBS executives. He launched a campaign of withholding his talent from the company. Rather than record new material, which would benefit Sony, he devoted his time to raising money for AIDS projects. First he began writing three tracks for a charity album to be released by Chrysalis to raise money for AIDS research, *Red, Hot & Dance* (a sequel to the heralded 1990 album *Red, Hot & Blue*), a collection of Cole Porter classics by contemporary artists, on which Michael agreed to waive royalties.

Without coming out as gay, Michael increasingly began to associate himself with homosexual causes. In October he halted the first of two shows at the Great Western Forum in Los Angeles to hit out at California Governor Pete Wilson's veto of a gay rights bill, set to outlaw discrimination against homosexuals. A protest rally had been staged earlier in the day, in nearby Santa Monica. During his concert, Michael voiced his support, saying: 'I know some of you were out marching today. For all those protesting up there, I'd like to add my voice to theirs.'

Michael's political comments were better received by the local press than his performances. The *Hollywood Reporter* declared he was neither 'spontaneous or inspiring – two lacks that conspired to make his 2½-hour-long show something of a trying, restless affair.' It was, it claimed, 'very pat and over-produced' while some of the lighting effects were deemed to be 'cheesy'.

The *LA Times* offered praise: 'emotional expression, not glitz, is his real stock in trade', but the tone of the review soon soured. 'When the curtain rose, Michael was posed as the moody pop icon sporting his trademark sunglasses and five o'clock shadow. But in what might serve as a metaphor for his self-liberation, he soon scrapped the male-model attitude and spent the rest of the show smiling and chatting with unpretentious warmth. While the concert highlighted Michael's range as a musician, it showed his limits as a performer. Without the heartthrob image to exploit, he spent most of the show running from one side of the stage to the other, where he mounted staircases and sang to the fans at the sides. Like his incessant pointing of the microphone towards the crowd for the audience participation effect, it didn't stay interesting very long. He also adopted a self-congratulatory tone ("Can you think of another of my songs that starts with the letter F?") that conflicted with the thoughtfulness and generosity he displayed elsewhere (a ringing endorsement of the current demonstrations against Governor Pete Wilson's gay job-rights bill veto).' His political outburst was reported around the world, which did not go unnoticed by CBS and Sony executives in New York.

The following month, on 24 November, Freddie Mercury, the lead singer of the rock band Queen, died at home of AIDS-induced bronchial pneumonia, the first major rock star to die from AIDS. Michael was in Los Angeles when he heard the news. On his return to London, he told reporters: 'I was very, very sad to hear of Freddie's death. I am still deeply upset by it – it's a tragedy. I had always admired Freddie and his music.' Michael agreed to front the remaining members of the band in an emotional send-off tribute concert to the memory of Mercury, to be staged at Wembley Stadium the following April.

That November Michael also helped save a struggling commercial radio station in London. Under the headline 'The Boy Doner Good', the *Sun* reported that London Greek Radio, which was struggling to stave off mounting debts of over £250,000, was a favourite of Michael's dad Jack. The singer had donated two gold discs for the station to auction and they raised £20,000 each.

Michael hardly missed such trophies. That month alone he scooped another clutch. The Music Video Producers Association Awards, held at the Troubadour Club in Los Angeles, gave three awards to the makers of the video for Michael's song 'Freedom 90', for editor Jim Haygood, art director John Beard and for Mike Southon's cinematography. A few weeks later Michael became the youngest recipient of the Golden Note Award, given by the American Society of Composers, Authors and Publishers (ASCAP).

Although pop journalists and writers were unaware of the extent of the rift between Michael and CBS, they began to comment upon the fact that there were very few new Michael songs on the way. Stories began emerging that Michael had scrapped his next album after recording just four tracks. The agreed line in CBS was that Michael had changed his mind on the album's content. It was announced that Michael had originally intended half of the tracks to be his own, the other half covers of other people's work. Now he was said to be writing all the tracks himself, in an album to be released in the spring or summer. The story was quite false. Michael was merely following the form of words chosen by CBS and Sony to explain the lack of product.

On 7 December, 'Don't Let The Sun Go Down On Me', the duet by Michael and Elton John, recorded live on the last night of his Wembley Arena dates earlier in the year, was released as an AIDS fundraising single. Bernie Taupin's lyrics never seemed more apt than in the context of the fight against AIDS. The climactic chorus struck a suitably haunting note with anyone who had ever been caught up in the traumas of the cruel illness, likening losing everything to the sun setting on life.

The single entered the British charts at No. 1 on 7 December and stayed there for a fortnight, suitably ousted by Queen's 'Bohemian Rhapsody', which was also released to raise money for AIDS causes. 'Don't Let The Sun Go Down On Me' hit the top in America at the beginning of February, two months after its release. It was Michael's tenth American No. 1, and John's fifth. The single went on to top the charts in a further thirteen countries. In the UK, profits were given to the London Lighthouse hospice and the Rainbow Trust Children's Charity; in America they went to the Dana Farber Cancer Institute.

Elton John was relieved at the success of the single because he had at first been reluctant for it to be released, sensing that it would flop. He said: 'I actually told him not to release it. I rang him and said: "George, the timing is a very critical thing. You've just had an album in the States which hasn't been as successful as the other one, *Faith*.

Maybe you should think twice about putting a live single out." I was worried about his career. He said: "Nah. It's going to be fine." It was a No. 1 hit in every country in the world.'

Michael's persistence in ignoring his own material had given him a stick with which to beat Sony. He continued to clash with the management of the media conglomerate throughout 1992, claiming that they had done little to promote his Elton John duet for AIDS. Michael let it be known that he believed 'Don't Let The Sun Go Down On Me' had been a smash hit despite Epic, CBS and Sony.

It is believed that the company, meanwhile, made it clear that it was not happy with his open support for homosexual causes, anxious that it might damage the rugged 'Faith' image which had proved so successful with the public in America. If he were to too openly draw attention to his homosexuality, perhaps Sony believed it would deter women fans and depress sales. Michael was to remain unimpressed by such commercial arguments and considered it an infringement of his rights as an individual to support which causes he pleased. By this time he was regularly branded a gay artist in the press and it was common for pop journalists to comment on the singer's large following among gays. Reporters were commissioned by their editors to stand up the story that Michael was in love with a man, Anselmo Feleppa.

Michael was in no mood for sharing the secrets of his sexuality with his public and he quickly acted to squash reports that he would soon be 'revealing all' in an American magazine. At the end of March, he took the unusual step of issuing a statement to the press about his private life via his solicitor, Tony Russell. It read: 'George wishes it to be known that a report emanating in America suggesting he is considering giving an interview about his private life is wholly without foundation and, as in the past, he will not be giving interviews on the subject.'

However, Michael continued his association with homosexual causes and, on 20 April, 1992, appeared in the 'The Freddie Mercury Tribute: Concert for AIDS Awareness' at Wembley Stadium. The bill was an odd mix of heavy metal, pop and R&B acts. It saw Guns 'N' Roses, Metallica and Def Leppard sharing the bill with Elton John, U2, David Bowie, Robert Plant, Roger Daltrey, Bob Geldof, Annie Lennox, Seal, Lisa Stansfield, Liza Minnelli and Elizabeth Taylor. The emotional send-off, televised in seventy countries, was a touching occasion for everyone taking part. At the end of his set, David Bowie recited the Lord's Prayer in tribute to Mercury and others who have suffered from AIDS. When a heckler in the crowd shouted at Elizabeth Taylor to get off stage, she retorted: 'I'll get off in a minute – I have something to say.' She then issued a blunt safe sex warning: 'Protect yourselves. Every time you have sex, use a condom. And if you use drugs, don't share the needle.'

The second half of the concert was a marathon of twenty Queen hits, backed by the remaining members of Queen – John Deacon, Brian May and Roger Taylor – and ending in the traditional spectacular burst of fireworks above the stadium. Of all the artists appearing that night, it was Michael who came closest to matching Mercury's flamboyant, semi-operatic style. He sang 'Year of '39', 'These Are The Days Of Our Lives' duetting with Lisa Stansfield, and 'Somebody To Love', accompanied by the London Community Gospel Choir. His performance that night confirmed Michael's reputation as the most distinguished balladeer of his generation.

Although Michael had not released any new original material for eighteen months, his income was still rolling in in large quantities. But his dispute with Sony was having an effect. His earnings in America had crashed. A few years earlier he had jostled with Steven Spielberg, Mike Tyson, Sylvester Stallone and Michael Jackson as the best-paid entertainer, but now he had slipped out of sight. By the end of 1991, *Forbes* magazine declared that Michael's American income had plummeted so low that his name did not even feature in the list of the country's Top 40 entertainment earners. He had been massively out-sold by New Kids on the Block, Bill Cosby, Oprah Winfrey, Madonna and Michael Jackson. And he had fallen below British names like the Rolling Stones, Paul McCartney, Sean Connery and Andrew Lloyd Webber.

Michael was unaffected by the figures and remained indifferent about money. He had too much to spend, no matter how generous he was to those around him. In 1992, he was named as Britain's most generous star in a survey by the *Directory of Social Change*. It claimed Michael had given £500,000 to charity over twelve months, putting him in the country's Top 20 individual benefactors. It was topped by John Paul Getty II, then worth about one and a half billion pounds, who had given away £90 million a year. The survey explained that most of Michael's donations went to the Platinum Trust, a charity helping people with physical and mental disabilities.

Michael's wealth was so large and his lifestyle so modest that he liked giving his money away. He found he positively enjoyed the act of giving. It suited him. Michael had set up the Platinum Trust charitable foundation and in its first five years he quietly gave £3 million to it. He was said to have paid off a dance student's £3,000 debt, incurred when putting herself through college. When it emerged that he was suing Chancery Financial Management to recover £1 million lost in a pension fund crash, he vowed that if he won back the money he would give it all to charity.

His continuing friction with Sony became evident when the *Red, Hot & Dance* venture came to fruition. Michael wrote and recorded his three new songs for it – 'Do You Really Want To Know', 'Happy' and 'Too Funky' – and other contributors included Madonna, Seal, P.M. Dawn and Lisa Stansfield. As usual, Epic did little to promote the record and Michael did little to disguise his anger at them. The British and American music press welcomed the new Michael offerings, but they also began speculating about why his own record label seemed so hesitant to discuss him and his work. The company seemed to be in the dark over the future plans of one of their biggest artists. And before long the clash between the singer and his record company became common knowledge.

'Too Funky' was released as a George Michael charity single on both sides of the Atlantic in June, with a fourth Michael original on its B-side, 'Crazy Man Dance'. The 'Too Funky' video was filmed in a studio near the Bois de

Bologne, in Paris, and Michael co-directed it with the French fashion designer Thierry Mugler, best known for leather and plastic catsuit creations. A fashion catwalk was the setting for the video, which again featured a string of glamorous and beautiful models, among them Linda Evangelista, Tyra, Emma S and Shana Zedrick, all modelling Mugler creations. And one of the women was a man, John Epperson, better known as Lypsinka on the New York drag queen circuit. A hundred or more chic extras made up the glossy audience.

While Mugler had strong ideas for the way the video should be shot, he was quickly overwhelmed by the scale of the project. After two days the video fell badly behind schedule and on the third day Michael stepped in in an attempt to salvage it. Michael got his revenge on Mugler. In the final version of the video, approved by Michael, the catwalk models are seen to be harrassed by Mugler's fantasy creations. According to the *Los Angeles Times*, the look was Mugler's 'tribute to the internal combustion engine'. 'A series of heavy metal outfits that seem part Harley chic and part '63 Chevy Impala,' it reported. 'One metal bustier even sprouts breast-mounted rear-view mirrors and hip-mounted handlebars. There are also strapless gowns that defy gravity and physiology, and even a white ostrich feather mane for that lion-in-drag effect.' Fully aware of the controversy it would spark, Michael filmed Evangelista and Zedrick in an intimate clinch. The tabloids quickly dubbed it a 'lesbian fantasy scene' and once again BBC TV censored the video for British screenings, agreeing to show it only in a truncated version.

Despite these business set-backs, Michael was enjoying himself. To celebrate his tenth anniversary in the music business he laid on a private holiday for twenty friends and employees. All the old crowd were there. They met up at a villa in Nice before flying by private jet to Necker, Richard Branson's private holiday island in the Caribbean. Guests included David Austin, Andrew Ridgeley and his new partner Keren Woodward, from the all-girl band Bananarama, and sister Melanie. Nor did Michael forget his family. He spent a great deal on a racing stable for his father, Theobald Stud, in Hatfield, Hertfordshire. Michael joked that he wanted his father to breed a Derby winner. He was also generous to his extended family. The same year he put up money for his aunt and uncle, Andrew and Stella Panayiotou, brother and sister-in-law of his father Jack, to open a designer clothes shop, Bolero, in Bromley, Kent, selling exclusive Italian and French designs.

In the UK, 'Too Funky' entered at No. 4 but fell out of the Top 10 after four weeks. In America, it entered at No. 41 and climbed over eight weeks to No. 10. Despite the single's impressive performance in the charts, Michael was bitterly disappointed with his record company, believing that the charity single would have topped the charts on both sides of the Atlantic had they provided a decent marketing campaign. As it turned out, the *Red, Hot & Dance* album sold a mere 60,000 copies.

Sony were no more enthusiastic about his next project, the so-called *Trojan Souls* album, which he was writing and producing. To avoid working for CBS, Michael would not sing but leave the vocals to Elton John, Aretha Franklin and Anita Baker. Epic passed on the deal, leaving rivals Warner Bros to provide the backing.

There was an attempt to break the deadlock between Sony and Michael with a top-level meeting at which all outstanding matters were to be settled. But when Michael finally came to meet Michael Schulhof, chairman of Sony Music Entertainment worldwide, they failed to reach a satisfactory outcome. It was a bizarre meeting, by all accounts, more sterile than combative, with Schulhof seemingly unaware of the importance of the event – an impression confirmed when, at the end of the meeting, he asked Michael for autographs for his children. During this time Michael turned, as in the past, to Dick Leahy, who sympathized with him. He told colleagues that Michael felt Schulhof 'wasn't getting the message'.

Having reached deadlock with the chairman of Sony, Michael asked for an urgent meeting with Norio Ohga, the world president of Sony, and one was arranged with him in New York. Michael flew in from Los Angeles to attend the mid-morning meeting on 26 October 1992. He was accompanied by his American manager, Rob Kahane, and his British publisher, Dick Leahy. The three of them rode the lift to the executive offices on the forty-third floor of Sony's Manhattan headquarters and entered a conference room. There, alongside Ohga, were the chairman, Schulhof, and Paul Russell of Sony Music UK. Michael shook hands with all three, then outlined his grievances. They listened in silence.

He told them that despite the fifteen-year contract with Sony committing him to provide a further six albums by the year 2003, he had decided that he would never work for them again. He said he was tired of being treated like 'little more than software' by a company which he felt had shown scant respect for long-term creative development and artistic integrity. As he came to the end of his statement, he asked them to release him from his contract.

Michael believed he had made his case well and that, for the first time, Sony fully understood his problems. As he left the meeting he was convinced he would be released from his contract and he flew back to Los Angeles. But before long he discovered that, on the contrary, Sony had decided to fight to keep him. They told him of their decision and on 30 October Michael, via his lawyer Tony Russell, promptly issued a thirty-page writ at the High Court in London, claiming his contract with Sony amounted to a 'restraint of trade'.

By providing a detailed account of his dealings with the company to back his case, Michael lifted the lid on the rigidly hierarchic way the multimillion dollar record industry handles its affairs. He described his contract as 'professional slavery' and, amongst a wealth of illuminating detail in court documents, claimed that for each CD sale of his album *Faith* he had 'inequitably' received just 69p, compared to Sony's £3.38. On vinyl album releases Michael saw 57p, while Sony made £1.83.

The writ also claimed that Sony owned all of Michael's recordings, even though he had always paid for recording costs which were deducted from his royalties. And he claimed that 9 per cent of his album sales earned him nothing because of the high level of 'free' units given to wholesalers and retailers. It further claimed an imbalance of business power. Since Michael had no right of audit over Sony outside the UK, he was put at a disadvantage. The company had the right to veto any music he might want to release, which was a restriction on his artistic freedom. And Sony insisted that he should not appear in any film produced by a third party, which was a restraint of trade.

Michael's legal team also made clear they would be citing European law – Article 85 of the Treaty of Rome – which prohibits agreements affecting trade between member states. As an example they suggested that if Sony decided not to release Michael records in France, he would be forbidden from working for any company that would.

Michael released a statement to the press. 'Since Sony Corporation bought my contract, along with everything and everyone else at CBS, I have seen the great American company that I proudly signed to as a teenager become a small part of the production line for a giant electronics corporation which, quite frankly, has no understanding of the creative process. With CBS, I felt I was believed in as a long-term artist, whereas Sony appears to see artists as little more than software. Musicians do not come in regimented shapes and sizes but are individuals who evolve together. Sony views this as a great inconvenience.'

Dick Leahy told the *Independent*: 'His dispute is not about ego or money. George has enough money for all his needs. It's about the style of management. Under the old management there was an understanding that their top worldwide artists would develop over time, and change direction when they needed to. Now it's all short-term thinking.' Leahy described Sony's approach as 'dictatorial' and explained that since Michael was effectively a one-man hit factory, 'all a record company has to do is market what he gives them – and he feels he wasn't marketed adequately.'

Returning the broadside, Sony too issued a coolly worded statement: 'Sony has a clear and unwavering commitment to George Michael. Together our relationship with him has been mutually fruitful. Our contract with George is valid and legally binding. We are saddened and surprised by the action George has taken. There is a serious moral as well as legal commitment to any contract, and we will not only honour it, but vigorously defend it.' So battle commenced.

11

A Day at the Races

The year 1993 began peacefully enough. George Michael, in his thirtieth year, set out with Anselmo Feleppa to the Caribbean for a New Year break. The holiday was the calm before what was to be months of the most turbulent private and public storms. On his return to Britain he began preparing for his legal battle with Sony. Although the case would not reach the High Court until the autumn, Michael spent much of the year in meetings with lawyers. He also began preparing himself for the strain of many weeks of gruelling mental bombardment in the full public gaze of the courtroom.

With the court battle scheduled for October, the press and media now considered Michael public property. Each day wildly speculative stories of his supposed plans appeared in the papers and the music press. They mostly ignored the odds stacked against any artist attempting to undo their contract and often suggested he would ultimately win his fight with the Japanese company. There was little successful precedent in the High Court for annulling a contract on the grounds that the very exclusivity was a restraint of trade – although in a similar case the Manchester group the Stone Roses was freed from its Silverstone Records contract in 1991 after a British court considered their particular recording contract an unjustifiable restraint of trade.

Typical of the way the story was treated was the coverage in the *Los Angeles Times* of 24 January, which declared: 'They're Off and Running in the George Michael Derby'. The writer went straight to the point, assuming that now it was simply a matter of time before Sony and Michael would agree severance terms. The story was therefore less concerned with the court verdict than which company would pick up Michael's contract when the case was settled. 'Even though the English pop thoroughbred can't break free of his Sony Records contract for another nine months at the earliest, record labels are already courting him.' Michael's American manager Rob Kahane was more realistic. He knew that the result of the court case was not a foregone conclusion. He believed Michael would have to fight to the very end. 'Every major label executive has called me saying, "Just want you to know we're interested and would offer a ton of money," but there has been no discussion at all about a deal because we're not free.'

Still, most industry observers were placing their bets on Burbank-based Warner Brothers Records signing Michael, although Kahane offered caution. The company was already working with Michael on the release of the *Trojan Souls* album, to be produced by Michael.

Beyond the court case, which was taking up considerable amounts of Michael's time and energy, he was preparing to release a record, and one which the combined might of CBS and Sony was powerless to prevent. It was to be an EP of tracks recorded live at the Freddie Mercury Tribute Concert the previous year. The record, which had on its label 'George Michael and Queen', was to be released to raise funds for the Mercury Phoenix Trust, 'for the distribution to AIDS charities worldwide in memory of the incomparable Freddie Mercury'. Because the record was for charity it was outside of Sony's grasp. And it was to be released instead by Hollywood Records in America and by EMI in the rest of the world (the owners of the rights to Queen's catalogue).

The two main tracks were 'Somebody To Love' and 'These Are The Days Of Our Lives', recorded live by Michael and Queen at Wembley. 'These Are The Days Of Our Lives', on which Michael sang with Lisa Stansfield, was the song with which Mercury had bowed out. Mercury was in the final stages of his illness, so when the video for his last record was being shot he was heavily made up in a bid to disguise his condition. The record was released posthumously in Britain in December 1991, just a month after his death, as the B-side to the re-release of Queen's best-known song, 'Bohemian Rhapsody'.

Mercury's lyrics for 'These Are The Days Of Our Lives' revealed his sadness.

The other tracks, which Michael had recorded during his 'Cover to Cover' tour, were similarly poignant in an AIDS context, in particular the highly charged medley which combined 'Papa Was A Rolling Stone' with the Adamski hit 'Killer'. Its lyrics appealed to the listener, asking for an affirmation of life and for an indication of a desire to make a contribution to it.

'Papa Was A Rolling Stone' had been an American chart-topper for Detroit's Temptations in the early Seventies, with a chorus that dwells on death and loss. 'Calling

You' had a celestial sound, a slow and harrowing song better known from the soundtrack of the film *Bagdad Café*. The final track was 'Dear Friends': a soft, hymn–like lullaby performed by Mercury alone.

The finest track on the EP remained Michael's reading of the Mercury classic 'Somebody To Love'. Michael's rendition at the Wembley tribute concert had been immaculate, even hitting a high A with the operatic ease of Mercury himself.

As the EP was going to the presses for its spring launch, Michael was still shunning the limelight. In private he was given a great deal of support by Anselmo Feleppa. In two years they had forged an extraordinary friendship. It was trusting and honest. Feleppa's Brazilian roots meant he approached life in a more open and sentimental way to the introverted Michael. Although brought up among Greek-Cypriots, Michael had adopted many of the constricting attitudes of the English male. Michael found he could always rely on Feleppa to bolster his spirits and make him laugh. When they were together, they were inseparable. When they were apart, they spoke regularly on the telephone.

But then tragedy struck. One night in March Feleppa, in Brazil, suffered a brain haemorrhage and died. Feleppa's death was a dreadful blow to Michael. He had come to depend upon the Brazilian as a diversion from his European and American life in music and business. He felt lost without Feleppa to anchor his life. He felt lonely and some days drifted into a morbid depression.

Talking years later about Feleppa's death, Michael said: 'It was a terrible shock. The grief is always there and sometimes it comes back. You feel it every bit as painfully as if it was yesterday, and other times you think of the person and how fantastic the experience of knowing them was. It was the most enlightening experience that I have ever had. The minute someone you really love is irretrievably lost you understand life in a different way. Your perspective changes. You understand how short life is, how incredibly painful it can be. But once you've seen the worst of things you can see the best of things, so that experience was very painful at the time but very positive in its outcome.'

Michael had taken measures to prevent his grief turn into rampant pessimism. He said: 'After he died I went through bereavement counselling which helped me a lot. I'm not naturally depressive. I mean, I've suffered from depression in depressive circumstances, but I don't have a tendency towards it. I'm not very good at wallowing. If I'm going to feel bad, I distract myself.'

Feleppa was buried in a Catholic cemetery on a mountain ridge in his home-town of Petropolis, fifty miles from Rio. His grave was marked with a large black marble tomb inscribed, in Portuguese, 'The tears of the interred will turn to joy in Heaven. Love has made your life eternal.' Michael did not attend Feleppa's funeral, fearing that his presence might bring out hoards of news photographers. Instead, he slipped out of Britain a few days later, flying to Rio to make his own discreet pilgrimage to Feleppa's grave with Feleppa's mother. She remembered, 'We wept together.'

Returning to Britain and feeling at an all-time low, Michael went ahead with interviews he had promised to give to help promote the release of the Mercury charity EP. The press had not yet caught up with the news of Feleppa's death, but it soon became obvious to interviewers that Michael was deeply upset. For once, even behind his trademark sunglasses, he found it impossible to hide his true feelings. In one interview while talking about Feleppa's sudden death he broke down in tears.

It was inevitable, perhaps, that when the press found out about Feleppa's death, they began speculating upon Michael's close friendship with the young Brazilian and jumped to conclusions. Sweeping aside the explanation that Feleppa had died of a brain haemorrhage, some reported that he had died of complications brought on by 'an AIDS-related illness'.

Michael's sexuality was raised by an MTV reporter on 20 April: surely the work he did for AIDS charities was a response to his own sexuality? Michael remained calm and turned the question from himself into a safe-sex message. 'It's really sad to me that people think in order to work towards a cure, you have to be afflicted yourself. If people look at me and they think I'm a gay man – fine. If they look at me and think I'm straight – that's fine, too. It makes no difference. The important thing for the kids, whether they be straight, bisexual, gay, whatever, is to be aware, there's a definite threat. They are all going to come into contact with people who are afflicted by this disease. There are plenty of people who will die because they felt it was something that was never going to happen to them.'

The *Daily Mirror* voiced what many were thinking when it ran a Michael story, based on the MTV interview, across two pages under the headline 'So What If They Think I'm Gay?'. The piece acknowledged that to be deemed gay was a dangerous thing for a singer, for still great numbers of the public were homophobic. The press, too, were deeply prejudiced against gays. In the *Mirror* the reporter Rick Sky wrote a story about Michael that described the AIDS virus as a 'gay-plague' and referred to the 'stigma of being gay'.

But if in public it suited George Michael to dodge the question of his sexuality, he was more open among friends. It was clear to all who knew him that Michael was homosexual, but in recent times, because of his affection for Feleppa, he had spent even less time with women. Later, in a rare response to a question about his sexuality, he replied: 'Someone like me, who sits there with this big neon question mark over my head and openly invites those questions, is [therefore] a thing of fascination. If people fit very neatly into one sexual category or another, they are immediately rather boring to the media. I talk to both gay men who want me to be gay and straight women who want me to be straight and a lot of people who are not sure of their sexuality. All the biggest pop stars have unanswered questions over their sexuality, it's what draws people to them.'

The singer concluded: 'I think everything about me has always been ambiguous, from the way I look to the tone of my voice. I mean, let's face it, I'm not exactly Bruce Springsteen. Anyway, my sexuality is no one's fucking business. Who really cares whether I'm gay or straight? Do they think they've got a serious chance of shagging me or something?'

The MTV interview gave Michael the chance to pay tribute to Freddie Mercury, who had died of AIDS. 'I only met him a couple of times, but Freddie Mercury had such a profound effect on me as a child. I kind of drank in everything he did.' Michael dedicated the EP 'to Freddie, who probably saved me from life as a waiter.'

After MTV, Michael's next big media interview was with Simon Bates for Radio One. At that recording, Michael found it impossible to completely disguise his sadness at the loss of his friend Feleppa, and he had to take time during the interview to compose himself. Simon Bates remembered Michael arriving at Radio One, in Portland Place, adjacent to Broadcasting House, and he was alarmed to see that the singer was drained of colour. He told Bates before the interview started that he had recently suffered the biggest tragedy of his life.

In the interview Bates asked Michael how he was coping with Feleppa's death, without referring to him by name. Michael became a little choked and looked uncomfortable as he searched for words. There were a few mumbled words, then silence, and he stopped the interview to compose himself. After the recording, Michael asked Bates to edit out his remarks about Feleppa. Bates was impressed at Michael's strength of character and that he went ahead with the interview when he was so clearly upset.

In the interview with Bates Michael revealed an unlikely interest in British politics. He had voted Liberal Democrat, he said, but was prepared to vote for any party which was prepared to tax rich people more. He especially loathed the Conservatives. 'Thatcher ruined the lives of many,

many people. When I see her on television, I think: "You silly cow. You really think there's some chance you're going to be back." She fooled people into thinking that they could attain their own little version of America. I think she was mad because her dreams are all set in the days of the British Empire.'

Michael was equally outspoken about the state of British music, lamenting that he 'had never heard so much bad music on the radio' and that record companies were too interested in old bands. And, ironically, he criticized companies who released cover versions of old songs, though because of his dispute with Sony, that is exactly what he was obliged to do. He traced the malaise to Live Aid in 1985, when 'so much attention, time and money was spent on revamping bands' rather than investing in new talent. The result was boredom. The same old faces, the same old tricks.

'I don't think there has ever been so many faceless and talentless people on television and radio,' he said. 'I don't believe anything I hear means much, other than people finding a way of making a bit of money and getting a little bit of glamour for ten minutes. We're all the losers, because pop music is the most incredibly exciting thing when it means something.'

Although Michael's message was not welcome in a music industry which was struggling to find a new direction, his words could not be ignored. Michael's understanding of the industry was complete and he knew what he was talking about. That intimate knowledge had made him a very rich man. In April that year he was the youngest of Britain's ten wealthiest entertainers. In a *Sunday Times* poll of the richest 400 men and women in Britain, of the entertainers Michael was once again placed fourth, with an estimated unchanged fortune of £80 million, after Paul McCartney (£400 million), Elton John (£120 million) and Mick Jagger (£90 million). After Michael came Keith Richards (£70 million), Mark Knopfler (£60 million), Cliff Richard (£45 million), former Eurythmic Dave Stewart (£30 million), George Harrison (£25 million) and Rod Stewart (£25 million). And all the others were in their thirties, forties or fifties and had been in the industry a decade or more; George Michael was still just twenty-nine.

On 1 May 'Somebody To Love' entered the British singles charts at No. 1, his ninth British No. 1 single, and stayed there for the next three weeks. The sleeve notes for the record carried in full Michael's comments on AIDS made at the Wembley concert the previous year: 'I think a lot of people, not necessarily people who have anything against gay people, are probably taking some small comfort in the fact that although Freddie died of AIDS he was publicly bisexual. It's a very, very dangerous comfort. The conservative estimate for the year 2000 is that forty million people on this planet will be infected by HIV, and if you think that those are all going to be gay people or drug addicts, then you are pretty well lining up to be one of those numbers. So please, for God's sake and for Freddie's sake, and for your own sakes, please be careful.'

Michael celebrated reaching the age of thirty with a double bout of celebrations. Festivities began on the afternoon of Saturday 26 June, three days after his birthday, when an invited party of family and friends were taken to the races in Newmarket, Cambridgeshire. Michael hired a marquee and laid on a party. Andrew Ridgeley was there, and gave Michael a pair of gold-plated ice-tongs in the shape of a goose, a reference to his old buddy's ability to lay golden eggs. Two horses from his father's stud farm in Hertfordshire were racing that afternoon, Mr Devious and Nikita, named after the Elton John song. Both were pipped to the post by Saihat, ridden by Lester Piggott. Had they gone to Haydock Races a week later they would have seen Mr Devious win its first race.

That evening a second, bigger event got underway at his father's stud farm, where Michael had invited 200 family and friends. The party had a 'Heavy Seventies Vibe' theme, so Afro wigs and bell-bottom flares mingled with the latest Versace fashions. The night was a demonstration of Michael's exceptional organizational skills. All the guests sat down to supper in a giant marquee, followed by dancing late into the night. Michael was anxious to avoid publicity and hired a small army of security guards to patrol the grounds, adjoining lane and fields, to keep unwanted fans and paparazzi at bay. The location was even kept secret from many of the guests, who were instructed to rendezvous at a spot in Watford where they were collected and driven off into the night.

Michael was on good form that night, jumping up on stage at one point in an Afro wig to give an impromptu rendition of 'Carwash'. Among the guests were Michael's parents and sisters and music colleagues, including his former Wham! backing singers Shirlie Holliman and Pepsi DeMacque. And the party included a smattering of pop's camper glitterati, such as Pet Shop Boys Neil Tennant and

Chris Lowe, Paul Young, Paul Rutherford of Frankie Goes to Hollywood and Elton John's manager John Reid.

Another guest at the party, one-time member of the Sheffield pop group, ABC, Fiona Russell Powell, claimed in an article that the party was awash with 'buckets' of Ecstasy tablets.

She also revealed in the same article, to the annoyance of Michael, and in of all places the British satirical magazine *Punch*: 'All the boys were snogging each other, which greatly upset George's Greek-Cypriot father. George had to run around looking incredibly embarrassed, begging everyone to tone it down.'

While the Michael/Queen EP went straight to the top of the British singles charts, in America its success was dampened by being deemed an album rather than a single and therefore obliged to compete against the massive weekly album sales of other artists. The record failed to make any headway past its entry point at No. 46. A decision was taken to release the four tracks as two singles, the 'Somebody To Love' track from the EP reaching No. 30, while the medley 'Killer'/'Papa Was A Rolling Stone' peaked at No. 69.

The video to accompany 'Killer'/'Papa Was A Rolling Stone' was well received by American critics, the *Los Angeles Times* praising it for taking a satirical shot at 'crass overmarketing of street-smart styles'. The paper's Maureen Sajbel reported: 'George Michael's new video "Killer"/ "Papa Was A Rolling Stone" is such a perfect example of 1993's melange of rave/grunge/hip-hop and thrift fashion, it could be put in a time capsule. The video is a satiric look at how street fashions have been marketed to death.

As kids dance and ride the subways – in crochet vests, flag shirts, lace bell bottoms, knit caps, knotted hair and pain-ful-looking pierced lips and noses – the words to the songs become household product ad logos that float through the sky. Andy Warhol would have been proud.'

'Killer'/'Papa Was A Rolling Stone' stayed on the American chart for seven weeks. It fell out of the singles charts in America at the same time that the EP 'album' did the same, in the middle of August. Together, they signalled the end of Michael's appearance on the record charts for almost three years.

Michael's legal team notched up an early advantage over Sony in July, when the Chancery Division of the British High Court of Justice, in the Strand in London, ruled in Michael's favour. Sir David Nicholls, vice chancellor of the Supreme Court, directed that a request from his legal team be made to the New York Federal Court to compel Sony Music Entertainment to produce their highly confi-dential recording contracts with such superstars as Michael Jackson, Bruce Springsteen, Mick Jagger, Billy Joel and Barbra Streisand. This was in order for Michael's own legal team to strengthen its arguments by comparing them with the contracts Michael signed with Sony. They hoped this would enable them to do one of two things: either to demonstrate that Michael was being poorly treated and that his contract was out of line with other artists working for Sony, or to show that Sony exploited all its artists.

Sony were uncomfortable with the request, believing their biggest stars would be incensed at having their private financial arrangements revealed to the public. In fact such details would not automatically become public knowledge, as they were subject to the confidentiality of the court.

It was not only the financial details of other stars that Michael's team hoped to use to his advantage. There were also unlikely promises of rewards in kind if certain sales figures were reached – again, incentives which did not apply to Michael. Some of the sub-clauses in other artists' contracts would have made spectacular reading, such as promises of ranches for reaching certain sales goals or, in the case of a certain indie band, the promise of a bubble car if they reached a specific chart position. Other clauses were simply embarrassing and therefore an irritation for Sony to reveal, such as the many profanity clauses, insisted upon by Sony to keep wild drug-fuelled rock bands in check when they were on the road and likely to trash hotel rooms.

Michael's legal team believed Sony executives did not wish to reveal its contracts with artists because it would reveal them to be exploitative. And there was a public relations dimension to the revelations which Sony also wished to avoid. They were aware that if the record-buying public discovered the true levels of reward enjoyed by artists with whom they otherwise identified, they might take a more sober view of the artists concerned and the music business in general, which could hit sales. This was especially the case in countries, such as Britain, where the cost to the public of CDs was excessive.

Michael spent much of the remainder of the summer out of Britain and he enjoyed some much-needed privacy. The only public sightings reported were that he had helped a friend celebrate at a birthday party in the south of France; that he had to be bailed out over a bill of a little under £20 by a fellow diner at a Los Angeles pizza parlour, and that he was back in London in September to give a boost to his former backing singer Pepsi DeMacque at the opening of a revival of the rock musical *Hair*, in which she had a lead role.

As summer turned to autumn, Michael braced himself for the court case. The impending proceedings prompted a rash of stories in the British press. With George Michael in the news, they wished to cash in on renewed interest in the singer's private life. A few days ahead of the start of the trial, Britain's tabloids again speculated about Michael's relationship with Feleppa. The *Sun* recounted a story running in Brazil's *Interview* magazine. 'George showered his new chum with gifts – including a Mercedes car and a gold Rolex watch,' it reported. 'It also says that he paid for him to have private accommodation in Beverly Hills and Rio. The magazine says the two men were virtually inseparable by the time Anselmo died and that grief-stricken George flew straight to Brazil to be at his graveside. *Interview* claims all this suggests a deeper relationship between the two men than just a normal friendship.'

What the British paper did not report was that the original article revealed Anselmo Feleppa had been a fan of Michael who had stalked him, deliberately setting out to effect a meeting between them, then befriend the singer. Feleppa, a well-to-do country boy from a town near Rio, was being groomed to work in his father's clothing factory and set about winning over Michael with fanatical precision. When Michael played Rio that January, Feleppa turned himself out immaculately and bought tickets in the front row for both shows, hoping to catch the singer's eye.

Michael did not notice him and, according to the report, Feleppa resorted to hanging around the foyer of Michael's hotel, the Copacabana Palace, hoping to bump into him. When this failed to throw up a meeting, Feleppa discovered that Michael was moving from Rio to a hotel on a private island reached only by boat. Although closed to everyone but Michael and his party, Feleppa managed to get a reservation by claiming to be a famous visiting Italian designer. Once established at the hotel, Feleppa stage-managed a successful meeting. However, that Michael, himself a master manipulator and wary of strangers, would then have allowed a cranky fan to become one of his closest friends remains unlikely.

At the beginning of October, Sony made an approach to Michael's lawyers, offering a settlement. The case was due to start at the High Court on 11 October and was expected to last a number of weeks thereafter. Sony were anxious to avoid the expense of a protracted legal action and proposed a speedily negotiated settlement. The company agreed to terminate the contract with Michael at a price, the exact sum to be agreed as quickly as possible, perhaps with Sony retaining a stake in the singer's future earnings. The dispute was damaging Sony in the eyes of the public and also agitating other artists, who could not believe that a settlement could not be found. Sony were aware of the value of Michael as a recording artist, but they were prepared to forego directing his recording career themselves, so long as they retained a financial stake.

Sony waited some time for a reply. The lawyers put the offer to Michael who was asked for his direction and he in turn asked his manager, Rob Kahane, for advice. It would not be the first time that Kahane encouraged Michael to make an aggressive response. The two men came to the conclusion that Sony were running scared and were hoping to hang on to a piece of Michael. They thought, wrongly as it turned out, that Sony were admitting that their case was not good enough and expected to be defeated in court. The Michael team refused the offer of more detailed talks and awaited the court hearing.

On 11 October, Georgios Kyriacos Panayiotou *v.* Sony Music Entertainment UK Ltd reached the High Court in London and was promptly postponed for a week due to a lawyer's injury. Seven days later, on 18 October at Court 39, the case finally got under way. It was to be a watershed case for Michael and for all creative artists tied to exclusive deals. If Michael won this case, record contracts would never be the same again.

The High Court, with its cold, Gothic warren of corridors, rarely hosted celebrity events. But as Michael's case began a number of other rock stars were appearing at the High Court. In one room, Boy George was laughing his way through a paternity suit announcing proudly to have 'never penetrated a woman' in his life. In another, Elton John was pummelling the *Sunday Mirror* after suing for libel over claims that he once contracted a bizarre eating disorder.

But eyes were mostly focused on the central court, where Michael's fight with Sony was a case of real substance. This was no domestic tiff over a petty libel; this was big business. As the case progressed it would draw worldwide attention and reveal the inner workings of the recording industry. The music business soon split down the middle over the case and divided between those who backed Michael in his David and Goliath fight for artistic freedom and those who thought Sony and the sanctity of the contract should prevail.

Michael turned up in person for the start of the trial and

his arrivals at the court always attracted media attention. News crews and photographers were kept firmly behind metal barriers, but pandemonium broke out as soon as Michael's limousine pulled up. The photographers broke into frenzied activity. Each day Michael stepped out of the car and walked into the High Court in silence, accompanied by a number of burly bodyguards. Each day he sported a healthy growth of thick, black stubble and wore dark glasses. He wore a dark Versace suit, with a red AIDS ribbon pinned to his left lapel, over a white shirt open at the neck or a £120 black Versace T-shirt. Most days he wore silver-tipped cowboy boots. Once inside the High Court he swapped his sunglasses for the more scholarly, horn-rimmed clear-lensed glasses he wore for everyday use and he remained bespectacled throughout the proceedings.

Alongside his legal team, there to support Michael most days were his American manager Rob Kahane, Gary Farrow and Michael's parents, who smiled back in reassurance each time he looked their way. The upstairs public gallery was crammed with Michael fans, mostly young women. Those at the front clung to the railings, all willing him success and hoping to catch an occasional glance from their hero. They rarely got it. Michael sat impassive as the proceedings ground on at a snail's pace. Much of the argument revolved around impenetrable technical matters of contract law, beyond the grasp of most of those who looked on.

Sinead O'Connor turned up one day to support Michael. They exchanged smiles across the frosty courtroom and she wrote a note to be passed to him. She told those outside that she had simply gone for 'the laugh'.

Justice Jonathan Parker presided over the case. Michael's QC, Mark Cran, opened with a statement to the court about the rift which had grown between Michael and his record label when the singer announced that he wanted to stay out of the limelight that accompanied his heartthrob status. Mr Cran told the court: 'He wanted to play down his image as a sex symbol and play up the quality of his music. To that end he entitled his next album *Listen Without Prejudice*. He was determined not to associate his image with the record. No picture of him appeared on the sleeve. But unfortunately he feels that CBS American Division did not support him, which led to considerable unhappiness. In the UK, after a delay, Sony put their backing behind it and it outsold *Faith* [in the UK].'

Michael was patient and polite when called to give evidence. He took the stand for three days, starting on 28 October. Questioned by the barrister for the defence, Mr Gordon Pollock, the exchanges often became tough and personal. Pollock questioned the singer on everything from the trashing of the original Wham! contract with Mark Dean's fledgling Innervision label to the sexually frank content of many of his videos. During questioning, Michael was obliged to admit he pressurized Innervision to renegotiate his contract by stealing the tapes to the first Wham! album, *Fantastic*.

Michael was also asked why he had demanded a change of image after *Faith* when the *Faith* image had proved so successful. The singer said: 'As long as the quality of music was maintained they [his mostly female fans] would have moved along with me. I believe that, regardless of my public position or possible financial ramifications for Sony,

I have the right to change as a person and artist. I had hoped that, having been a great asset for almost a decade, I would be supported in these changes. Sony have, by and large, refused that support.'

Pollock asked Michael how much he was worth. Michael refused to say, acknowledging simply that he was extraordinarily wealthy. He agreed to write down the figure for the judge to read. On seeing the total, Pollock quipped, 'That is supposed to be a decimal point?'

At one point Pollock put it to the singer that 'the real reasons for this action have little to do with the legal pleadings; you just don't get on with Sony/CBS any more, do you Mr Michael?' Michael admitted as much, leaving Pollock to suggest that he was no worse off than any other artist in Sony's stable. This line of questioning caused Michael's advocate, Mark Cran, to counter that the singer's worth was not at stake in the action, it was the imbalance of his deal with Sony. The court was told that on Michael's sales grossing £99.5 million, Sony had made £52.45 million outright profit and the singer just £7.35 million. Michael had also borne the recording costs.

Cran explained further: 'He is getting the same rate for CDs as he would be for vinyl. It may be that the vinyl rate is inappropriately low.' Cran said the complexities of the recording agreements caused them to be manipulated to the advantage of the record companies and the contract was to the 'detriment of the artist and the benefit of Sony'.

Sony took a very different view of the case. As the relationship between the creative artist and a record company was at the heart of the company's profitability, they had been anxious that the case never reach court and they had tried everything they could to settle. They felt confident that the court would uphold their contention that the contract was unbreakable.

They thought it incongruous that Michael, who had always protested that his dispute was about creativity, not money, should sue them for, of all things, restraint of trade. The notion of exclusivity was the essence of an exclusive contract and he could hardly claim that he had not known that when he entered the agreement.

They suggested that the reason Michael had taken such a large advance from Sony, in a lump sum of $11 million, an enormous amount even by music industry standards, was that he was on a tour of the world and would therefore be outside Britain long enough to be exempt from income tax. Sony felt that having received the advance, Michael was reneging on his part of the bargain – to record songs and market seven albums.

Michael had tried to suggest that his cosy relationship with CBS was shattered by the purchase of CBS by Sony. Yet all the other artists, including major stars like Bob Dylan and Michael Jackson, were perfectly content. Michael's assertion that Sony was incapable of managing creative artists was far-fetched.

Michael had suggested that Sony refused to back *Listen Without Prejudice, Vol 1* with adequate marketing. But, countered Sony, Michael had refused to appear on the cover of the disc or in the video, he had refused to take part in any personal promotion and had refused to go on tour to bolster the album.

They also took to task another suggestion from the Michael camp, the allegation that the Sony management were homophobic and had therefore deliberately not backed the album. But they admitted the existence of a tape recording of a telephone conversation between the president of the Columbia Broadcasting System, or CBS, Don Ienner, and Michael's manager Rob Kahane, in which Ienner referred to Michael as 'that faggot client of yours', which backed Michael's contention. Michael's response had been to show his contempt for Ienner at every opportunity. Sony suggested that it was the breakdown in that key personal relationship between Michael and Ienner which was at the basis of the action, not an argument about contracts.

Outside the court, Sony offered another explanation for why Michael had set out on such a self-destructive course. They suggested he was suffering from writer's block and that the court case was simply a distraction from his inability to compose any more. Michael had taken to recording cover versions of others' songs because he was unable to write new songs of his own. And the boycott of new material was a front to cover his lack of inspiration. They said Michael had taken tapes, thought to be his still-unreleased *Trojan Souls* project, to Warner at a time when Warner were interested in buying him out of the Sony contract. According to Sony, the reason the tapes had never seen the light of day was because Warner executives thought they were poor. And they quoted a Warner executive saying, 'There is no chance of us releasing them.'

The Michael/Sony case generated thousands of television reports and miles of newspaper columns. The *Guardian* featured Michael in its snappy Pass Notes column, dubbing Michael 'Andrew Ridgeley's social worker'. Under 'What others say about Michael', it wrote he was a 'calculated, efficient, well-blended confection, hardworking, Thatcherite rocker, Lloyd-Webber with a beard, Manilow without the nose'. The secret of his success, continued the *Guardian*, was 'OK looks, the occasional good tune, the occasional good line – "Guilty feet have got no rhythm". You must remember, we live in an age when John Major can become prime minister and George Carey is Archbishop of Canterbury'. Pass Notes concluded Michael was not to be confused with 'George Gershwin, Boy George, Andreas Papandreou, Michael Ignatieff'. He was most likely to say, '"Wake Me Up Before You Go-Go". It was a pop tune m'lud. Top of the hit parade about five years ago.' And the singer was least likely to say, 'Listen Andrew, I think I've made a terrible mistake. Let's dust down our shuttlecocks and reform Wham!'

Michael's ego also fielded blows from papers such as the *Sunday Times* which, on 24 October, followed the line put out by Sony in an anonymous profile, and declared, 'There are those who believe Michael's litigation is not a way of asking for a nice life, but a way out, that he has dried up and peaked at thirty'. Even the singer Billy Bragg was drawn into criticism of Michael. He said drolely: 'I think he [Michael] would have got more joy if he had sued his hairdresser.'

The same day, the *Mail on Sunday* returned to speculating upon Michael's sexuality in a report which referred to Michael's High Court trial only in passing. 'What is it about Michael's life that has given him the resolve to fight this ground-breaking legal case?' it asked. 'The answer may lie in the remarkable and poignant story of Anselmo Feleppa.'

It repeated the *Interview* material that the two men were inseparable and went on, 'Anselmo's death earlier this year from an AIDS-related disease deeply touched Michael. In this country [Brazil] where homosexuality is still viewed by many as a curse, Anselmo's family are now trying to distance their dead son from George Michael.' In reality, Michael was openly received as part of the Feleppa family. And over the long months Michael and Feleppa's mother had drawn strength from one another in equal measure over their shared loss.

The *Mail on Sunday* report, which left its readers in no doubt that Michael was gay, ended on a note inserted by the paper's lawyers. It read: 'Although striking up a friendship with Anselmo, Michael, of course, is not gay and has always denied he was such.'

Despite a report in the *Daily Star* which claimed that Michael was planning to start his own new label and to that end was trawling nightclubs to sign up new bands, Michael was returning each night to his home in Hampstead, where he mostly kept his own company. Each day he returned to a crushing solitude where he found he was unable to write songs. Feleppa's death continued to cast a dark shadow.

The only short respite he got from his private anguish was work. He made a rare appearance at the 'Concert of Hope' at Wembley Arena on 1 December, to mark World AIDS Day. The Princess of Wales, who attended the show as patron, had asked Michael to help with the event. David Bowie played master of ceremonies. After a half-hour set from k.d. lang, wearing white muslin and hob-nail boots, and half an hour by Mick Hucknall belting out Simply Red classics, Michael took top billing and performed for an hour, poignantly dedicating his song 'Freedom 90', as 'a last-minute joke', to Princess Diana, whose marriage was coming to its end. He said: 'I think she took it as it was intended. I knew she'd like it.'

Michael's set included 'Father Figure' and 'Papa Was A Rolling Stone' and closed, triumphantly, with 'Everything She Wants'. It was Michael's first appearance on stage in Britain for almost two years and he won a rapturous ovation from the sell-out crowd of 11,000.

12

Wasting Assets

George Michael spent six months waiting for the verdict of the court. The case ended on 13 April 1994 (after 178 days in which the court sat for 75 days), and there was a further two-month delay while the judge reached his verdict and wrote the reasons for the judgement.

On 21 June, Michael, looking solemn, returned to the High Court to hear Mr Justice Jonathan Parker give his deliberation. Michael's parents were in court, as usual, his father dressed in a grey pinstripe suit and wearing glasses. After seven months of reflection, Michael was pessimistic about the result and felt by intuition that Mr Justice Parker was about to find in Sony's favour. The road to this moment had been a long and expensive one. Not only was his personal equilibrium tested by the prolonged break in his career while the court deliberated, but the legal fees were high. Michael's barrister in court alone cost a minimum of £500,000.

Any hope Michael held that he was to be freed from his contract quickly faded as the judge began slowly to read a summary of his judgement. The full summary of the case and the reasons behind his judgement were contained in a 280-page document.

Mr Justice Parker told Michael that Sony's agreement

with him was legal and binding. He believed that since Michael had repeatedly renegotiated the terms of his contract through the course of his career the contract was 'reasonable and fair' and fairly entered into. Michael's agreement with Sony was not a restraint of trade, he said, nor did he believe that the contract, totalling $11 million, was weighted in favour of the corporation. Michael shook his head in disappointment as Mr Justice Parker's words sank in.

Michael's action failed, according to Mr Justice Parker, on four counts. First, the contract had been renegotiated. Second, Sony had paid a request from Michael for a million-dollar advance. Third, in 1988 Sony had agreed to pay in stages a further $11 million. Fourth, Michael's constant access to and use of legal advice to shape and contest the contract showed that the contract had been fairly entered into.

In his deliberation Mr Justice Parker singled out for lengthy criticism Michael's American manager Rob Kahane. He described Kahane as 'a thoroughly unreliable and untrustworthy witness, whose evidence was coloured by an intense dislike of Sony. Had Sony seen more of Michael and less of Mr Kahane from 1990 onwards, events might have turned out differently'.

The verdict was a bitter disappointment to Michael. He listened to it in stony silence then promptly left the High Court, looking tight-lipped and tense, to face the waiting news cameras. Outside the court, in an impromptu pavement news conference, representatives of Sony told reporters that the company looked forward to resuming its relationship with Michael.

Michael responded by addressing a hastily arranged press conference at the Howard Hotel in Temple Place, near the Law Courts. There he told reporters: 'I am shocked and extremely disappointed.' Then he hinted that he would appeal against the judgement: 'It means that even though I both created and paid for my work, I will never own it or have any rights over it. And perhaps most importantly, I have no right to resign. In fact, there is no such thing as resignation of an artist in the music industry. However, I am convinced that the English legal system will not support Mr Justice Parker's decision or uphold what is effectively professional slavery.'

Although the verdict had gone against Michael, he announced that he would continue to pursue his aim of breaking with Sony. Despite the set-back, Michael was confident that a resolution of the dispute could work in his favour if he kept up the expensive assault on Sony a little longer. He consulted with his legal advisers and decided to up the stakes on his hugely expensive gamble to effect a break with Sony.

At the press conference he restated his determination never to record for Sony again, even if it meant waiting in silence until his contract expired in nine years' time, in 2003. And he announced he would be challenging Mr Justice Parker's ruling through the courts. He would first take the case to appeal, but if that failed he would bring the matter before the European Court of Justice in Strasbourg. The spiralling cost of litigation would not prevent him from pursuing his belief that his agreement with Sony was unfair and curbed his artistic freedom. So far Michael had already spent between three and four million pounds on lawyers' fees and Sony's costs were much the same. The judge had yet to award costs in the case and he might have to pick up the legal bill for both sides.

Back home that night, Michael changed the message on his telephone-answering machine. Those who rang to commiserate with the verdict were greeted to Michael singing to the tune of 'Careless Whisper', 'I'm never gonna sing again. Bastards. Bastards.'

On the West Coast of America, those in the music industry woke up to a headline in the *Los Angeles Times* announcing, 'Michael's Pact With Sony Upheld'. The story read: 'In a decision that should make the record industry sleep easier, the British High Court of Justice ruled Tuesday that superstar George Michael cannot walk away from his contract with Sony Music Entertainment Ltd.'

Depending where you asked, there was a mixed reaction to the verdict in the music industry. For many on the creative side it was thought that business had once again triumphed over creativity. Sony and the other Japanese technology giants had had a bumpy ride in the complex and often hostile creative environment of the entertainment industry. Many commentators had predicted that if they suffered many more set-backs they might even withdraw their investment and sell back to domestic investors who could manage the switch-back industry more profitably. To lose the Michael case might have been one such blow; winning meant that they would be sticking around.

The businessmen running the music industry looked on the verdict with relief. It may never have seemed likely that Michael would succeed in tearing up his contract with Sony, for they had faith in the English interpretation of contract law. But on the outside chance that Michael did win, the principle of the judgement would have under-mined the whole sector. They would have faced artist after artist asserting their right to abandon their existing and often disadvantageous agreements with record companies and attempting to strike better deals with their competi-tors. At stake was the artist's standard contract of seven years.

As the *Los Angeles Times* made clear, 'Although a favourable ruling for Michael in the British Court system would have no legal bearing in the United States, insiders predicted that a pro-Michael verdict could have been used as grounds to raise the same issues for artists in US courts.'

A few days after the hearing, Michael agreed to be interviewed for television by Sir David Frost. The singer explained that he had effectively only ever signed one deal, his initial contract tying him to Innervision Records. Subsequent contracts with Epic, then CBS and finally Sony were all updates of the same original deal. The amounts of money, too, had never been an issue for him.

'I will completely agree they are massive amounts of money,' he told Sir David, 'and I am fully aware that I am in a business which pays amazing amounts of money. But CBS signed Wham! in 1983. Everything I have been given by Sony, whether it was in 1984, whether it was in 1988, 1990, they have never been giving me anything above the royalties that I had already earned.' He added: 'No one ever did me a favour and said, "Here, George, here's $11 million. You know, let's see what you can make back." They were always working in the black, as it were.'

Whilst he was part of an industry with amazingly rich pickings, he complained to Sir David that he did not have the same freedom as ordinary workers. 'The trouble is that this business is not like working in an office, or working for a company. If you really fall out with people who control your professional life, you have a right to walk away. That is the right of every individual, and the music industry takes away that right from every artist it signs.'

Michael described the High Court ruling against him as 'bizarre'. 'I thought it was a very strange judgement,' he said. 'The judge was kind enough to point out that he believed I was very honest and candid in the witness box, so I did my best to be truthful and at the same time he completely accepted everybody on Sony's side. If they were all telling the truth about the events that happened between 1990 and the time the writ was served, then why was I not lying? Someone was lying.'

The interview was directed as much to Sony as to the public at large, warning the company that the court verdict was not an end to the matter. Michael would still use any means at his disposal to avoid recording another song for them.

He said that the case should never have reached the High Court and he had hoped at first that the corporation was so rich from its control of some of the biggest names in the music business that they could be persuaded to release him from his contract without much trouble. He was happy for any such deal to be kept confidential, to prevent other artists from using it as a precedent.

'If they had been reasonable I could have said, "I don't want to tell the world that this is going on. Please let me go. I've been with you for ten years. I've made you hundreds of millions of dollars. And people will believe the deal is over, you know, I've been here this long."'

Instead, Sony 'wouldn't come close to accepting that'. He confessed that he had no reason to expect Sony to come to an agreement with him before the next round of court battles and he was resigned to letting the case go to appeal.

Back in his home in Hampstead, Michael became convinced that his continuing obduracy in the face of an immensely expensive legal action would prove to Sony that he was in earnest about his demand for freedom and that they must concede that the only option for them was to agree to the terms of a divorce. He had made his declaration after the case that he would never record for Sony again in the full knowledge that it left the way open for other record companies to start the complex bargaining process with Sony that would eventually bring his release. Michael was soon vindicated, as before long it became apparent that a number of companies thought his talent so considerable and so potentially lucrative that Sony received and began to assess a number of approaches.

Trevor Dann, the BBC's head of music, summed up: 'It was one of those things where pride was involved more than anything on both sides. It was very, very difficult for George having made this great play of "I'm a slave" and so on to ever back down. So even though I'm sure on many occasions he was advised to give up, he just couldn't. And he's that kind of stubborn bloke. And Sony couldn't give up either because every single person signed to them would have said, oh well, this is this then, it doesn't matter. I can sign any old thing and it doesn't matter. So neither of them could afford to back down and that was it really.'

Between the end of the first court case and the

prospective appeal, Michael tried to write songs, but he found it difficult to concentrate. So he turned instead back to his *Trojan Souls* album, made up of material recorded by others. He worked on the project in a north London studio throughout July, but otherwise mostly stayed at home.

In August his legal team lodged an appeal against the earlier ruling with the Court of Appeal and the case joined the long list of civil suits queuing to be heard. No date for a hearing was given. Michael waited patiently, relaxing at his homes in Hampstead and Santa Barbara.

However, there was one part of Mr Justice Parker's extensive deliberation which Michael agreed with. The judge had gone out of his way to criticize the poor behaviour of Rob Kahane, and Michael's relationship with Kahane came to a swift end. Just four months after the deliberation, in October, Kahane and Michael parted company. He was leaving Michael's inner circle, it was said, 'to start his own record company'.

Reporting that Michael had 'broken away from his long-time manager Rob Kahane', the *Los Angeles Times* declared: 'It looks as if Michael is going to manage himself for a while. His publicist, Michael Pagnotta, said the British singer has no plans to sign with new management until after the dispute with Sony is resolved, either through appeals or a settlement. Meantime, Michael's recording career remains on hold, with no release plans for either himself or the long-planned *Trojan Souls* album.'

Michael did manage to write one new song, a highly emotional ballad which he performed for the first time in November, at the first MTV European Music Awards in Berlin. The event was hosted by Tom Jones, with the city's Brandenburg Gate as a backdrop, and reached a television audience of up to 250 million. While Michael singing a new song for the first time was considered one of the most exciting aspects of the show, and might have been seen as a blow against Sony and all the other large companies who dominated the music industry, a more sensational protest against the big companies was made by The Artist Formerly Known as Prince. He upstaged Michael by making a public protest against record company exploitation by appearing with the word 'slave' written on his cheek.

Prince had telephoned Michael several times during his lengthy legal battle with Sony to express his concern, but Michael was not interested in sharing the bad experiences Prince felt he was having with his record company. 'I just never rung him back,' he said. 'We weren't exactly in the same boat. All I really wanted to say to him was, "Wipe that fucking word [slave] off your cheek, you're not exactly doing me any favours." The only time I really spoke to him, we had this forty-five-minute conversation about God. Maybe I got him on an off day.'

For his part of the show, Michael first sang 'Freedom' on stage with a clutch of supermodels, Naomi Campbell, Karen Mulder and others. Then, as he was left alone to stand in the spotlight, he sang for the first time 'Jesus To A Child'. The song was based on his own experience and seemed to be exorcising a private grief. It was filled with raw tenderness, overshadowed by suffering and inspired by the death of his friend Anselmo Feleppa. The *Sun* suggested '"Jesus To A Child" was a highly personal love song about a lost partner, and is bound to fuel speculation about Michael's love life.'

It was difficult not to believe that the powerful lyrics were a direct reference to Feleppa's death. Michael later explained, had been written in only a few hours. He said: 'It is a song about bereavement. But it is also a song about hope.' He added: 'It's a special song, one of those songs that just felt like it was handed to me.'

The performance of the song on MTV prompted an immediate avalanche of interest from fans, who besieged Sony with the same question: when will 'Jesus To A Child' be released as a single? Michael remained silent, content that the new song showed that the court case had dulled none of his songwriting ability.

In December, Michael's legal team was back in court trying to speed up the appeal. Michael thought that Sony were still prepared to defend their actions and that some new condition was needed to force through a deal with the company. Charles Gray, representing Michael at the Court of Appeal, tried to persuade Sir Thomas Bingham, the Master of the Rolls, that it was imperative that Michael's appeal be heard quickly. Mr Gray described Michael's career as 'blighted' by the uncertainty over the outcome and that blight could only be lifted by an urgent appeal hearing.

He told the court that Michael's career was 'a wasting asset' and that it was not only Michael who was suffering but the general public. 'Millions and millions of people all over the world listen to this man's music. There is deprivation over a huge field.' Sir Thomas, not a music lover, was unmoved, declaring that the appeal would be heard sometime the following year but would not be brought forward.

While Michael's career once again seemed to be on hold, there could be no doubting his continued drawing power in music. In January 1995 listeners of London's Capital Radio voted his ballad 'Careless Whisper' their favourite single of all time. Eleven years after its first release in 1984, the title proved Michael's enduring appeal.

In February Michael teamed up with Eric Clapton to help the family of Nigel Browne, a bodyguard they had both employed, who had been killed in a helicopter crash in 1990. Browne had been one of Michael's inner circle on his global 'Faith' tour in 1988. According to the *Daily Express*, by underwriting their legal expenses, the two superstars had 'battled to win £500,000 compensation' for Browne's partner Sonia and her eight-year-old daughter Michaela in their legal battle with the insurers of the US helicopter company Omniflight.

When Sonia Browne finally won her claim, her lawyer, Eddie Johns of Frank Charlesly and Company, said: 'Eric Clapton and George Michael have been tremendously helpful and Sonia is eternally grateful to them. I cannot make any comment on financial help, but they have both done as much as they could in terms of giving their own time and energies to the matter. I was very impressed by them. It is unusual for people to be so selfless.'

In February, too, it was reported that Michael and a handful of rock stars were teaming up to open a rock theme restaurant in London. Michael was evidently thinking of teaming up with Phil Collins, Bono and Slim Jim Johnson, the former drummer of the Stray Cats, who were said to be in talks with Jake Panayiotou, owner of Brown's discothèque. There was a high-minded aspect to the putative business: a share of profits from the venture would apparently go to charity. The story was, however, later dismissed as fabrication.

Michael's better nature was again evident when, in April, he paid a visit to Sarm West studios in west London and ended up contributing to a new version of his old hit 'I'm Your Man', one of his songs from the Wham! days. Michael turned up at the recording studios for a technical check on specifications. He had used the studio in the past and had found its atmosphere conducive to good music. When he learnt that a version of his 1985 hit was being recorded in one of the studios he decided to eavesdrop on the session. He and his friend, the producer Jon Douglas, who was running the session, watched through the studio glass as an unknown British artist, Lisa Moorish, sang a cover of 'I'm Your Man'. Moorish became nervous when Michael first took an interest, in case he took exception to the recording and withdrew his permission for the song to be recorded. But Michael instantly offered to sing a verse and provide backing vocals on the track.

Michael agreed to sing on condition that his contribution remained totally secret. It was also understood that the song could not be released as a single until, if at all, he was freed from Sony. Moorish noticed that, after months of inactivity, the singer was raring to get back to work. 'He just seemed really excited to be back in a studio again,' she said. 'He was totally relaxed and brilliant to work with. He was itching to get behind a microphone and sing with feeling again – and his enthusiasm was infectious.'

In the annual Capital FM Radio Awards ceremony that April, held at the Royal Lancaster Hotel in Bayswater, west London, Michael was voted Best Male Vocalist for the second year running. Michael had a long association with Capital Radio, London's premier commercial pop station, and had been known to support the station's regular fundraising event, Help A London Child, held over the Easter Bank Holiday weekend. At the awards ceremony, Michael revealed that he would support the upcoming Capital radiothon by allowing them to give the radio première to his new song, 'Jesus To A Child', which he had first performed at the MTV European Music Awards in Berlin the previous November. He added that he would match listeners' donations to hear the track with a cash gift of his own.

The airing of the epic six minutes and fifty seconds recording proved to be the star attraction of the fundraising weekend. While there was still no suggestion the song was near to being released as a single – the terms of any possible divorce from Sony were still being hammered out – it was confirmation that he had at last committed a clean version of the song to tape and that it could be swiftly released when there was a break-through. He had played all the instruments on the recording himself, except for the acoustic guitar, which was played by Hugh Burns.

Michael's song finally raised £70,000 for the charity, with listeners bidding £20,000, a mobile phone company giving another £20,000 and Michael adding a further £30,000. The airing of 'Jesus To A Child' sent Michael's fans into a frenzy of activity. Although only heard within the limits of Capital's transmitters, London and the south-east of England, there was soon a healthy market in bootleg copies. If nothing else, the unsatisfied demand showed that, despite the long court case and the enforced period of silence from Michael, his image with the public remained intact and he still enjoyed an enormous following.

The sudden burst of activity by Michael fed through to high street tills, even though no recording of 'Jesus To A Child' was yet available. There was such a surge in demand for his old recordings that his first solo album, *Faith*, re-entered the British chart on 29 April and remained there for a month. It entered out of the blue at No. 60, then hit Nos. 70, 74 and 65 before disappearing as quickly as it had arrived.

In early July it was rumoured that Michael's career might be about to take a most unlikely new direction, with overtures being made to the singer by the remaining members of the band Queen, who had been crippled by the death of their lead singer, Freddie Mercury. According to a report in the *Sun*, Queen's drummer, Roger Taylor, considered Michael the only singer with enough character to take Mercury's place on a Queen tour planned for later in the year. It was merely wishful thinking on Taylor's part. Michael's hatred of going on tour would ensure that he would never agree to such a thing. The fact was that, without Mercury to front them, Queen were finished as a live touring band.

13

Older and Wiser

Michael's musical career, then, remained active within the constraints he had put on it. But his life was dominated through the first half of 1995 by negotiations with Sony to reach a compromise and thereby bring the legal wrangle to an end. It soon became clear that there would be no need for the case to go to appeal. And the person who brought about the break-through was David Geffen, the American music and film industry billionaire, whom Michael considered a trusted friend.

They had been friends since first meeting in the Wham! days and had soon begun talking in detail about old records. Trevor Dann, head of BBC music, described how the friendship between the two men was based on 'sitting and talking about records, because David Geffen is the consummate businessman but loves nothing better than to sit and tell stories about producing Joni Mitchell albums. And he just loves the music.'

To Michael, Geffen was the most impressive business-man working in the music industry. His sureness of touch in picking talented young musicians, then transforming them into pop superstars through his record labels was awesome to someone with business ambitions like Michael. Geffen had sold his company at the top of the market to MCA for $730 million. Since then he had turned the sum into a personal fortune worth an estimated £1.2 billion.

Michael admired everything he knew about Geffen's influence on the music business. Having had mixed experiences with his managers in the past, Michael was impressed by Geffen's record as a manager and agent, and he was in awe of Geffen's extraordinary wealth. When, in 1990, he sold his company to MCA (the entertainment conglomerate that owns Universal Pictures), he took ten million shares of MCA stock. Then, when MCA was acquired by Matsushita, Geffen's stock was suddenly worth more than $700 million. The year he cashed it in, he is said to have paid more taxes than any other American. Remaining as chairman, he earned a salary of $600,000 a year, much of which he gave to his charitable foundation.

Michael was at ease with Geffen's ambiguous sexuality. The billionaire had once had a torrid romance with Cher and later dated Marlo Thomas, but in 1980 he came to terms with his homosexuality and by the early nineties had become one of the most important forces in the gay rights movement in the United States. At an AIDS Project benefit in Los Angeles, he and Barbra Streisand were honoured for their contributions. The *Advocate*, the nation's leading gay publication, named him Man of the Year. Geffen was a strong voice in persuading President Clinton to consider lifting the ban on gays in the military. He lobbied Washington DC and took out full-page newspaper advertisements in favour of the cause.

To Geffen, George Michael was an undoubted talent whose career had been handled badly. He thought that to allow a master songwriter like Michael to down tools and compose no songs while the dispute ran its course was a terrible squandering of an asset. He therefore approached Michael with a deal to put to Sony. Michael should be released from his current recording contract and his work would be handled and released by Geffen. First, though, Geffen needed to get the two sides talking. He acted as a go-between, arranging a meeting between Michael and Mickey Schulhof, the chief executive of Sony Entertainment, at Schulhof's apartment in midtown Manhattan. After a tense start, the conversation became reasonable and it was quickly established that the way forward was for Michael to begin negotiations with other record companies to explore the value put on Michael's contract.

The Geffen connection was reported first by the *New York Times* and picked up in Britain by *The Times* as a relatively minor part of a much more important story for the American entertainment industry, the foundation of a new company by three of America's most successful entertainment moguls. Dreamworks SKG was made up of Steven Spielberg, the most brilliant and successful director in Hollywood, Jeffrey Katzenberg, the former Disney studio head who had transformed the company's fortunes, and David Geffen, the record industry billionaire who had founded his fortune upon the highly profitable Geffen Records label. And, through Geffen, the new company started to negotiate with Sony over Michael's contract.

The unexpected headline was therefore not 'Geffen to bid for Michael', but 'Spielberg may rescue George Michael'. 'Hollywood's newest knights in shining armour may be preparing to ride to the rescue of pop star George Michael by freeing him from a contract he described as "professional slavery",' said *The Times*. 'Under the banner of their recently formed entertainment company, the recording tycoon David Geffen, the film director Steven Spielberg and the former Disney executive Jeffrey Katzenberg are reportedly considering a deal that would release the singer from his present contract and allow him to join their record division.'

Dreamworks SKG were already well advanced in their plans. Premises had been bought and studio buildings were on the point of being erected on the site of Howard Hughes's old aerodrome in the south of Los Angeles, by the international airport. (They were eventually to build elsewhere.) Their intention was for a fully integrated film and recording studio which would be in total control of its output, including feature films, television films and music and the studio would also administer its own product exploitation of computer games and the like.

What the trio needed fast was creative people willing to work hard across the board. In George Michael Geffen saw a prodigious talent who had been frustrated from expressing himself by insensitive management – just the sort of creative person whom the three men thought would prosper under their direction. What Geffen offered Michael was the ultimate in freedom to write songs, working across the board in as many mediums as he wished. Geffen hoped that Michael would write songs for Dreamworks movies, perhaps for an animated feature, as in the traditional Disney feature formula, just as Elton John wrote songs for Disney features like *The Lion King*. Geffen promised that whatever Michael wished to do in whatever field would be seriously considered. And if he simply wanted to write and record songs, that was fine too.

In fact Michael had no intention of writing a Disney-like soundtrack and he thought his friend Elton John had made a mistake by writing the soundtrack of *The Lion King*. 'I wish Elton hadn't done that,' he said. 'I just don't really think that a great musician can be done justice by cartoon characters really. And you know, I know Elton loves the stuff and he's thrilled with it and it's sold very, very well because lots and lots of people loved it and it's great, but my own feeling is that I don't really want to hear Elton John's voice and think of Simba the Lion. I have too much respect for what he does as a musician without any of the stuff. I think the album that he followed it up with was the best album that he'd made in years and years and I think a lot of people didn't take it particularly seriously because of the Disney record. And, he'll really hate hearing this – I'm really sorry to say this – but I thought it was beneath him.'

The arrangement Geffen was offering was the sort of sweetheart deal which had allowed the producer in the past to win over the confidence of some of the most successful and profitable pop musicians and translate their talent into good business. His company Asylum Records had dominated the Seventies with music from Linda Ronstadt, Jackson Browne and The Eagles. Geffen kept on working his way through the fashions in music. He was the business brain behind Guns 'N' Roses, Nirvana and Aerosmith and he had presided over the work of Elton John, John Lennon and Peter Gabriel.

In 1975 he was misdiagnosed as having cancer and took four years out, returning to the music business in 1981 when he founded Geffen Records. Alongside his work with musicians, he had produced a number of unusual but successful films, among them Martin Scorsese's *After Hours*,

Little Shop of Horrors and *Risky Business* and theatrical productions including *Cats, Miss Saigon* and the 1988 Tony Award-winning *M. Butterfly*. In 1993–94 Geffen Records declared profits of more than $500 million. Geffen had followed the Michael *v.* Sony case closely from his many homes in the United States – a $47.5 million Beverly Hills fake Georgian mansion that once belonged to Jack Warner of Warner Brothers, a beach house in Malibu and an apartment in New York.

Anyone who fell into Geffen's embrace was treated to great charm. He was a tough but generous employer. A loyal secretary retired and reportedly received a cheque for $5 million. He led the most extraordinary life, commuting between Los Angeles and New York in his private jet. His homes were like modern art galleries, housing works by David Hockney, Jackson Pollock, Andy Warhol and Roy Lichtenstein. Geffen had become so wealthy that even Hollywood moguls like Steven Spielberg, whose career had proven the most consistently profitable over the previous two decades, were in awe of the fortune Geffen's business deals had brought him.

Spielberg, with colossal earnings from *Jaws, Close Encounters of the Third Kind, Raiders of the Lost Ark, Back to the Future, E.T.* and *Jurassic Park*, all of them record-breaking films at the box-office, was worth just $150 million. Geffen had amassed around $1 billion and he was several times richer than Spielberg, proving that music can be more profitable even than pictures. It was this fact which had finally goaded Spielberg into taking a plunge into film and record production by teaming up with Geffen and Katzenberg on Dreamworks SKG.

With such a generous approach to Michael's output,

David Geffen soon established Dreamworks SKG as the
front-runner among the companies bidding to take
Michael off Sony's hands. They were closely followed by
the US entertainment giant Time Warner, who felt that
their interest in the still unreleased *Trojan Souls* album gave
them an advantage.

As the talks about Michael's future made progress, it
was clear that the singer favoured any outcome which
resulted in Geffen taking an interest in his career. With
Geffen there was unlikely to be a return of the tensions
between personalities which had soured relations with
Sony. And Geffen was genuinely interested in creativity.
Before long it emerged that Time Warner and a syndicate
of Dreamworks and Virgin were the only names talking to
Michael.

Then Time Warner spectacularly fell out of the running.
They convened a special meeting to introduce Michael to
the top Time Warner executives, to reassure the singer
that any relationship with them would set off on a firm
and friendly footing, but the strategy quickly went off the
rails and turned to farce. According to a report in the
Sunday Times: 'Bob Morgado, then head of Warner Music,
made a series of *faux pas*; the worst was appearing confused
about Michael's name, let alone where he would fit into
the organization, which was wracked by power struggles.
"He kept calling him George Michaels," says one person
involved with the meeting. "It's like talking about Barbra
Streisland."'

At the heart of the negotiation was Michael's severance
terms with Sony. At stake were a number of factors: the
meeting of the legal costs; the shape of the future deal with
the new record company; and the exploitation of existing

Michael work in the extensive back-catalogue in Sony's hands. In talks about extant material Sony had the upper hand as the work clearly came under his deal with them. In a bid to force the pace of a deal, Sony announced plans to rush-release a George Michael greatest hits album, based on his back-catalogue which they already owned.

On Sunday 25 June, the *Sunday Times* was first to reveal that a settlement in the long-running dispute between Michael and Sony was imminent. Michael had fought one of the fiercest battles the music business had ever witnessed, but the end was far from dramatic. On Tuesday 11 July Michael's lawyer, Tony Russell, arrived at the singer's home in Hampstead bearing a 400-page proposed settlement. The two men sat down and spent the next five hours poring over each clause. Often it was left to Russell to explain the exact meaning of certain details or translate impenetrable legalese.

It was being proposed that Michael should agree to a two-album deal with Geffen's Dreamworks SKG, who would be the distributor of the records in North America alone, with Virgin Records taking the rights in all remaining worldwide territories, including the UK. Dreamworks and Virgin would between them pay a one-off sum of $40 million to Sony and Michael would receive an advance against royalties of $10 million. He was set a new royalty rate of 20 per cent – a record high for the industry. Sony would retain a 2 to 4 per cent royalty from sales of both proposed albums and would be free to release a George Michael greatest hits package, which would include tracks taken from the two new albums. And Michael's legal costs of £4 million were to be met by Dreamworks and Virgin.

There was little in the document to surprise Michael,

because in the course of negotiations he had been actively involved in and approved every major decision. Michael could never again claim that he was unaware of any aspect of the new deal. He was about to agree to a contract he knew he would never be able to break. He signed the contract, with Russell as a witness, and briefly enjoyed the euphoria of release. His miserable years with Sony were finally over. He would now put the legal world behind him and concentrate on music.

The public announcement of the Michael/Sony divorce was made two days later, on 13 July. Michael was in no doubt that the credit for ensuring his divorce from Sony went to David Geffen. 'I think that his [Geffen's] relationship with Sony was good enough to spur things on. I honestly think that without David Geffen it's very possible that I would have been in the Court of Appeal,' Michael said.

'I'm contracted to both labels for two albums,' explained Michael in the same radio interview. 'You've got to remember they [Dreamworks SKG/Virgin] had to pay somewhere in the region of $50 million just to get me out. If I'd really been in a position where I was free I would have done a one-album deal with Virgin and a one-album deal with Dreamworks in America, simply because I believe that that's the way business should be done. At the end of a business project, if one partner has failed or the relationship is not good, I think people should be able to walk away.' But Michael knew that he had as good a deal as he could achieve this time round. When he came to renegotiate his contract, he would attempt to forge a one-album deal only.

Trevor Dann remembered the feeling in the music

industry at the time. He said, 'I think everybody knew it would get settled eventually and it was just a question of stubbornness until they agreed to sit down and hammer out some kind of compromise. I think George Michael feels that he's been dreadfully exploited over the years. That all the things that have ever happened to him that have been good have been because of him, and all the bad things have happened because of somebody else. If you're in the record business this rings very hollow because George was just like any other young pop star years ago, saying oh of course I was dying my hair, oh of course I was singing a load of old bollocks, of course I'll go skiing for the video and in the Wham! days he did everything he was told and they got it right for him. And then of course he turned around and said, I want to be taken seriously.'

The return of George Michael to recording caused some in the music industry to denigrate him. Jonathan King, a veteran commentator on the music scene, wrote a caustic column in the *Daily Mail* suggesting that Michael's 'self-imposed exile will ultimately see him off as a major recording artist.' King went on: 'George has, in some ways, become the Howard Hughes of pop music. Sitting in a darkened room brooding. Or, suitably attired in trademark shades and designer stubble, walking his dog in lonely misery. Or chained to a hot computer, a prisoner of contracts, slaving over a stained keyboard.'

King revealed that he had once tried to lure Michael back into songwriting. 'It could all have been different. I approached George to write A Song For Europe. I thought it would appeal to his patriotism – to compose the winning Eurovision tune for Britain. To his charitable instincts – to donate a hit to an up-and-coming band or hopeful young future star and kick-start a career. To his ego – to prove he could still do it better than anyone else. And to his well-documented greed – he would have made a fortune from backing a new act. But George wasn't interested in the idea.'

Another who seemed to be gunning for Michael was his former manager, Simon Napier-Bell. The *Guardian* reported Napier-Bell saying: 'I haven't met anyone in the industry who cares about George Michael any more.'

While it would take some time for Michael to release any material of his own, there was one record that could now be released – Lisa Moorish's cover version of the Wham! hit 'I'm Your Man'. The single was released in the middle of August and entered the chart at No. 24, but quickly faded. Although the song did not carry a credit for Michael, his voice is so distinct that his contribution was obvious to all who heard the single. And when he was asked whether he had sung on the record, he found it hard to deny.

Although the single was not a great success, Michael's work with Moorish and her producer Jon Douglas did lead to a very valuable collaboration with Douglas for Michael's next album, his third, which would eventually be called *Older*. They would come to write two songs together, both released on the album and as singles.

Now free from Sony, Michael was eager to get back to work and he began writing songs again, sharing his time between London, Los Angeles and St Tropez. When a batch of songs were ready for the album he was preparing, he booked sessions at Sarm Studios West. The new album was provisionally scheduled for release in the spring.

Michael was regularly using soft drugs to help him write

songs and relax, 'around twenty-five joints a day' he claimed. '*Older* was pretty much recorded on cannabis. I wasn't drinking at the time – basically because I was too stoned.' He told Adrian Deevoy of the *Big Issue*, 'I started smoking grass because it was either that or some kind of medication which I really didn't want to take. I was a complete and utter pot-head. I know it's lunacy, but the horrible truth is that the grass really helped me. It got me through making *Older*. I was under more stress than I'd ever been. This had to amount to something substantial to justify the wait. And grass really helped me with the lyrics. I'd know there was something that I really wanted to say but I wouldn't know how to say it, so I'd have a few drags and stand behind the mike and in a few minutes it'd be there. It's bad because I don't want to smoke, but I can't see myself giving grass up as a writer.'

Michael's fondness for cannabis was all the more remarkable given his inability to roll a decent joint. As he was dependent upon others to do it for him, he usually only smoked with others around. He believed that had he been able to prepare the dope himself, he would have taken much more of the drug. 'I can't go home with a bag of grass and sit and get stoned out of my head,' he said. 'I have to have someone smoking with me.'

Some days at the Sarm Studios West, Michael worked away on his own with just a recording engineer in the studio to man the machines. Among the engineers on the sessions were Chris Porter, Paul Gomersall, Ben Swan and Charlie Brocco. On other days Michael was joined by Douglas and they worked closely together. Michael wrote two songs with Douglas and he co-wrote another with his friend David Austin, but the other eight tracks were written by Michael alone.

With his career and creativity back on course, Michael turned to finding a manager. After a number of names had been suggested he chose Andy Stephens, a former vice-president of Sony Music Europe and head of Epic, who Michael had known since 1984 when he had first asked him to manage Wham!. After the problems of dealing with Michael through the abrasive Rob Kahane, the music industry welcomed the change. Trevor Dann remembered Stephens as 'a very pleasant man indeed. He's nothing like a manager. He's just a smart, well-spoken, intelligent bloke and he very rarely uses the old management cliché about, oh I don't think George will be interested in doing that. He doesn't do all that. And he will sometimes side with you and he'll go, look, if you want him to do that just ask him to do so and so and he'll come round. So I think he's probably a really good bloke.'

In August 1995 Michael bought another home, in the south of France. The house, which he was to name Chez Nobby after one of his nicknames, was set on a cliff top above St Tropez with a clear view over the Mediterranean. It cost £1.8 million.

Towards the end of the year, Michael made a rare public appearance at the MTV European Awards, held in Paris. Michael joined U2's Bono and bands like East 17 and Take That, at the city's Le Zenith nightspot before a 5,000-strong audience, to lambaste the French government for nuclear tests in the South Pacific.

Michael was there to present Greenpeace with the Free Your Mind award and took time out to criticize the

French behaviour. 'As one of several Englishmen here this evening, I'd like to relay a message from back home, not just from the people here tonight,' he said. 'We all know Europe is a big issue at the moment and is a business idea, not a cultural idea. If business means looking the other way while your business partners endanger the future of the planet, I think we're better off going it alone.'

Meanwhile, Michael was still hard at work completing his album. A new Michael sound was emerging from the recordings, the rugged sound of his earlier solo albums giving way to a more mature and rounded soul feel. The most commercial track on the album was 'Fastlove' (co-written and co-produced with Douglas), thanks to a slick sound and even slicker lyrics. Michael, Douglas and Dave Clews played keyboards and Andy Hamilton played saxophone. Douglas also co-wrote and co-produced another prominent track from the comeback album, the brass-heavy 'Spinning The Wheel'. As well as the trio on keyboards, there were six other musicians, five of them on wind instruments. Alan Ross played guitar, then John Thirkell and Stuart Brooks played trumpet and flugelhorns, Chris Davis and Phil Smith saxophone and Fayyaz Virji trombone. The lyrics told of a doomed relationship, and in parts were interpreted as a jibe against Sony.

Michael's collaboration with David Austin, 'You Have Been Loved', was a slow and gentle ballad about a mother losing her son. In some ways, it nodded towards his encounter with the mother of Anselmo Feleppa, particularly its opening.

It was clear from the song that Feleppa was still on Michael's mind and as confirmation the *Older* album on its release carried a dedication to his Brazilian friend, 'who changed the way I look at life'. It was around this time, according to later reports, that Michael turned to another gay man for support – Kenny Goss, a tall, handsome Texan four years older than the singer. They met in a Los Angeles restaurant and quickly became good friends. Goss would eventually become Michael's lover and, later, his live-in lover.

George Michael planned his long-awaited comeback in 1996 with meticulous precision and he decided to use the occasion to reveal a new look. As he had once shed his Wham! skin to emerge as a soberly stubbled solo performer, with similar ease he shed his robust hirsute look for a more stylized and delicate image. From now on he would wear his hair in an oddly shaped crew cut, coming to a widow's peak like a member of The Addams Family. The facial stubble gave way to a neatly manicured, skinny goatee beard. And the golden tan had faded forever.

At the end of 1995 Michael was preparing to release 'Jesus To A Child', his first single for two and a half years. Two weeks before Christmas, the song was distributed to selected radio and television stations ahead of release, to encourage demand when the discs reached the shops in early January, but Michael insisted that the near-seven-minute song – far longer than the average song on radio station play-lists – be played only in its entirety. His demands were met by the grateful chosen stations, and air-time of the single was guaranteed throughout the holiday and New Year period.

Michael had deliberately decided to release his comeback single after Christmas. The biggest sales of the pre-

Christmas market saw the fiercest competition between artists since 1955 as The Beatles, Michael Jackson, Oasis and others competed hotly for sales. Michael was considering a January release, traditionally the quietest month of the year for new material, as, without such tough competition, it was the time most likely to attract the largest sales. Lesser bands managed decent sales in January which pushed them up the charts. An established name like George Michael should be guaranteed a blistering hit.

Michael had been away from the business so long, he was anxious to make an unfaltering return with a perfect chart comeback. He decided to release two CD versions of 'Jesus To A Child' with different extra tracks – a ploy used to effect the previous summer to help Blur beat Oasis to the top of charts with its 'Country House' single. And as an added incentive to set the bandwagon rolling, the first batch of CDs would be put on sale for just 99p – up to £3 cheaper than rivals' records.

Over the New Year holiday, Michael's comeback made headlines and some papers were quick to point out the pitfalls ahead of him. In the *Independent*, Jim White wrote: 'Five years is a long time to be away. Things have changed out there. Members of the Live Aid generation of which he was the greatest talent are now cast as laughable has-beens, and for the first time in his professional life George Michael is way out of kilter with the prevailing fashion. Compared to Noel Gallagher, Damon Albarn or Jarvis Cocker, the big players of the mid-Nineties, George is too slick, too well-coiffured, too concerned with his looks. His style is all cappuccino, glossy magazines and well-tailored suits.'

In a profile taking a sideswipe at Michael as he re-entered the market, the *Sunday Times* showered Andrew Ridgeley with praise and attributed much of the success of the Wham! years to him. 'What everyone always suspected about the pair's working relationship has since been acknowledged: that the singer was the sole musical force, while Ridgeley, the more sophisticated of the two, the stylish one who loved *pop* as opposed to just music, took responsibility for image matters, creating the "casual chic" look that was intrinsic to their early success. Ridgeley was the natural-born pop star, something George wasn't then and isn't now.' The paper summed up: 'Bjorn Borg may have invented the designer stubble, but Michael, on *Faith*, turned it into a lifestyle issue. The look was meant to suggest ruggedness and intensity. In the event, it became known as Michael's "fairy biker" look. Ridgeley, you have to feel, would not have allowed it.'

On 1 January 1996, Michael began the New Year as he would continue: back at the top. He again led the Capital Radio listeners' poll as all-time favourite performer with his song 'Careless Whisper'. It meant he had now topped the list seven times in ten years. Over 300,000 listeners took part in the poll to compile the chart of the capital's top 200 songs. Michael had five songs in the chart: his duet with Elton John, 'Don't Let The Sun Go Down On Me', the Freddie Mercury cover 'Somebody To Love', 'A Different Corner', and 'Father Figure'.

While waiting for the release of 'Jesus To A Child' Michael set about completing songs for *Older*. The songs emerging from the sessions were proving to be as good as any of Michael's finest work. Although there was a fair amount of bleak and meditative downbeat material, the album as a whole was revealing Michael as a more

271

sophisticated and accomplished singer-songwriter and producer. When it came to putting the songs in order on the
album, he gave to 'Jesus To A Child' pride of place, first
track first side.

The single topped the sales chart the moment the record
shop doors opened on 20 January, dislodging Michael
Jackson's six-week run with 'Earth Song'. The 'Jesus To
A Child' video was delicate and dark and loaded with
symbolism and a glossy Hollywood movie lustre. It opened
with a pile of dust knocked over by a suspended chair.
The camera then panned past the figure of a naked man
prostrate on the floor. Then ballet dancers appeared,
showing their nipples, caged in crates. Michael, shot only
from the neck up, sang the song without moving. The
video was directed by Howard Greenhalgh and filmed at
locations around London. When the BBC came to screen
it on *Top of the Pops*, it asked that the nipples be painted
out.

Michael stayed at the top of the singles chart for just
one week. It was a brief reign, but it reassured Michael
that he had not lost his touch in the five years he had
spent in the wilderness. 'Jesus To A Child' stayed on the
chart for seven weeks. The song went on to make No. 1
in sixteen countries.

In America, Michael planned the same marketing
approach for 'Jesus To A Child' as in Britain. The record
was distributed to radio stations on 3 January, with a
release date set for one month later (though it went on
sale late, on 24 February). It received saturation air-play.
The *Los Angeles Times* reported: 'Radio programmers
haven't lost faith in George Michael. The English pop
star's new single, the melancholy ballad "Jesus To A

Child", is receiving widespread air-play on a variety of formats. This early reaction seemingly belies speculation that Michael's audience would dissipate in the six years since he released his last album – a period that he spent, in part, fighting a bitter legal battle with Sony Music. "Radio has opened its arms and embraced this song," says Tony Novia, an editor at *Radio & Records* magazine, a Los Angeles-based trade publication that keeps tabs on the play-lists of the nation's key radio stations.'

The single entered the Billboard singles chart at No. 7 and held the slot for a fortnight before slipping to Nos. 12, 20 and, finally, 39. The single topped several regional American charts, including the lucrative market reflected in the *Los Angeles Times*' Southern California listing, where it was No. 1 for three weeks. The paper's review of the record echoed the common judgement among American observers of the music scene on Michael's comeback: 'George Michael may have spent much of the past few years in a legal battle winning his freedom from Columbia Records, but his return to the pop arena feels confident and assured.

'"Jesus To A Child", a ballad about the bliss of pure love, may not be the best single out there right now, but it shows that the Grammy-winning artist still has a pop touch. In this seven-minute ode to rediscovering love after a period of darkness, Michael delivers one of his most affecting ballads since "Careless Whisper". His smouldering, nicely restrained vocal and the song's subtle, almost effortless groove capture the bliss of unexpected romance.'

The video, with its naked bodies, was declared obscene by some American TV stations. Some refused to play it unedited; others refused to even run it at all. MTV only played the video late at night, deciding it was too hot for a young audience.

At the Capital Radio Awards in April, Michael again received the favourite song accolade for 'Careless Whisper', and a ball-shaped award for his 'outstanding contribution to music'. On the podium at the Royal Lancaster Hotel, Michael poked fun at Liam Gallagher, of Oasis, who at the BRIT Awards had pretended to poke a trophy up his bottom. The Capital award was a lumpy statuette. 'Liam would have had a bit of a problem with this one,' Michael said. 'We might have needed an ambulance for him.' Michael had regained his public confidence.

As 'Jesus To A Child' slipped out of the charts, Michael had already prepared his next single, 'Fastlove', to be released in April and his long-awaited album would quickly follow on. 'Fastlove' was very different from 'Jesus To A Child'. The record accurately reflected Michael's state of mind immediately after Feleppa's death and it revealed a deep pessimism. 'Fastlove' was in sharp contrast: upbeat, fun and wildly infectious. It proved to be one of the biggest dance tracks of the year, then one of the biggest dance tracks of the decade.

The 'Fastlove' video was shot over two days at Pinewood Studios, in Buckinghamshire, with a budget of £250,000. It was directed by Vaughn Armell and Anthea Benton, two TV commercial directors who had worked on Levi ads, and was slick and stylish, combining state of the art computer graphics with slight-of-hand visual trickery by Michael. The video showed male and female models, among them Rachel Williams, Angie Grgatt, Deborah Shaw and Pearle Danquin, acting as if operated by Michael with a television remote control gadget.

Michael is seen seated and striking thoughtful poses, cross-legged in a high-backed swivel chair which is slowly spinning. Then he is briefly seen strutting sensually in an indoor downpour of rain, his wet designer suit clinging to his torso.

The video also showed that Michael still harboured some animosity towards his former bosses at Sony. A pair of silver headphones are fleetingly seen twice in the video, bearing the letters FONY in a swipe at Sony's logo. Executives at Sony were furious.

'Fastlove' entered the British charts at No. 1 and remained there for the next three weeks. It reached No. 1 in fifteen more countries. It only reached No. 8 in America, although by the end of the year, at the MTV Video Awards in New York, Michael picked up the MTV Europe Viewers' Choice Award for the song. On 13 May, the week after 'Fastlove' dropped out of the British singles chart, Michael released his third solo album, *Older*, on both sides of the Atlantic.

14

Loss Adjustment

Older sold in huge numbers, entering the British album charts at No. 1. It became Virgin Records' fastest-selling album ever, selling ten times the number of its nearest chart rival, *Jagged Little Pill* by Alanis Morissette. It started with advance orders for 500,000 copies and in the first week sold more than all the other artists in the Top 20 album chart put together.

In Dubai, the country's biggest record store stayed open all night to meet demand. In Sydney, Australia, HMV reported that it had sold more copies of *Older* than any record since it opened five years before. Similar sales records were broken around the world where the album went to No. 1 in a dozen more countries.

By the end of the first week, *Older* had sold two and a half million CDs worldwide. Calculated at the new 20 per cent royalty rate, it earned Michael more than £4 million. According to figures lodged at Companies House, Michael's income fell from over £14 million in 1988 to less than £900,000 in 1993. With the success of *Older* it was clear that Michael was about to revive his flagging fortunes. He still had little interest in material things. He had no yacht, no fancy lifestyle. But to celebrate his return to the charts after such a long period of absence he bought himself a Jaguar XK8.

The album was dedicated to Anselmo Feleppa. But Michael also devoted it to Antonio Carlos Jobim, the Brazilian songwriter who in 1963 had written 'Garota De Ipanema', better known as 'The Girl From Ipanema', 'who changed the way I listened to music'. Jobim had died the previous year. And Michael added a line for his fans: 'Thank you for waiting.'

As well as 'Jesus To A Child' and 'Fastlove' there were nine new songs. 'Spinning The Wheel' and 'Star People' were fast, upbeat dance songs, the latter becoming for many the favourite track of the album. The title track, and 'Move On' both borrowed jazz styles. 'You Have Been Loved', another song inspired by Feleppa's death, was melancholy and sober. Also fairly bleak was 'To Be For-given', in which Michael was 'drowning in depression', in the words of one critic. 'It Doesn't Really Matter' was generally considered the weakest song. 'Free', which con-tained the line 'Feels good to be free', was another aside aimed at Sony.

In Britain the album got a rave review from the *New Musical Express*, which rated *Older* nine out of ten. But it was not without its critics. Simon Mayo and Chris Evans, both Radio One deejays, dismissed the album as irrelevant and uninteresting. The *Daily Telegraph* joined in. 'Gone is most of the zest and bravado that made him a global pin-up,' it wrote. 'In its place he serves up an understated, sensuous confection of late-night moodiness, fake jazz and melancholic soul. The music is uneventful, something to play in the background on a quiet night in.'

In a satirical account of Michael's second coming, the

veteran Radio One deejay John Peel made fun of Michael's reputation for humourlessness and pomposity: 'This is plainly a work of great seriousness. On the front cover is George, frowning, half in shadow. He looks, just for a second, like Frank Zappa. "Older," we read, "And wiser," we breathe. Inside is a small picture of the back of George's head. Alongside is written, "thank you for waiting". And thank you for saying thank you George. There are more pictures in the booklet: George frowning, George smiling angrily, George looking, well, very Eastern Mediterranean. Alongside these pictures are George's lyrics. These are sour, disdainful, petulant, humourless. The performances are seamless, unhurried and at their best when the credits read "All Instruments: George Michael." Odd that.'

Music critics in America were divided over the album and, by the end of the year, the general verdict was that after such a long wait it was something of a disappointment. Elysa Gardner in the *Los Angeles Times*, one of the most astute observers of recording artists, awarded *Older* two and half stars, rating it between fair and good. She wrote: 'Michael's sober quest for maturity and respect may have taken a toll on more than just his bank account. The quality that's always distinguished his best material, dating back to his bubble-gum days in Wham!, is a sense of pure pop transcendence. Even in expressing more troubling or sophisticated emotions, the hit songs from *Prejudice* and 1987's *Faith* were memorable for their radiant melodies and arrangements full of earnest passion and energy. In contrast, many of the new album's icily elegant, minor-chord driven tunes sound uninspired, effete, even cynical

– older indeed, but not necessarily in ways that one associates with creative growth.'

Gardner praised Michael for retaining his flair for 'incorporating savory accents of funk and soul into his pop brew' in 'Fastlove' and 'Star People'. But other songs, especially his ballads, 'suffer from the same lack of structure and overly tame production that afflicts a lot of contemporary R&B'. In 'Spinning The Wheel' and 'Move On' Michael had achieved 'a light jazz feel that also makes for good background music but should have no noticeable effect on your central nervous system'. And she concluded: 'At the rate this mature pop star is going right now, it seems he's never gonna dance again. And that would be a shame.'

People magazine also thought *Older* too miserable. 'Michael – once the butt-wiggling poster boy of pop – is also a new man, somber, mellow, restrained and, remarkably, dull.' It wanted more lively, optimistic songs. 'For much of this eleven-song CD, Michael delivers his compositions sotto voce, in a whispy style that makes his early-Eighties Wham! songs sound like Nine Inch Nails. Why is he reluctant to unleash his trademark thunder chops? And where is his trusty swagger?'

In America *Older* only reached No. 6 in the national Billboard album chart, though it topped many regional charts, again making No. 1 on the important *Los Angeles Times* Southern California chart.

In May 1997 Michael made a rare public appearance and relaxed his impeccable control of his public image by risking an appearance on Manchester's Key 103 radio station with the satirical chat-show host Mrs Merton, alias Caroline Aherne, who affects to be a plain-speaking and tactless northern middle-aged woman. 'I'm glad you're making a comeback,' she joked. Referring to his carefully manicured beard, she asked: 'Do you still have your goatee?' Michael replied: 'Yes, but it's been rearranged. Did you ever see the Village People? It's kind of reminiscent of that.' Mrs Merton suggested that, 'You'll look back in five years at pictures of yourself and you'll kill yourself laughing and think, Why?' Michael, unphased by the assault, said he had been laughing at himself 'for the last ten years'.

He said he liked the Spice Girls and Mrs Merton advised: 'Don't go getting tempted by them. They're all slappers. Their lyrics are so trite. You know, "I'll tell you what I want, what I really, really want." I remember in your day you wrote really good lyrics, like "Wake Me Up Before You Go Go".' Michael roared with laughter.

In the summer Michael took a break and kept himself out of the public eye. On a rare outing he went to Wembley in June to watch England play Germany in the Euro 96 football semi-final. Michael joined Mick Jagger, Chris Evans, Frank Skinner and David Baddiel to watch England lose after a tense penalty shoot-out. Friends say Michael was now very relaxed due, in no small measure, to greater security in his emotional life. His Texan chum Kenny Goss had become his lover and that summer Goss started living with Michael as his partner. In time, they would exchange – and wear with pride – gold wedding bands.

During July Michael watched with wry amusement as the former Take That singer Robbie Williams released his debut solo single, a remake of Michael's 'Freedom 90'. The relentlessly commercial Take That had often been compared to Wham!. And there were striking similarities. They were both pretty-boy bands popular with young girls which had split whose members tried to work on as solo artists. The songwriter responsible for Take That's success was Gary Barlow and Barlow and Michael were regularly compared in the music press. Take That's Robbie Williams was more like Ridgeley, good-looking and flirtatious. And like Michael and Ridgeley, Williams entered into an ill-fated High Court action against his record company, but later backed down.

In August Michael released another single from the album, 'Spinning The Wheel'. The video, shot in black and white, had a moody retro feel, with Michael seated behind a microphone on a stand. He was wearing a satin designer suit and hiding his eyes behind dark glasses. It was with quiet satisfaction that Michael noticed that when the single entered the British chart at No. 2, it ousted Robbie Williams's cover of his 'Freedom 90'. But neither could take the No. 1 slot from the Spice Girls' 'Wannabe'.

Working with Dreamworks and Virgin for the first time, he was pleased to discover that they respected his wishes to only take part in the minimum of publicity. But some Virgin executives were disgruntled. Tours and personal appearances sold records and it went against the grain that Michael did not put himself out to sell his record. Michael, too, realized that concerts were necessary, it's just that he was still determined not to tour.

By the end of the summer he came up with a plan. He decided take part in two solo concerts, one for television – for MTV's 'Unplugged' series – the other for radio. Nigel Sweeney, his record-plugger, approached Trevor Dann, head of music at the BBC, to propose a concert for

Radio One, Britain's most popular music station. Dann remembered: 'Nigel Sweeney said George was thinking of doing a TV show and that he'd quite like to do something for the radio. He asked what I thought. I said he should do a gig at the Radio Theatre in Broadcasting House.

'Next thing I was told George Michael had rung. He said he was really interested in the radio bit and asked if he could take a look at it. So he came over and we showed him around.' Michael visited the minute Radio Theatre and seemed to like what he saw. It is an art deco jewel in the core of Broadcasting House, Portland Place, and had played host to dance bands, radio drama and quizzes in BBC Radio's earlier years, until the corporation moved to the larger Paris Studios in Lower Regent Street. Miraculously, the Radio Theatre has survived despite the BBC's trend in more recent times to sell off many of its greatest assets. Michael thanked Dann for showing him around and left the building.

Next Dann heard back from Michael, via a third party. The singer invited Dann and Matthew Bannister, head of Radio One and managing director of BBC Radio, to meet for lunch at Morton's, a Mayfair club. He would bring his manager, Andy Stephens, and Sweeney.

On the morning of the lunch, Nigel Sweeney rang Dann. Dann remembered: 'I said, I know what this will be, this will be cancelling. I answered Nigel, saying, "Oh hello, what's the reason then?" And he said, no – actually we are cancelling it but it's not what you think. George only wants you and Matthew to go. He's blown out me and his manager. So Matthew and I turned up at Morton's and were shown to Mr Michael's table.

'He was the most affable man and terribly curious about what we did. All he wanted to know was what Radio One was doing and kind of saying, are you ever going to play my records or am I too old? I don't mind either way but I'd like to know. You could see that this was a man coming off the back of that whole Sony court case, who had completely taken control of his career and probably didn't trust anybody. I thought he's just not going to take anybody else's advice any more.'

It was proposed at the lunch that Michael would record an exclusive concert for Radio One, to be performed in the intimacy of the Radio Theatre. He telephoned Dann himself to confirm that he wanted to go ahead. He invited Dann and Bannister to join him for lunch a second time, at The Avenue, in St James's Street. Michael was more relaxed than before. Dann remembered: 'He doesn't want to talk about himself, he's just terribly inquisitive about other people. That, of course, makes him very not just charming, but disarming because most people at that level just love to talk about themselves. And when he does talk about himself, he talks about his music. If you ask how he's getting on you get a very bland response. But if you say, I love the horn section in the last whatever–it–was track then he'll talk about that for ages.'

During the lunch, Dann and Bannister raised the idea of Michael granting Radio One an exclusive interview, to be transmitted when the concert was eventually aired as a highlight of the Christmas holiday schedules. Michael seemed happy with the idea and they began discussing who would interview him. Dann said they started with the safe hands, 'the Paul Gambaccini, Johnnie Walker end of the market or maybe Dave Pearce or one of the younger jocks'. Michael said he would give the matter further thought.

He took the Radio One concert in October very seriously and rehearsed with musicians for four weeks. Michael arrived at Broadcasting House the day of the concert to find a small audience of about two hundred, made up of Radio One invitees, BBC bigwigs, record company VIPs and around sixty members of Michael's fan club. He delivered a faultless set which included 'Father Figure', 'One More Try', 'Waiting For That Day', 'Freedom', 'Fastlove', 'Older' and 'Star People'.

Dann recalled: 'It was an absolutely electrifying performance because he knew that he was on the radio and didn't have to perform. He just sat on his stool and sang. And then, as he warmed up, he began to give it some. By the end he was up clapping and the audience was clapping along. He really began to enjoy himself and did three or four extra songs. I was completely swayed, in the sense that I'd always sort of admired his records but never really liked them. I thought he was terrific because he really can sing. He's got a fantastic voice yet sometimes he likes to sing songs that do not always stretch it. But when you actually hear him in the flesh it's a very commanding vocal style.'

Michael later said of the radio concert: 'I enjoyed it hugely. It's exactly the type of thing that I wish I had been doing for the last thirteen to fourteen years. I wish that I'd had that kind of experience as a singer and I think that had I been playing in this type of situation for my career I'd be a much better singer than I am now.' He added: 'One of the things that I intend to do in let's call it the second phase of my career – or the second half of my career – is make sure that when I sing, I sing in situations that I enjoy. And this was definitely, definitely, the first of those.'

When Michael confirmed that he wanted to go ahead with the Radio One interview, his choice of interviewer surprised Trevor Dann. 'Andy Stephens rang me up and said, you're not going to like this but George has decided that he wants Chris Evans to do the interview. I said it's up to you but I think it's a suicidal move. Andy said, no, George is quite adamant that he can handle it and that from his career's point of view that's the interview he needs to do. If he's going to make himself attractive to younger people without going on the old children's telly bandwagon, as it were, he's got to do the Chris Evans show and then young people will think he's groovy.'

The interview with Chris Evans turned out to be a relaxed affair. Michael said he was now resigned to the constant tabloid stories about his life and that only once had he sought legal redress over a newspaper story. He told Evans: 'The only time I sued the *Sun* was over this ridiculous story that said that I'd gone into the Limelight Club and thrown furniture around, and said, 'Don't you know who I am?' Then, apparently, I threw up over some poor girl. I hadn't actually entered the club. I hadn't actually done anything. I had walked up to the club, seen that there was a private party for, I think, Andrew Lloyd Webber or something, and walked out again. So everything that they put in there was fabricated. It's incredible. The *Sun* has this way of rephrasing things so you're not even sure whether you said it or not, you just know that you don't remember sounding as stupid as that. They have "*Sun*-speak".'

285

He described what he did in a typical day. 'I get up about ten o'clock normally and I go through the thirty or forty messages I received since I last picked up my messages, and then decide slowly who to call back because I'm normally extremely tired in the morning. I've got quite a wide circle of friends but my close, close friends [that] I spend most of my time with is a very small number of people.' He looked forward to his life. 'I want to go all the way,' he said. 'I want to be working 'til the day I die. I want to have something creative to do, some way to take things creatively. I want to drop dead in the studio.' He revealed that there was one last chore he was expected to do for Sony. He said: 'Getting out of my Sony contract involved promising three new tracks for the greatest hits album, so that's the first thing that I can remember in a long time that I have to do.'

He spoke about smoking marijuana and cannabis, explaining that he was still incapable of rolling a decent joint, so he rarely smoked alone. However, when the craving struck him when he was alone, he was capable of making a 'really nasty-looking sausagy thing'. He said he was not happy with his smoking habit and would like to give it up. He explained: 'I don't like anything that has control of me.' He had undergone hypnotism to try to stop smoking, but it had made no difference.

Evans, who was well aware that Michael was homosexual, asked whether it was 'better for business' if he avoided making his sexuality known. Michael replied: 'I think a lot of people think that I play with it for that very reason. I don't think it would make any difference to business. I really don't think my sexuality has much to do with my business any more.'

In November, Michael gave an interview to the *Big Issue*, a magazine sold by the homeless. To choose such a magazine for one of his rare interviews was a political statement which he was happy to expand upon. He explained: 'I do actually believe that there shouldn't be people with their hands out on the street in this country these days. Half of me thinks the next government has to do something about it and half of me thinks no government's ever going to be able to do anything about this ever again. Sometimes I'll put my hand in my pocket, nine out of ten times I don't have any money on me. I really think it's a great idea in any situation to encourage self-help as opposed to charity. So I think the *Big Issue* is a good idea and it was a way of me doing a print interview without it being with the actual mainstream press – and obviously I'm not a big fan of the mainstream press.'

To back up his sentiments, Michael became a volunteer at a London soup kitchen. The *Big Issue* reported: 'According to volunteers at the centre in Holborn, the casually dressed singer quietly hands out food and drink prepared in his Hampstead home before talking to some of the capital's rough sleepers.' Quoting a spokesman for Michael, the magazine said he was 'acutely aware how the desire to help could be wrongly interpreted as a publicity gimmick. "All this Saint George stuff you hear is rubbish, he just wants the same freedom as anyone to help."' Before long, however, the press had been tipped off and he was forced to abandon his efforts which had become the centre of attraction for a gang of photographers and reporters.

He disclosed to the *Big Issue* that he had a new partner, referring to Kenny Goss though he was careful not to say who it was. After enduring the horror of the press's hounding of Anselmo Feleppa, he was not about to invite speculation on his private life a second time. Asked about the state of his love life, the singer replied: 'Fantastic. Absolutely fantastic. That's all I shall say. I've got everything I want at the moment which is quite a scary position for me to be in. You automatically look for something to go wrong.' And after years of advocating safe sex and AIDS awareness, he explained he always used condoms. 'If I'm in a relationship, I make sure we end up getting tested [for HIV]. I don't really think condoms are enough. And they're not reliable enough. They break.'

Michael threw a party in January for his mother, Lesley, who was seriously ill. The *Daily Star* reported she had been 'given the all-clear after hospital treatment for diabetes'; in fact she was not suffering from diabetes but cancer. At the MTV Awards that month, Michael was named Best British Male and Elton John collected the award on Michael's behalf. The singer could not attend the ceremony since he and his family were now keeping a bedside vigil with their mother, whose health was deteriorating rapidly.

As he nursed his mother through her last few weeks, Michael heard for the first time 'Waltz Away Dreaming', a tender song written and performed by Toby Bourke, the first artist signed to his new label, Aegean. When his mother died in February, Michael went into the studio with Bourke to record the song again, with Michael on backing vocals and Bourke singing an extra verse reflecting Michael's love for his mother. The recording helped Michael come to terms with his mother's death.

On 27 March Michael attended the Capital Radio

Awards at the Royal Lancaster Hotel, where he picked up two awards, for Best Male Vocalist and Best Album. When Michael went up to collect his trophies he dedicated them both to his mother. He told the audience, made up of people in the music industry, 'My mother was a woman of great compassion. She felt we were living in a world which was being drained of that.' His voice quivered as he spoke. Then he promised the station the first playing of Tony Bourke's 'Waltz Away Dreaming' at its Easter fund-raiser, Help A London Child. He pledged to treble every £1 donated by listeners.

A few days later, that debut performance of the song helped swell the profits past £1 million, making it the station's most successful weekend since the event was launched seventeen years earlier. Listeners pledged £35,000 to hear Michael's collaboration with Tony Bourke. Michael then surpassed his own pledge to match listeners' pledges threefold, finally giving £166,000 to the fund.

In April Michael released the next single to be taken from the *Older* album, the 'Star People '97' EP, a re-recorded version of the album track with new lyrics and a revamped rhythm track. The EP also included four dance remixes and live tracks recorded during the MTV Unplugged concert in 1996.

Michael began lending his name to another cause he felt worthwhile: music education. He was invited to be a 'surprise guest' in the annual VH1 Honors concert, at Los Angeles Universal Amphitheatre, hosted by Stevie Wonder, who had dedicated the event to music education. The show included James Taylor, Stevie Winwood, Sheryl Crow, the Wallflowers, Prince and Emmylou Harris. The

Los Angeles Times reported: 'It was Wonder – on the day in which Speaker of the House Newt Gingrich had argued that the entertainment industry, not the government, should fund public arts programmes – who best cut through the rhetoric to get the evening's point across.

'Fittingly, Wonder's music has already done much to demonstrate music's power to inspire and unite. His first spontaneous chant came tagged on to the end of his enduring urban portrait "Living In The City", during which he was joined by surprise guest George Michael. That teaming was emblematic of the evening, which transcended the standard awards show format via spirited collaborations. Each performer – save for Prince, who is notoriously individualistic, and Celine Dion, whose performance was pretaped – made at least one appearance with another.'

The show, which was premièred on the cable music channel a few days later, raised $150,000 for VH1's Save the Music programme, which collects instruments to donate to schools and to expand music education.

Inspired by the LA concert, Michael became concerned about musical facilities for British schoolchildren. Two weeks later he met the leader of the Labour Party Tony Blair at his home in Islington. Michael readily agreed to act as an 'ambassador' for Labour's plans to link all British schools to the Internet. And he agreed to join a commission charged with implementing Blair's pledge to give every child in the country access to a computer. Michael's commitment might even include turning up unannounced in schools, to monitor the project. Within a week of the meeting the Labour Party won a landslide victory in the general election and Tony Blair became Britain's first Labour prime minister for eighteen years.

Michael picked up more awards in May. At the BRIT Awards (the annual event of the British Academy of Songwriters, Composers and Authors) he picked up two trophies, Best Songwriter and Most Performed Work for 'Fastlove'. He received the awards from Brian May, of Queen, saying: 'I would like to thank my mother whose soul is in every note I have ever written.'

Michael at first appeared to be well able to cope with his mother's death. After the pain he had endured in the months following Anselmo's death, he had built new strengths of character which helped him deal with the loss. He found it best to throw himself into work rather than try to make sense of his emotions.

But preoccupying himself with his music could only go so far in blocking out the grief. His songs, which in the past had been inspired so much by his love for his mother, were still dependent upon her memory. Rather than confront his loss, he found that working was merely aggravating his sorrow. After several months' hard work he suffered a mental collapse and explained that by trying to control his emotional response to his mother's death, the sorrow had been magnified.

He should have spent more time mourning. 'Your grief still takes you by surprise week after week,' he said. Michael cited debilitating sadness over his mother's death as the reason behind a request later put to Sony asking for a delay in meeting his contractual 'divorce' obligations of new songs intended for inclusion in a greatest hits package. Sony was in no mood for a further disagreement with

Michael and they agreed to the delay; the scheduled release date of the album was put back twelve months to autumn 1998.

At the end of the summer of 1997 Michael was preparing to release another single to be taken from the *Older* album, 'You Have Been Loved'. The tender ballad turned his own recent experience on its head, explaining the acute sadness of a recently bereaved mother who has lost her son and had originally been understood by fans to be a tribute to Anselmo's mother. Now the lyrics, with their gentle refrain, seemed to apply as much to Michael's own mother. Before long the song became associated in the public mind with the sudden death of another mother, Diana, Princess of Wales.

George Michael woke up on Sunday 31 August, 1997 to the news that Princess Diana had been killed in a motor accident in Paris. Michael had met Diana about a dozen times and while he could count himself among her friends and featured on her Christmas card list, he had always kept his distance from her. He explained: 'I could have kept in a lot more contact with her because we really got on well. But I was always reluctant to call her up. It was almost like a mate of mine who doesn't want to call me up too much in case it looks strange – because he thinks that everybody else is calling me up. It was the same equation with Diana and me.'

Kensington Palace invited Michael to Diana's funeral, to be held in Westminster Abbey the following Saturday, 6 September, and he accepted. He arrived at the Abbey with Elton John and his boyfriend, David Furnish. The service was charged with high emotions and, with the memory of the deaths of his mother and Anselmo still clear in his mind, he found it difficult to hold back the tears. At one point he was unable to hide his feelings, and he broke down sobbing. As Michael explained: 'I bawled my eyes out at the service. There was a [television] camera on me for most of the time but they were obviously not broadcasting images of people who were really in distress. I had forgotten my hanky and I was really streaming. I was one of the few people in that part of Westminster Abbey that was really blubbing. It was almost like I was reliving my mum's funeral. It wasn't as if I didn't get upset at my mum's funeral, but it was just too soon after her death and maybe it hadn't sunk in.'

The next day Michael was due to make a promotional appearance, by phone, on the Pepsi Chart Show, the most popular programme on commercial radio in the UK. Paying tribute to the Princess, he declared that 'Diana was a gift from God. She had the ability to give us hope'. He also echoed the sentiment expressed so bluntly in the Abbey the previous day by Diana's brother, Earl Spencer, voicing his concerns for the future of Diana's sons, Prince William and Prince Harry, and demanding that the press leave the princes alone for the next couple of years. In particular he felt Prince William needed protection, so that in time he could 'become an ambassador' for Britain. Michael urged the public to boycott publications which took advantage of the young prince and intruded upon his privacy, explaining, 'if you loved her, that's the greatest favour, the greatest respect you could show her'.

He said of the princes: 'I pray that after time they will feel her presence in everything they do – and know their mother's love will never leave them. There are no words that can adequately describe the loss that Princess Diana's passing represents to the world. She was truly the greatest ambassador for compassion and humanity in modern times.

'We can only hope that her memory will inspire many of us to pursue those qualities in our own lives. On a personal level, I truly believe some souls are too special, too beautiful to be kept from heaven, however painful it is for the rest of us to let them go.' He then dedicated his single 'You Have Been Loved' to her.

This unexpected boost for 'You Have Been Loved' soon took Michael's album *Older* into the history books – no fewer than six songs taken from the album reached the top three in the singles charts, an unprecedented feat. The previous single reached No. 2 but was just kept from the top – as had been 'Jesus To A Child', 'Fastlove', 'Spinning The Wheel', 'Older' and 'Star People'. And 'You Have Been Loved' was similarly to be obstructed, but by another record-breaking single, Elton John's 'Candle in the Wind 1997'. It was a reworking of his tribute song to Marilyn Monroe, with new lyrics written by Bernie Taupin in memory of Princess Diana, which he had sung at her funeral. The record quickly became the biggest-selling single of all time, with over thirty-three million sales worldwide.

With Michael's greatest hits album delayed, Sony released a lucrative alternative, a compilation album of Michael's Wham! chart-toppers, reworked by Michael, who was anxious to ensure that the recordings were up to his standards. During September he re-recorded and re-edited some of the original tracks for the album, to be called *If You Were There – The Best of Wham!*. It was scheduled for release in November and was to include

'I'm Your Man', 'Everything She Wants', 'Club Tropicana', 'Wake Me Up Before You Go Go', 'Freedom', 'The Edge of Heaven', 'Wham! Rap! (Enjoy What You Do?)', 'Where Did Your Heart Go?' and 'Last Christmas'.

Sony was about to start earning huge sums again from George Michael and the company must have enjoyed a headline in the *Sun* on 4 November: 'George Falls Out With Label No. 2'. The paper reported that relations between Michael and his American employers at Dreamworks SKG were becoming strained. He had clashed with the embryonic record label over its failure to promote *Older* in the immense North American market, where it had sold a mere half a million copies, less than a third of the sales in the much smaller UK market, where the record was still selling well. Michael urged Dreamworks to re-release it in America and promote the album more wholeheartedly. It was like his dispute with Sony all over again.

Michael put out a statement to his fans on his internet site, (*http://www.aegean.net*): 'So far my time with Dreamworks has been frustrating and disappointing. I would like to apologize to many of my fans, especially those in America, for the lack of availability of my work. I hope you all realize the relative dismissal of *Older* in America is as bewildering to me as it is to you. In the New Year I have asked Dreamworks to release a new double CD package of *Older*. It will include my re-mixed versions of the singles "Star People" and "Strangest Thing".'

To help promote the release, Michael agreed to give a single newspaper interview, to Tony Parsons, who had ghosted his autobiography, *Bare*. The interview, for the *Daily Mirror*, was conducted at Michael's Hampstead home. Parsons recorded that, as well as his familiar Range

Rover, Michael now boasted a new Aston Martin sports car in the garage. Michael, his beard 'slightly longer than in recent photographs', wore an Adidas tracksuit, and remained curled up on a sofa sipping tea as he spoke. He told Parsons that in recent months he 'no longer smoked dope' and had cut down on cigarettes.

He acknowledged that his reaction to the death of Anselmo had contributed to the sombre tone of *Older* in which 'bereavement tinges the whole album' and he promised his next album 'is not going to be down. I want to make some great pop music before I'm too old. And for it not to be about the pain in my life. I know some people think I am a miserable old git – I want to show people that, though I have had a hard time, I am not a miserable git. I am tired of transmitting pain.'

An era in Michael's life was clearly coming to an end. He had spent too long grieving over the loss of Anselmo and 'that period is over'. He had also been changed by his mother's death and even his feelings about living in London were different. He said: 'The last couple of months have been pretty tough but I definitely feel as though I am coming through the other end of it.' And he went on: 'I don't love this country any less than I did before my mum's death, but my ties with Britain are definitely less now that my mum's died. It's hard to work out if that's because she's gone or because there are too many memories here. Here I am surrounded by things that represent my childhood and her.'

In fact, in recent months Michael had endured a great deal of pain, not all of it mental. He had undergone a hernia operation in North America, a surreal side-effect of which was that his testicles swelled to twice their normal size. He said: 'Now the swelling has gone down and they have returned to normal – unfortunately! In fact, I think they might even be a bit smaller than they were before.'

Michael's interview with Parsons drew comments from his old sparring partner Boy George, who pounced upon the remarks about his love for Anselmo to conclude that this was hard evidence that Michael was homosexual.

By the end of 1997 Michael had passed through a most turbulent period of his personal and professional life and, if not unscathed, he had certainly survived the bruising experience of personal loss and business battles with his equilibrium intact. As 1998 began his friends reported him as particularly warm-hearted to those who stood by him during the difficult period. To some extent he had recovered the intimacy of the group who surrounded him in his early days. His former Wham! backing singer Shirlie, who had been declared bankrupt, was once again employed by him, organizing the information service for his fans at his internet site.

In January 1998 Michael let it be known that he was unlikely to appear later that year in a concert at Althorp House being organized by Earl Spencer to celebrate the life of Princess Diana. While the Princess had let it be known that he was one of her favourite pop stars, along with Sir Paul McCartney, Sir Elton John and Eric Clapton, none of them would agree to Earl Spencer's plans. He and the others were anxious not to become drawn into the controversy surrounding what many people thought was the Earl's exploiting of his sister's memory for his own ends.

George Michael's return to the top of the world's music charts was assured by the release of *If You Were There – The Best of Wham!*, which made the UK's Top 10 bestselling albums list for 1997, although it had only been released a matter of weeks before the end of the year.

Tuesday 7 April 1998

In the early months of 1998, George Michael was making quiet progress with the songs for his new album. He was taking it easy, enjoying the Los Angeles sunshine and hanging out. He was also slightly bored. Some days he would drive himself to a nearby park to stretch out on the grass and see who was around. Tuesday 7 April 1998 was such a day.

Michael got up in a blue T-shirt and blue Adidas sweat-pants and spent the morning at home, a rented salmon-pink luxury house on Calle Vista Drive. And in the afternoon he chose to ignore his boyfriend's black Range Rover Discovery and instead drove his black Mercedes 190 saloon, its California number plate reading 2 ZEW 565, to the Will Rogers Memorial Park. It is a neatly manicured public space lined by palm trees on Sunset Boulevard in Beverly Hills, just opposite the Beverly Hills Hotel, and had been named as an act of homage to a great silent-movie comic whose most famous phrase, it was amusing later to recall, was: 'I've never met a man I didn't like.' Michael parked his car and walked across the road to a public restroom. He was familiar with the place, a notorious homosexual haunt, and had in the past stopped to check it out. This time, however, Michael's appetite for adventure was to end in embarrassment.

That Tuesday afternoon, at 14.50, according to the police account, Michael made eye contact with a tall Spanish-looking young man. He was well built, about thirty years old and he followed Michael into the toilet. No word was exchanged between them then or at any time. The police version of events reveals that George stands at the urinal and ushers the young man to go into the cubicle next to him, which he does. Michael begins masturbating and walks back towards the entrance, where he leans against the wall and exposes his penis to the man. Michael starts lowering his pants, revealing a nicotine patch on his bottom. After watching Michael masturbate for a while, Marcelo Rodriguez, the young policeman standing in the cubicle, brushes past Michael and walks outside.

The details of the arrest are a matter of public record, handed out to the press by the police department on North Rexford Drive on paper headed with a picture of the Beverly Hills Town Hall. Rodriguez reported Michael's actions to his colleague on the beat, Beverly Hills Police Department officer Shan Davies, who approached Michael in the toilet and told him that he was to be charged with committing lewd conduct in a public place. Michael protested, 'This is entrapment!' He was asked for identification and, as he could not provide any, he was handcuffed and with tears of anger welling in his eyes was placed on the back seat of a police car by a sergeant summoned to the scene, Sammy Lee, who took him to the Beverly Hills County Jail. There Michael was photographed and fingerprinted, given an official Californian criminal number, BH9802756, and charged with violating 647 (A) PC of the California penal code under his real name, Georgios Panayiotou. The police asked him to turn out his pockets and found Michael in possession of the prescription drug Prozac. He was dismissed with a summons to appear before the Beverly Hills Municipal Court house on 5 May at eight thirty in the morning.

By the time that Michael had procured bail, of $500, it was past eight in the evening. He went home with the certain knowledge that before long the incident would leak out to the press and all hell would break loose. Indeed, Lt. Edward Kreins of the Beverly Hills Police had already made plans to hold a press conference the following morning to announce their celebrity catch. In a deadpan Californian whine Kreins gave the official version of events, which neatly met head on any criticism that the police action was hostile to the gay community of Beverly Hills. It was the police department's duty to protect children in the park. Kreins said that 'members of our Crime Suppression Unit do routinely monitor the parks throughout the city which are all public parks. The parks have a lot of family members and children located in them. Members of our Crime Suppression Unit were monitoring the park yesterday. They did go into the restroom area of the park and did observe Mr Michaels engaged in a lewd act. He was by himself. The officers observed the act and arrested Mr Michaels.'

A reporter asked whether Michael was aware that he was being observed, Kreins replied: 'I believe to my knowledge he was aware that he was being observed, yes.' Kreins was asked whether Michael had propositioned the officer concerned and replied, 'No. He did not.'

Michael returned home in a desolate mood. The incident

had shaken him and he was now obliged to think fast.
News reports of the affair were already playing on television. Michael decided he would put up the shutters and
stay where he was. He telephoned his lawyer, Tony
Russell, and his manager, Andy Stephens, both in London,
who without hesitation booked flights to Los Angeles to
take charge of events. Until help arrived it was decided that
Michael would not make himself available for comment.
He needed a little time in which to plan a way of managing
the impact on his career of making public the one aspect
of his life which had so far remained unresolved: his
undeclared homosexuality. He took the precaution of
hiring a local lawyer, Arthur Barens. He looked out of the
window to the reporters and photographers and TV crews
camped outside his house, hoping to catch a glimpse of
him. Television news helicopters circled overhead, training
their cameras on the windows. He later described it as like
'living in a circus'.

After spending the whole of Thursday holed up at
home, on Friday Michael agreed to a television interview
with the NBC television network, but thought better of it
and cancelled at short notice. And in the evening Michael
ventured out, dressed in a black Armani jacket and black
open-necked shirt. He made the short limousine ride to
Spago, the show-business restaurant on Sunset Boulevard,
and ordered a prime filet mignon tartare steak with arti-
choke and Maine lobster. He had determined to meet his
embarrassment head on and was reassured to discover that
other celebrities dining at Spago felt it important to come
up and wish him well. Tony Curtis came to his table and
told him to 'keep smiling' and Michael went on to join
Lionel Ritchie and his friends for half an hour, where he

clearly appeared relaxed. At the potentially awkward moment when Michael needed to go to the men's room, the door was discreetly watched over by two of the restaurant staff. As he returned to the table, even George could not suppress a smile. After a group of reporters had noted Michael, they approached him for a comment on his arrest. Michael told them he had nothing to say and that he would be grateful if they left him alone.

On Saturday morning, Michael was taken by limousine to the studios of the 24-hour cable television news channel CNN. Russell and Stephens had approved of a single television interview on the unsensational news station in order to make a definitive statement on the charge against him and the personal implications of the arrest. Michael was quietly defiant as he faced CNN reporter Jim Moray. 'I don't feel any shame,' he said. 'I feel stupid and I feel reckless and weak for having allowed my sexuality to be exposed this way. But I don't feel any shame whatsoever and neither do I think I should.' He described his experience as 'humiliating, embarrassing and funny to a degree'.

He admitted to having cruised lavatories many times before. 'The truth is I put myself in the extremely stupid and vulnerable position, especially because I am in the privileged position that I am. I won't even attempt to deny . . . I won't even say that it was the first time it ever happened. You know, I've put myself in that position before. And I can only apologize.'

Michael said he did not find it easy to describe why he did such things. 'I can try to fathom why I did it. I can try to understand my own sexuality a bit better, but ultimately at the end of the day part of me has to believe that some of the kick was the fact that I might get found out. You know, deep down I truly believe that and, well here I am, I got found out. I don't suppose it'll be that exciting any more.'

Then came the admission which Michael had so long postponed. He would declare that he was homosexual and that he felt no shame about it. He told Moray, 'My sexuality was not cut and dry. I spent the first half of my career being accused of being gay when I hadn't had anything like a gay relationship. In fact, I was twenty-seven before that happened to me. So I spent my years growing up, being told what my sexuality was really, which was kind of confusing, and then by the time I'd kind of worked out what it was and I'd stopped having relationships with women, I was just so indignant at the way I'd been treated until then I just thought, "Well I'll just hold on to this, I don't think they need to know, I don't think I should have to tell them." But, you know, this is as good a time as any.'

The importance of what Michael was announcing seemed to elude Moray, who sought further explanation. 'So in unambiguous terms,' he asked, 'what is it that you want to say?' Michael replied, 'I want to say that I have no problem with people knowing that I am in a relationship with a man right now. I have not been in a relationship with a woman for almost ten years. I do want people to know that the songs that I wrote when I was with women were really about women and the songs that I've written since have been fairly obviously about men.'

It was a telling moment for Michael, for in being honest he was risking a great deal. He was about to discover who his true fans were. So much of his appeal was to young women, who believed his songs spoke to them, as women.

Would they accept the sentiments of a homosexual Michael, singing about men? The decision to come out as gay had been forced upon him and Michael hoped to turn his embarrassment to his advantage, if he could. He hoped that his fans might give him credit for his openness and honesty in the face of such humiliation and that they would feel sympathy for him. The fans' verdict would be given when they came to buy his next album. From now on the quality of his performances and of his songs would be put severely to the test.

Michael used CNN to apologize to his fans for obliging them to follow such a sorry story and he appealed to them to understand his state of mind. 'I just want to tell my fans, who I feel to some degree I have, apart from embarrassing myself, I have embarrassed them to some degree, and I just want to let them know that I'm OK. I know a lot of them realize that I've had a very tough time over the last five or six years and I want to let them know that this is not going to finish me off. This is really nothing compared to the bereavements I've had to deal with, some of the other stuff, even compared to the legal situations I've had to deal with. This is kind of, I was going to say a walk in the park, but I don't think that would work very well!'

After the interview, Michael and his lover Kenny Goss went out to dinner with friends to The Ivy in Beverly Hills, to celebrate his coming out and the end of an extraordinary few days.

Michael's adventure in the Will Rogers Memorial Park made headlines around the world and none more so than in Britain, where the tabloid press had a field day at Michael's expense. The story displayed Britain's tabloid press at their most hypocritical, faking indignation at the heinous crime while milking the story of the arrest for every salacious detail. And amid the pages of coverage which wallowed in each last scrap of information about Michael's undignified arrest there were some more sober commentators who came to Michael's aid. Chief among them was *The Times*'s columnist Matthew Parris, writing in, of all places, the *Sun*, the paper which had most revelled in the exposure of Michael's secret vice. Parris was unfazed by the likely prejudices of his readership when he wrote of the offence: 'Nobody dies. Nobody is assaulted. Nobody is robbed. Nobody is hurt. Nobody bleeds. Nobody suffers. Except the poor fellow caught.' Parris went on to declare, 'I do not think what he's done is so dreadful', and he asked, 'When is this country going to grow up?'

Support came from an unlikely quarter in the shape of the gay rights campaigner Peter Tatchell, who had indulged in the 'outing' of public figures in the past; he offered a most understanding explanation of Michael's plight. 'I think George was under a lot of pressure from people in the pop industry. He was a star who appealed both to young teenage girls, to an older audience and to gay men and I think the record company wanted to keep him onside with all his different fan-bases. But in the process they forced him to hide his sexuality. To be honest. To not tell the truth. And that really put him under an enormous and intolerable burden.'

Support came too from his old sparring partner Boy George, who said, 'I hope that George is not prosecuted and I don't think he has done anything to be ashamed of.' When all was said and done, he said, 'we are sisters under the skin'.

An unlikely critic, however, turned out to be Tony Parsons, the *Mirror* columnist who had become Michael's regular official conduit to the tabloid press. Michael counted Parsons a friend and had trusted him with the delicate task of writing his autobiography, *Bare*. Yet Parsons felt free to strongly criticize Michael's behaviour. While he sympathized with Michael's depressed state, Parsons could not disguise his horror at the incident in the toilet. 'What is truly shocking to those of us who know him is that he would risk the scandal of being caught in a public place,' he wrote. 'If these charges are true, then George has been bloody stupid.' And he concluded, 'He is way out of line. Nobody wants to see this kind of thing when they pop to the loo after feeding the ducks. George has made a huge mistake.'

For many in London, however, the whole affair seemed little but a joke. Victor Lewis-Smith, in the *Mirror*, found humour in the lewd act itself. 'What I want to know is: how can you commit a lewd act by yourself? As an investigative journalist, I felt it was my duty to find out so I've spent the last forty-eight hours trying out various scenarios involving a satsuma, a tawse, three tubs of Swarfega, a Mars bar, cling film, lipstick, potty putty and a car battery. I tried everything I could think of, but didn't feel lewd, just ridiculous.'

Back in Los Angeles, Michael was preparing for the court case and its attendant publicity. He wanted the best representation in court and took advice on who would best suit his case. He stood down Arthur Barens in favour of a show-business lawyer of some repute, Ira Reiner, who had had some success in keeping his celebrity clients out of jail. He represented Robert Downey Jr. when the actor was up on drugs and gun charges. He successfully prosecuted the infamous Menendez brothers for murdering their parents, a trial that had gripped America and made Reiner a national celebrity.

Reiner began making overtures to the police for a deal. George would most likely be able to avoid appearing at the trial. It might even be possible to avoid a trial altogether if a guilty plead was entered, with the judge merely passing sentence in his chambers. And the prospect of a jail sentence also seemed dim. As a first offence, and with the evident public embarrassment caused to Michael and his reputation, a fine would be more in order, perhaps as little as $2,000.

When the case, which was postponed for a week, was heard on Thursday 14 May, Michael did not attend the court. He was lying low back in Britain and allowed Reiner to act on his behalf. In the brief fifteen-minute hearing at Beverly Hills Municipal Court, three blocks from the park where Michael was arrested, Reiner entered a no-contest plea, which under Californian law is equivalent to pleading guilty. Judge Charles Rubin first mispronounced Michael's Greek name, then referred to him throughout as Michael George, before fining the singer $810 and sentencing him to twenty-four months 'informal probation', during which time he was banned from the Will Rogers Memorial Park. Michael was also ordered to attend five one-hour sessions of sexual counselling with a psychotherapist, a course which he had already begun, and he was sentenced to perform eighty hours of community service in the Los Angeles area before November 1998. What at first seemed an ordeal became a chastening process for Michael, then a strange rite of passage. The incident in the park brought out so much into the open that he could now relax completely, almost for the first time in his life.

By the end of the nineties George Michael was well established in the third, independent phase of his career. He had released an album, *Older*, under his new contractual conditions for new record companies and, if not quite as dazzling as *Faith*, the songs on the album set the markers for the quality of what might be achieved before long. Although *Older* did not do well in the United States, reflecting the fact that little effort was made by Michael to promote it there, selling little over 700,000 copies in 1996, it did well in the rest of the world, picking up thirty-five platinum or gold discs.

The songs on *Older* showed Michael in wistful mood, dwelling on the tragedies in his own life and the lessons of life's disappointments. As the material suggests, it was a mature album from an artist who had plainly learnt a great deal from his career so far. Of all the songs since his break with Sony, his single 'Jesus to a Child' quickly became a classic ballad, ideal for radio play around the world. A second album for Dreamworks/Virgin was expected with keen anticipation. The critics were gentle with Michael and gave him some credit for breaking away from Sony. And while they were prepared to accept George in the most sombre of musical moods, it was hoped that the release of pent-up frustration evident in *Older* would give way to some more cheerful, upbeat music.

For a career to have reached so successfully into a tertiary stage, as Michael had achieved, suggests an artist of some considerable talent. The stages of change in an act and style are critical in the continuing success of recording musicians and few pass beyond their first incarnation. Most typical is a one-hit wonder, or a band with little staying power and a repetitive string of hits before chart failure and oblivion. Some succeeded in making the break from their band, merely to enjoy a brief spell of success before diminishing returns set in. A few like Michael managed to make a second career shift.

In this third phase Michael pushed out to stake his claim to some of the territory occupied by the most eminent singer-songwriters in the world. As an established independent artist with a free brief, he found himself recording his own songs and competing with the giants of the industry, Elton John, Burt Bacharach and Bob Dylan, on an even footing. It was a long journey from his bedroom, strumming out songs on a guitar. It was even a long way from the fizzy days of Wham!, which were so crammed with promotional activity. By *Faith* there was more than a hint that Michael had a special talent. And his subsequent songs showed a depth and consistency which suggested that Michael was now capable of writing good songs into the foreseeable future. It was the ultimate position a songwriter might hope for.

The foundations of Michael's song-writing skills were built in his years with Andrew Ridgeley. While it was undoubtedly George Michael's musical creativity that drove the success of Wham!, Ridgeley made a significant contribution to the success of the band. He was the ambition, the driving force, the nagging member of the duo who was determined to make some distance in the lower reaches of the music industry. Michael rode along behind Ridgeley's enthusiasm and has come to admit that he owed a great deal to Ridgeley. Ridgeley made Wham!

happen, which gave Michael's songs the most exciting showcase.

Had the duo been less successful, had Ridgeley not insisted that they make every effort, Michael acknowledges that he would have spent years clawing his way up as a songwriter. Ridgeley's hectic activity left Michael time to calmly write songs and work out in detail the style the band should adopt. The partnership was an extraordinary, instant success. Wham! added a brightness and freshness to a stale music scene and openly displayed a sincerity and energy which the cynical music industry had long forgotten. For all the time they remained together Michael and Ridgeley were faultless as performers. And driving the engine of the twosome were Michael's exceptionally commercial songs.

The contrast in the careers of Michael and Ridgeley is striking. While Michael drove himself to exploit his natural talent as a songwriter, ending up a multimillionaire in the process, Ridgeley's career stood still. He spent a great deal of the £2 million he earned at the break-up of Wham! as well as a further £17 million in royalties on, first, his failed solo career, then on failing to become a racing driver. He finally settled down with Keren Woodward of Bananarama and her son from a previous partnership in a Georgian rectory in Cornwall. The end of Wham! proved to be the end of Andrew Ridgeley the pop star.

The end of Wham! might well have been the end of George Michael, too. Switching from a stable partnership into a solo career is treacherous territory. Yet Michael made a confident transformation, and with the album *Faith* proved himself to be a songwriter of enormous talent.

'Careless Whisper' quickly established itself as a standard ballad. If *Listen Without Prejudice, Vol. I* was a shade disappointing, it was put down to tiredness after the *Faith* tour and the fact that Michael was beginning his business hassles with Sony. Both albums were written with skill, performed impeccably and produced with precision.

Michael was sitting pretty. He was by this time an established singer-songwriter with an impressive songbook and the certain prospect of many good songs to come. And there Michael might have remained, happily stuck on a plateau, turning out an album a year for seven years for Sony, had he not demanded to be allowed to return to the market and test how much his talent would now fetch. That, it appears, is what the battle with Sony was about. It was certainly what it achieved. For all the anxiety and the irritation that the court case caused for Michael, and the misery was far in excess of his worst estimates, by the end of the affair he had not only increased his worth but had installed himself as an independent artist, capable of working among the giants of the worldwide entertainment industry.

Formerly merely a pop star, he had become a man of substance with whom people queued up to strike deals. And Michael had it on his own terms. There would be no more tedious record company executives, no partner to carry, no hasty deals signed to sophisticated managers. Michael was firmly in control. Control of his business affairs was essential to maintain full artistic control of his records. He had taken control of the recording process when he began producing his own records. The process fascinated him and he was expert at it. It came as no surprise to the Radio One executives administering his

Broadcasting House concert that he should wish to remix the recording and approve the final version of the broadcast. It was all part of holding on to his work so that others could not spoil it.

But while his musical career was brighter than ever, the court case against Sony had placed attention upon the real George Michael rather than his public persona. And speculation began again over his continuing apparent single status. As the incident in the Will Rogers Memorial Park revealed, Michael was not averse to the dangerous habit of visiting public lavatories of questionable repute, popularly known for homosexual activity. Such behaviour was rash, but it afforded some anonymity, so long as he was not caught. In the meantime he lived a treacherous double life.

The deceit was an act of self-defence. Recording artists who do not show themselves to be heterosexual tend to have their private lives raked over by the press. To appear to be unconventional is a danger to the fan-base and only those whose public image is a complete confection can overcome the dramatic slump in sales. As Trevor Dann, the BBC's head of music, explained: 'Most of the people who get away with it, like Elton John or Freddie Mercury, are larger than life caricatures. For example, even Michael Jackson's fans know he's eccentric. When you see those little girls interviewed they all say, so what if he sleeps with llamas! They are cartoon figures. George has never played that game. He has always been a real bloke. He doesn't dress up. He certainly doesn't camp it up in any sense.'

The public scrutiny of George Michael during the High Court hearings against Sony confirmed that his private self was much like his public image. But what was the private

George Michael like? A great deal of Michael's appeal is that he is a good-looking, fit, available young man. To imagine him as anything other than straightforwardly heterosexual may come as a disappointment to many of his fans.

As Trevor Dann put it: 'His whole appeal is sex. It's slightly the Cliff Richard vibe. Cliff Richard did have male fans, though I don't think any of them would own up to it now. George certainly does. They think he's a sensitive and tender bloke. And his woman fans want to make love to him.'

George Michael has responded to the pressure upon him to account for his private life by shutting out all but a very small number of people. A rare breach in his solitude took place when a female fan broke into his home. Before he could say anything, the teenager muttered, 'You're real, you're real', then passed out. He made a cup of tea for her before sending her on her way.

Whichever home he is living in, Hampstead, Santa Barbara or St Tropez, he lives a quiet life. He is not a celebrity who likes to be stopped for an autograph in the supermarket or be seen attending chic parties. He is a private man and rarely goes to dinner parties or nightclubs. If he eats out it is rarely in the West End and more likely in small local Italian and French restaurants in Hampstead. In his way he keeps total control of what is said about him, because if there is nothing to see there is nothing to report.

There is good evidence to suggest that George Michael is now well on the way to becoming a memorable songwriter who will before long boast a great songbook of standard songs. But in other ways it is not easy to assess

Michael. To which recording artists should he be compared? There is no perfect parallel to what he has achieved. In his successful switch from membership of a duo to a solo artist there are many precedents. Cher and Tina Turner set up successful soulful solo acts after they split with their original partners, but they were mere singers. Of the singer-songwriters, only perhaps Paul Simon, who shed Art Garfunkel, writes songs to compare with Michael's. His mostly likely match as a songwriter who went his own way is John Oates, formerly half of the Philadelphia duo Hall and Oates, but Michael's songs are richer and more subtle.

And what of his public image? With his black leather clothes, his studied nonchalance, his sleek black hair, his abundant sexuality and his preference for torch-song, he is in a tradition which began with the young Elvis Presley and was later adapted in a peculiarly English way by Cliff Richard. George Michael has their fresh appeal, nimble figure and dancing step. And like them he has developed an obsession with the cultivation of an image which matches his personality. George Michael the singer is the perfect vehicle for George Michael's songs. Every now and then the image may be improved upon, but only to further articulate the mood of the music. Spray-on personalities adopted by regular make-over artists like David Bowie were not for Michael. The same trick plays in reverse. George Michael the private person is totally comfortable appearing as George Michael the singer, which allows him to sing with conviction.

George Michael is so well groomed, as if ever ready to perform, that, like a distinguished actor, he can sometimes seem like a caricature or carefully sculpted model of himself. Those who have spent time in his close company comment on his almost too perfect skin, his impeccably white and straight teeth and his firmly coiffed hair. There can seem to be an artificiality about him. He is instantly charming and makes easy conversation. He likes swapping facts and anecdotes about music and musicians. He is, by all accounts, a pleasure to be with. Yet nothing much is given away. He remains on his guard and is only happy to meet strangers under controlled circumstances, when he is paying the bill.

He is always anxious to avoid being taken advantage of and can cut off friends who he believes have taken liberties. This became clear when Michael was invited to the opening of a bar in the West End of London, the Capital Café, owned by the music station. Richard Park, the head of Capital, invited Michael to open it in a special ceremony. Michael declined, saying he was a singer, not a celebrity who opened bars. However, he said he would try to make the opening, so long as it was kept quiet. Michael set out from Hampstead, listening to Capital Radio in his car, and heard a disc jockey announce that George Michael was on his way to the party. Michael tapped the driver on the shoulder and told him to make for home.

A prolonged burst of activity by Michael is expected in the next couple of years. The George Michael greatest hits album is to be released by the end of 1998. And then there is his second album to satisfy the Dreamworks/Virgin contract. His fourth solo album is likely to emerge in 2000 when, after two decades as one of music's biggest players, he will still be just thirty-seven.

The need for independence, for freedom from control

by others, caused him to repeatedly question the contracts he made with his record companies. And the constant reassessment and renegotiation drove his career. He pushed himself artistically in order to be in a position to force his record companies to reassess his worth. By the end of 1997 he was free from any business interference. Yet his new companies, Dreamworks and Virgin, must wonder where their relationship with him will lead. They each have a two-album contract and Michael has let it be known that when that expires he will be looking for single-album contracts so that he can vary his output as he wishes. The test then will be whether Michael's songs continue to amuse the public.

As for the incident in the Will Rogers Memorial Park, it has at least caused Michael to leap the final hurdle in matching his public to his private persona. In some ways, despite the public embarrassment, the affair is a relief. Michael need no longer go through the charade of seeming to be heterosexual to please a section of his fans. The verdict on whether George Michael's unceremonious outing will affect his commercial success will be given in the sales of his forthcoming albums.

Bibliography

Bare: The Autobiography of George Michael by George Michael and Tony Parsons, Michael Joseph, 1990

George Michael: The Making of a Superstar by Bruce Dessau, Sidgwick & Jackson, 1989

Wham! Confidential: The Death of a Supergroup by Johnny Rogan, Omnibus Press, 1987

Wham! The Official Biography Part II Virgin Books, 1986

Thanks also to various newspaper reference libraries, including: *Hollywood Reporter*; *Los Angeles Times*; *Variety*; *The Times*, London; *Guardian*; *Independent*; *Sunday Times*; *Sunday Independent*; *Mail on Sunday*; *Mirror*, *Sun*, *News of the World*; *Star*; and *Time* and *People* magazines.

Index

Index

321

Index

Index